ADVANCES IN
GROUP PROCESSES

Volume 16 • 1999

ADVANCES IN GROUP PROCESSES

Editors: SHANE R. THYE
Department of Sociology
University of South Carolina

EDWARD J. LAWLER
MICHAEL W. MACY
HENRY A. WALKER
Department of Sociology
Cornell University

Series Editor: EDWARD J. LAWLER
Department of Sociology
Cornell University

Managing Editor: THERESA H. WOODHOUSE

VOLUME 16 • 1999

JAI PRESS INC.

Stamford, Connecticut

ISBN: 0-7623-0452-9
ISSN: 0882-6145

Manufactured in the United States of America

CONTENTS

LIST OF CONTRIBUTORS

Andreas Flache

Department of Philosophy
University of Bayreuth

Noah E. Friedkin

Department of Sociology
University of California at
        Santa Barbara

S. Alexander Haslam

Division of Psychology
Australian National University

Rainer Hegselmann

Department of Philosophy
University of Bayreuth

Nobuhito Jin

Faculty of Social Work
Shukutoku University

Eugene C. Johnsen

Department of Mathematics
University of California at
        Santa Barbara

Toko Kiyonari

Department of Behavioral Science
Hokkaido University

Peter Kollock

Department of Sociology
University of California at Los Angeles

Michael J. Lovaglia

Department of Sociology
University of Iowa

Penelope J. Oakes

Division of Psychology
Australian National University

Katerine J. Reynolds

Division of Psychology
Australian National University

Steven D. Silver   Laboratory for Social Research
                                    Stanford University

John Skvoretz   Department of Sociology
                                    University of South Carolina

Lisa Troyer   Department of Sociology
                                    University of Iowa

John C. Turner   Division of Psychology
                                    The Australian National University

Murray Webster   Department of Sociology
                                    University of North Carolina
                                       at Charlotte

Joseph Whitmeyer   Department of Sociology
                                    University of North Carolina
                                       at Charlotte

Toshio Yamagishi   Faculty of Letters
                                    Hokkaido University

PREFACE

EDITORIAL POLICY

Advances in Group Processes publishes theoretical analyses, reviews, and theory-based empirical chapters on group phenomena. The series adopts a broad conception of "group processes." This includes work on groups ranging from the very small to the very large, and on classic and contemporary topics such as status, power, exchange, justice, influence, decision making, intergroup relations, and social networks. Contributors have included scholars from diverse fields including sociology, psychology, political science, philosophy, mathematics, and organizational behavior.

The series provides an outlet for papers that may be longer, more theoretical, and/or more integrative than those published by standard journals. We place a premium on the development of testable theories and theory-driven research. Chapters in the following categories are especially apropos:

- *Conventional and unconventional theoretical work, from broad metatheoretical and conceptual analyses to refinements of existing the-*

ories and hypotheses. One goal of the series is to advance the field of group processes by promoting theoretical work.

- *Papers that review and integrate programs of research.* The current structure of the field often leads to the piecemeal publication of different parts of a program of research. This series offers those engaged in programmatic research on a given topic an opportunity to integrate their published and unpublished work into a single paper. Review articles that transcend the author's own work are also of considerable interest.

- *Papers that develop and apply social psychological theories and research to macrosociological processes.* One premise underlying this series is that links between macro and micro sociological processes warrant more systematic and testable theorizing. The series encourages development of the macrosociological implications embedded in social psychological work on group.In addition the editors are open to submissions that depart from these guidelines.

CONTENTS OF VOLUME 16

This volume of *Advances in Group Processes* includes a diverse array of chapters, beginning with two that extend and clarify theoretical research on social networks. In "Social Influence Networks and Opinion Change," Friedkin and Johnsen build on prior work by providing a generalized model of interpersonal influence which subsumes a range of extant models. This new theory incorporates intra-personal tendencies and broader patterns of social relations to explain how initially diverse opinions converge through social interaction. The new formulation is tested and supported with experimental data from two, three, and four person groups. In "Understanding Network Exchange Theory," Michael Lovaglia explicates the basics of network exchange theory for readers not well versed in this theoretical tradition. After laying out the fundamental concepts and assumptions of network exchange theory in clear and non-technical language, Lovaglia examines traditional and contemporary topics around which the theory has developed. Numerous illustrations and applications are provided throughout the chapter.

The next two chapters focus on the emergence of trust and cooperative norms under conditions of uncertainty. Flache and Hegselmann use computer simulations to explore the emergence of social support, when individuals have the option of leaving old networks for new ones. Focusing on two behavioral tendencies, individual altruism and rational self-interest, this work uncovers several non-intuitive findings. For example, the simulations reveal that dense social support networks can emerge among purely rational egoists; and that too much altruism has the potential to actually erode social support systems. Staying within the "virtual" realm, Peter Kollock examines how individuals overcome the risky business of Internet trading when negotiated agreements are not necessarily enforceable. His analysis catalogues both formal and informal mechanisms that have naturally emerged to promote trustworthy exchanges. Kollock finds that core sociological concepts such as identity, accountability, monitoring and sanctioning all play a role in the production of trust in online markets.

The next two papers bear on social identity processes. In "Part of Life's Rich Tapestry: Stereotyping and the Politics of Intergroup Relations," Oakes, Reynolds, Haslam, and Turner provide an interdisciplinary theory of stereotyping which bridges related strains of research from social psychology and social cognition. Their self-categorization theory suggests that the structure of intergroup relations will condition the propensity for people to categorize and stereotype. The authors report a range of empirical tests which support the basic theoretical predictions. Next, Yamagishi, Jin and Kiyonari challenge the basic tenants of social identity theory in their article "Bounded Generalized Reciprocity: Ingroup Boasting and Ingroup Favortism." The authors review a growing set of findings which question long-standing interpretations of the minimal group paradigm most heavily associated with Tajfel and associates. They provide experimental data which demonstrates that the classic "ingroup favoritism" effect hinges critically on two factors: (1) whether or not group members expect reciprocity, and (2) the degree of their interdependence. The authors conclude by posing an alternative theoretical formulation to reconcile these findings.

The two final chapters deal with emergent processes in discussion groups and teams. In "Status Orders in Task Discussion Groups," Skvoretz, Webster and Whitmeyer propose and experimentally test a formal model of participation in task groups. This model asserts that external status characteristics and emergent interactional processes (i.e., bystander effects) work in tandem to produce interactional inequalities in open task discussion groups. An analysis of coded discussions from groups of varying status composition were found to support the theoretical predictions. Lisa Troyer and Steven D. Silver break new ground by arguing for a somewhat broader perspective than is typically employed by researchers in the group processes tradition. In their "Institutional Logics and Group Environments: Toward an Open System Perspective on Group Processes," they assert team efficiency is partially determined by the environment in which the team is embedded. Drawing on diverse sources, from Lewin's classic field theory to modern research in organizations, they suggest organizational teams are most efficient when the institutional logic of the organization matches that of the team. Data from a provocative case study are presented in support of this thesis.

Shane R. Thye
Edward J. Lawler
Michael W. Macy
Henry A. Walker

Volume Co-editors

SOCIAL INFLUENCE NETWORKS AND OPINION CHANGE

Noah E. Friedkin and Eugene C. Johnsen

ABSTRACT

Social influence network theory, which is both cognitive and structural, focuses on the contributions of networks of interpersonal influence to the formation of interpersonal agreements and group consensus. It entails a cognitive process when it deals with how actors integrate conflicting influential opinions to form revised opinions on an issue. It entails a social structure when it deals with an influence network that is defined by the pattern and strengths of the interpersonal influences among the members of a group. This article extends our work on social influence network theory, develops a set of formal implications of this theory, and assesses the theory in small groups of dyads, triads, and tetrads.

INTRODUCTION

The process of interpersonal influence that affects actors' attitudes and opinions is an important foundation of their socialization, identity, and decisions. It is also

Advances in Group Processes, Volume 16, pages 1-29.
Copyright © 1999 by JAI Press Inc.
All rights of reproduction in any form reserved.
ISBN: 0-7623-0452-9

an important foundation of actors' efforts to shape their situations by modifying the attitudes and opinions of significant others with whom they interact. In groups, this influence process can produce shared understandings and agreements that define the culture of the group and frame the collective activities of its members. This process is also one of the key foundations of social control.

In classical sociological theory, social control refers to the occurrence and effectiveness of ongoing efforts in a group to formulate, agree upon, and implement collective courses of action (Janowitz 1975). The difficulty in arriving at a collective decision given actors with fixed discrepant preferences—as exemplified by Arrow's (1951) dilemma of social choice—is rendered moot when a social influence process produces consensus. The classical agenda on social control is not only to elucidate such social influence mechanisms, but also (taking the reduction of mechanisms based on coercive domination as an explicit value position) to discover conditions under which noncoercive mechanisms provide an effective basis of social control. Thus, the classical approach to the study of social control focuses on effects of noncoercive interpersonal influences arising from communication, social comparison, and bargaining.

Sociological theory on social influence mechanisms has addressed the origins of bargaining power (social exchange theory), the conditions of cooperation (rational choice theory), and the construction of role and status structures (expectation states theory). Surprisingly, however, there is not a well-developed formal sociological approach to the opinion formation process that may produce consensus in a group. The process of opinion formation can rarely be reduced to accepting or rejecting the consensus of others; typically, individuals form their opinions in a complex interpersonal environment in which influential opinions are in disagreement and liable to change. This article seeks to advance the classical sociological agenda on social influence and social control by showing how networks of interpersonal influence contribute to the formation of interpersonal agreements and consensus in such complex circumstances. Taking a formal approach, it extends the work of symbolic interactionists on the social construction of shared opinion and definitions of situations in dyads to address the problem of how N-actor agreements may develop.

Two interrelated theoretical problems must be solved to develop an account of how social influence networks affect attitudes and opinions and enter into the formation of N-actor agreements. The first problem is the development of a model of the *social process* that forms such agreements, that is, how actors modify their opinions taking into account their own circumstances and the influences of other actors. The second problem is the development of a model of the *social influence structure* that describes the configuration and strengths of interpersonal influences in a particular population, that is, the social structural context in which the influence process occurs. This article addresses both of these problems and builds upon previous work (Friedkin 1986, 1998; Friedkin and Cook 1990; Friedkin and Johnsen 1990). It extends the authors' work on social influence network theory, develops a set of formal implications of this theory, and assesses the theory in small groups of dyads, triads, and tetrads.

SOCIAL INFLUENCE NETWORK THEORY

The theory described in this article has been under development by social psychologists and mathematicians since the 1950s (DeGroot 1974; French 1956; Friedkin and Johnsen 1990; Harary 1959). This line of research began with French's (1956) formal theory of social power, which introduced a simple model of how a network of interpersonal influence enters into the process of opinion formation. Drawing on the algebra of a Markov Chain process, the theory was developed in a more general form by Harary (1959) and DeGroot (1974). These initial formulations described the formation of group consensus, but did not provide an adequate account of settled patterns of disagreement.[1] Friedkin and Johnsen's (1990) generalization of the theory addressed this limitation and integrated this line of social psychological work on opinion formation with another developing line of sociological work on network effects (Burt 1982; Doreian 1981; Erbring and Young 1979; Friedkin 1990; Marsden and Friedkin 1993). The distinguishing characteristic of this theoretical approach is that it attempts to model the flows of interpersonal influence that affect the opinions of actors; compare the work on social decision schemes (Stasser, Kerr, and Davis 1989) and social impact theory (Latane 1981).

Our theory postulates a simple recursive definition for the influence process in a group of N actors:

$$\mathbf{y}^{(t)} = \mathbf{A}\mathbf{W}\mathbf{y}^{(t-1)} + (\mathbf{I} - \mathbf{A})\mathbf{y}^{(1)} \tag{1}$$

for $t = 2,3,\ldots$, where $\mathbf{y}^{(1)}$ is an $N \times 1$ vector of actors' initial opinions on an issue, $\mathbf{y}^{(t)}$ is an $N \times 1$ vector of actors' opinions at time t, $\mathbf{W} = [w_{ij}]$ is an $N \times N$ matrix of interpersonal influences ($0 \leq w_{ij} \leq 1$, $\Sigma_j^N w_{ij} = 1$), and $\mathbf{A} = \mathrm{diag}(a_{11},a_{22},\ldots,a_{NN})$ is an $N \times N$ diagonal matrix of actors' susceptibilities to interpersonal influence on the issue ($0 \leq a_{ii} \leq 1$). Applying equation (1) iteratively, we obtain

$$\mathbf{y}^{(t)} = \mathbf{V}^{(t-1)}\mathbf{y}^{(1)} \tag{2}$$

where,

$$\mathbf{V}^{(t-1)} = (\mathbf{A}\mathbf{W})^{(t-1)} + \left[\sum_{k=0}^{t-2} (\mathbf{A}\mathbf{W})^k\right] (\mathbf{I} - \mathbf{A}) \tag{3}$$

for $t = 2.3.\ldots$.

Six of this model's process assumptions are fundamental. (1) *Cognitive Weighted Averaging*: Actors are assumed to form their revised opinions through a weighted averaging of the influences on them. Flows of interpersonal influence are established by the *repeated* responses of actors to the (possibly changing) influential opinions on the issue. However, actors are not only influenced endogenously by the opinions of other actors, but also exogenously, at each point in the process, by the conditions that have formed their *initial* opinions. The relative weight of the endogenous and exogenous influences for each actor is determined by $\mathbf{A} = [a_{ii}]$, the coefficients of susceptibility to social influence.[2] (2) *Fixed Social Structure*: The social structure of the group of actors is assumed to be fixed during the entire process of opinion formation. This social structure consists of (a) the set of actors, (b) the direct influence network among them, represented by the matrix $\mathbf{W}$, (c) the susceptibilities of the actors to interpersonal influence, represented by the diagonal matrix $\mathbf{A}$, and (d) the actors' initial opinions, represented by the vector $\mathbf{Y}^{(1)}$. (3) *Determinism*: Given the direct influence matrix $\mathbf{W}$, the susceptibility matrix $\mathbf{A}$, and group members' initial opinion vector $\mathbf{Y}^{(1)}$, the subsequent opinion changes in the group are completely determined. (4) *Continuance*: The process of opinion formation in the group continues until all changes of opinion that may occur have played themselves out. (5) *Decomposability*: The opinion formation process is decomposable into time periods, defined by the times $t = 1,2,3,\ldots$, that may not be of the same length in real time. (6) *Simultaneity*: In each time period, simultaneous linear equations yield an accurate prediction of all the influence events that occur during that period.

We work with the following version of this general formulation which stipulates that

$$\mathbf{W} = \mathbf{AC} + \mathbf{I} - \mathbf{A} \qquad (4)$$

where $\mathbf{C} = [c_{ij}]$ is an $N \times N$ matrix of relative interpersonal influences $(0 \le c_{ij} \le 1, c_{ii} = 0, \Sigma_j^N c_{ij} = 1)$[3]. That is, we have equated actors' lack of susceptibility to interpersonal influence with the weight that they place on their initial opinions

$$w_{ii} = 1 - a_{ii} \qquad (5)$$

for all i and have distributed the cumulative weight of others $(a_{ii} = \Sigma_j w_{ij}, j \ne i)$ according to the relative strength of the interpersonal influences, that is, for $i \ne j$

$$w_{ij} = a_{ii} c_{ij} \qquad (6)$$

Assuming the process reaches an equilibrium, that is, $\lim\limits_{t \to \infty} \mathbf{y}^{(t)} = \mathbf{y}^{(\infty)}$ exists, equation (1) becomes

$$\mathbf{y}^{(\infty)} = \mathbf{AWy}^{(\infty)} + (\mathbf{I} - \mathbf{A})\mathbf{y}^{(1)} \tag{7}$$

and hence

$$(\mathbf{I} - \mathbf{AW})\mathbf{y}^{(\infty)} = (\mathbf{I} - \mathbf{A})\mathbf{y}^{(1)} \tag{8}$$

If, in addition, **I-AW** is nonsingular, then

$$\mathbf{y}^{(\infty)} = (\mathbf{I} - \mathbf{AW})^{-1}(\mathbf{I} - \mathbf{A})\mathbf{y}^{(1)} \tag{9}$$

whence actors' settled opinions are given by

$$\mathbf{y}^{(\infty)} = \mathbf{V}\mathbf{y}^{(1)} \tag{10}$$

where,

$$\mathbf{V} = (\mathbf{I} - \mathbf{AW})^{-1}(\mathbf{I} - \mathbf{A}) \tag{11}$$

More generally, by equation (2) we can obtain equation (10) if

$$\mathbf{V} = \lim\limits_{t \to \infty} \mathbf{V}^{(t)} \tag{12}$$

exists. In either case, **V** is a matrix of reduced-form coefficients describing the total interpersonal effects that transform initial opinions into final opinions. The coefficients in $\mathbf{V} = [v_{ij}]$ are nonnegative ($0 \leq v_{ij} \leq 1$) and each row of **V** sums to unity ($\Sigma_j v_{ij} = 1$); hence, v_{ij} gives the *relative weight* of the initial opinion of actor j in determining the final opinion of actor i for all i and j. If $\mathbf{I} - \mathbf{AW}$ is nonsingular, then **V** can be derived directly from equation (11); otherwise, **V** can be estimated numerically from equation (3) for a sufficiently large t when $\lim\limits_{t \to \infty} \mathbf{V}^{(t)}$ exists.

Selected Special Cases

Our theory is developed for the *general case* in which there are individual differences in interpersonal influences and opinions, and it subsumes (as special cases) situations in which such individual differences are constrained. These special cases include certain classical situations:

1. A status order in which an individual is located in a stratified influence network,
2. A conformity situation in which a deviate is faced with a fixed consensus of others that the deviate either accepts (moves toward) or rejects,
3. A minority influence situation in which a deviate may change the majority consensual opinion, and
4. An intergroup conflict situation in which disagreement occurs between two factions.

In this section, we show how social influence network theory includes and integrates these special cases.

To see how various situations may be covered by the theory, consider the following example, which is taken from one of the tetrads involved in our experiments; we will describe these experiments later on in the article. In this group, each member (a) was presented with an issue on which opinions could range from 1 to 100, (b) independently formed an initial opinion on the issue, and (c) after a discussion of the issue, settled on a final opinion that may or may not have been in agreement with the settled opinions of certain other members of the group:

$$\mathbf{y}^{(1)} = \begin{bmatrix} 25 \\ 25 \\ 75 \\ 85 \end{bmatrix} \quad \mathbf{y}^{(\infty)} = \begin{bmatrix} 60 \\ 60 \\ 75 \\ 75 \end{bmatrix}$$

The influence network for this group

$$\mathbf{W} = \begin{bmatrix} .220 & .120 & .359 & .300 \\ .147 & .215 & .344 & .294 \\ 0 & 0 & 1 & 0 \\ .089 & .178 & .446 & .286 \end{bmatrix}$$

describes the distribution of relative interpersonal influences on the issue. The main diagonal of $\mathbf{W}$ are the actors' self-weights ($w_{ii} = 1 - a_{ii}$) and, therefore, $\mathbf{A} = \text{diag}(.780, .785, 0, .714)$ describes the actors' susceptibilities to interpersonal influence. The off-diagonal entries of $\mathbf{W}$ are interpersonal influences. For example, $w_{13} = .359$ indicates that the direct (unmediated) relative influence of actor 3 on actor 1 is .359. The total effects matrix

$$\mathbf{V} = \begin{bmatrix} .280 & .045 & .551 & .124 \\ .047 & .278 & .549 & .126 \\ 0 & 0 & 1 & 0 \\ .030 & .048 & .532 & .390 \end{bmatrix}$$

indicates the net influence of each actor on every other actor that arises from all of the flows of interpersonal influence (direct and indirect) among the members of the group. For example, $v_{13} = .551$ indicates that a little over 55 percent of the content of actor 1's final opinion is determined by actor 3. Comparing $\mathbf{W}$ and $\mathbf{V}$, we can see that the influence of actor 3 on the other actors has been enhanced by the flows of influence in this network. It also is interesting to note that actors 1 and 2, who were in final agreement, have relatively slight net interpersonal effects on each other. The predicted final opinions are

$$\hat{\mathbf{y}}^{(\infty)} = \mathbf{V}\mathbf{y}^{(1)} = \begin{bmatrix} 60 \\ 60 \\ 75 \\ 75 \end{bmatrix}$$

which correspond exactly to the observed final opinions. The ability of the derived model to exactly reproduce the empirical data is not always assured, but it is not surprising in this case. The fit is always exact when equilibrium opinions are in disagreement (as in the present case) and $\Delta_i \geq 0$; see equation (A6) in the Appendix.

The social structure of the group is described by the distribution of initial opinions $\mathbf{y}^{(1)}$, and the influence network, $\mathbf{W}$. The special cases described entail constraints on one or both of these components of the social structure of a group. These constraints can either be naturally occurring features of a group, as they were in the group described above, or they can be experimentally designed conditions under which subjects are placed in order to study a feature of social influence networks, process, or outcomes.

These special cases have an important property in common—they allow a simplification of equation (10),

$$y_i^{(\infty)} = \sum_{j=1}^{N} v_{ij} y_j^{(1)}$$

from which the total interpersonal effect of a subset of actors on another subset of actors can be described in terms of the initial and equilibrium opinions of other group members. This derivation is straightforward in a dyad:

$$y_i^{(\infty)} = \sum_{j=1}^{2} v_{ij} y_j^{(1)} = (1 - v_{ij}) y_i^{(1)} + v_{ij} y_j^{(1)} \tag{13}$$

and, hence,

$$v_{ij} = \frac{y_i^{(\infty)} - y_i^{(1)}}{y_j^{(1)} - y_i^{(1)}} \tag{14}$$

In larger groups a comparable formulation of interpersonal influence is

$$\tilde{v}_{ij} \equiv \sum_{j \neq 1} v_{ij} = \frac{y_i^{(\infty)} - y_i^{(1)}}{\bar{y}_i^{(1)} - y_i^{(1)}} \tag{15}$$

where $\bar{y}_i^{(1)} = \sum_{j \neq i} g_{ij} y_j^{(1)}$ and $g_{ij} = v_{ij}/(1 - v_{ii})$ for $v_{ii} \neq 1$ ($\tilde{v}_{ij} = 0$ for $v_{ii} = 1$). We will show how this general formulation simplifies in certain special cases.

One Actor Who Deviates from a Consensus

Our model captures, as a special case, the classical conformity situation in a group in which influence is exerted on an opinion of one member who deviates from the consensus of other group members. Consider equation (10) in scalar form

$$y_i^{(\infty)} = \Sigma_j v_{ij} y_j^{(1)}$$

with the *additional* stipulation of the existence of a consensus of initial opinions among all actors other than actor i. Let $\hat{y}_j^{(1)}$ equal the *consensus opinion* of all actors $j \neq i$. Hence, for, $j \neq i$,

$$y_i^{(\infty)} = v_{ii} y_i^{(1)} + \sum_{j=1}^{n} v_{ij} y_j^{(1)} = (1 - \tilde{v}_{ij}) y_i^{(1)} + \tilde{v}_{ij} \hat{y}_j^{(1)} \tag{16}$$

and equation (15) simplifies to

$$\tilde{v}_{ij} = \frac{y_i^{(\infty)} - y_i^{(1)}}{\hat{y}_j^{(1)} - y_i^{(1)}} \tag{17}$$

because $\bar{y}_i^{(1)} = \hat{y}_j^{(1)}$. The interpersonal influence is that of a *consensual collective other* on an actor. This formulation of the influence of a unanimous majority on a minority of one is identical to the measure proposed by Goldberg (1954), who referred to it as an "index of proportional conformity." While Goldberg proposed the index without theoretical justification, our approach provides a clear theoretical foundation.

Note that in this formulation, we have not assumed that the consensus is *fixed*. Hence, the initially deviant opinion may influence the opinions of other group members. The influence of the deviant member, actor i, on one of the other group members, actor j, determines the extent of that member's opinion change:

$$v_{ji} = \frac{y_j^{(\infty)} - \hat{y}_j^{(1)}}{y_i^{(1)} - \hat{y}_j^{(1)}} \tag{18}$$

Such influence is consistent with a situation in which the influence of a deviant breaks up the initial consensus of the other group members; it also is consistent with a situation in which the consensus of the other members is maintained, but changes as a result of the influence of the deviate. Such situations are the focus of a line of work on "minority influence" initiated by Moscovici (1985).

A further result is obtained by assuming so-called Asch (Asch 1951) conditions, in which the initial opinions of the other group members represent a *fixed* consensus, that is, where $w_{jj} = 1$ for all $j \neq i$. for all. For convenience, letting $i = 1$, the influence network for this Asch-type situation is

$$\mathbf{W} = \begin{bmatrix} w_{11} & w_{12} & w_{13} & \cdots & w_{1n} \\ 0 & 1 & 0 & \cdots & 0 \\ 0 & 0 & 1 & \cdots & 0 \\ 0 & 0 & 0 & \cdots & 0 \\ \vdots & \vdots & \vdots & \cdots & \vdots \\ 0 & 0 & 0 & \cdots & 1 \end{bmatrix}$$

indicating that, while actor $i = 1$ may be influenced by each of the other group members, these other group members are not subject to any interpersonal influence. In an Asch-type experiment, these actors are confederates of the experimenter who instructs them not to alter their initial opinions. In this case, because the deviate cannot influence the other actors, the only issue is the extent to which the deviate will be influenced.

Moscovici (1976, 1985) has argued that the influence of a minority on a majority entails *compliance* (both public and private acceptance) and that the influence of a majority on a minority entails *conformity* (public but not necessarily private acceptance); that is, the character of the interpersonal influence differs. Although it is possible that an actor will conform to a consensus without changing his or her underlying opinion, it also is possible that such conformity can occur based on a response to one of the other members of the group; that is, the mere presence of a consensus does not necessarily imply that a group-level normative pressure exists. Indeed, it may be that what has been thought of as group-level pressure to conform to a consensus is nothing more than the aggregation of separate interpersonal influences that are exerted by each member of the consensus on the deviate.

Stratified Influence Networks

Many sociologists view the influence process as a source of power inequalities and dominance. In studies of natural groups, it has been shown that groups often quickly generate a consistent or "consensual" rank ordering of group members in terms of prestige and influence. Expectation states theory (Ridgeway and Walker 1995) suggests that these status orders arise because of shared beliefs about the value of certain status characteristics; for example, because actors value expertise similarly, they will tend to rank order the members of a task-oriented group in a similar way. Hence, a stratified influence structure will emerge

$$\mathbf{W} = \begin{bmatrix} w_{11} & w_{22} & \cdots & w_{NN} \\ w_{11} & w_{22} & \cdots & w_{NN} \\ \vdots & \vdots & \cdots & \vdots \\ w_{11} & w_{22} & \cdots & w_{NN} \end{bmatrix}$$

in which all actors accord the same influence to a particular actor and in which an actor's self-weight corresponds to his or her interpersonal influences.[4] Our interest focuses on the consequences of a maintained status order for the resolution of issues.

Status orders include as special cases an egalitarian situation ($w_{11} \approx w_{22} \approx \cdots \approx w_{NN}$) and domination ($w_{11} \approx 1$, $w_{22} \approx w_{33} \approx \cdots \approx w_{NN} \approx 0$). As an implication of the stochasticity of $\mathbf{W}$, only *one* actor can be dominant in a status order (if, $w_{ii} = 1$, then $w_{jj} = 0$ for all $j \neq i$). In status orders with a dominant actor, a consensus will appear immediately at $t = 2$. Hence, status orders with a dominant actor are maximally efficient in producing consensus. This conclusion follows directly from equation (1) and the influence structure of a status order.

These implications have a particularly dramatic manifestation in a dyad. In a dyad, the formation of virtual agreement (regardless of $\mathbf{y}^{(1)}$) is consistent with two situations: (1) a status order in which one of the two actors is dominant or (2) an egalitarian influence structure in which $\mathbf{A} \approx \mathbf{I}$ (but $\mathbf{A} \neq \mathbf{I}$). In the former situation, the consensus will be the initial opinion of the dominant actor and will be formed immediately at $t = 2$. In the latter situation, the consensus will be the mean of the initial opinions of the two actors and will be formed very slowly. Indeed, in a dyad, for $\mathbf{A} = \mathbf{I}$, when both actors are maximally accommodating (place no weight on their own opinions) an equilibrium is unattainable.[5]

Influence Networks with Two Factions

Intergroup conflict often takes the form of a disagreement between *two* factions, each of which has a certain opinion (internal consensus) on an issue. In such a situation, the aggregate influence of the members of one faction on an actor in a different faction is

$$
\tilde{v}_{i[j]} = \frac{y_i^{(\infty)} - \hat{y}_{[i]}^{(1)}}{\hat{y}_{[j]}^{(1)} - \hat{y}_{[i]}^{(1)}}
\tag{19}
$$

where $\hat{y}_{[i]}^{(1)}$ is the initial consensus value for every member of i's faction, and similarly for j, and $\tilde{v}_{i[j]}$ is the aggregate influence of j's faction on i. The aggregate influence of a faction on one of its own members is $1 - \tilde{v}_{i[j]}$ or

$$
\tilde{v}_{i[i]} = \frac{y_i^{(\infty)} - \hat{y}_{[j]}^{(1)}}{\hat{y}_{[i]}^{(1)} - \hat{y}_{[j]}^{(1)}}
\tag{20}
$$

where $\hat{y}_{[j]}^{(1)}$ is the initial consensus value for every member of j's faction, and similarly for i, and $\tilde{v}_{i[i]}$ is the aggregate influence of i's faction (which includes i) on i.

MODEL VALIDATION

Our model of social influence captures various types of social influence situations and allows them to be viewed from a single theoretical perspective. Such theoretical integration is an important goal of a formal model. This section introduces the approach taken to examining the predictive accuracy of this model.

This assessment of the model will focus on three issues. First, we will analyze the fit between the observed and predicted equilibrium opinions of groups. This analysis is not only interested in the accuracy of these predictions, but also in an assessment of whether it would suffice to posit that group members' opinions converge to the mean of their initial opinions. The latter issue is not problematical to sociologists, who have long emphasized that social influences are stratified; however, it is an important issue to address in light of a continuing assertion among some psychologists (McGarty 1992; Turner and Oakes 1989) that the process of interpersonal influence entails a simple (as opposed to a weighted) averaging of group members' opinions. This assertion underlies a large body of work on group polarization (Isenberg 1986; Lamm and Myers 1978) in which it is assumed that the formation of a group consensus which is *not* the mean of group members' initial opinions is indicative of a process that is *different* from the process of social influence observed by Asch (1951) and Sherif (1936). Thus, our aim is to assess the importance of developing a structural (sociological) approach to opinion change, since if opinions do tend to converge to the mean of initial opinions, there is little call for the development of such an approach.

Then, we assess whether the parameter values that can be estimated from the pattern of initial and settled opinions of group members—the matrix $\mathbf{A}$ of individuals' susceptibilities to interpersonal influence—correspond to actors' subjective assessments of the extent to which their opinions have been influenced by the other members of the group. Such subjective reports are prone to systematic biases (e.g., actors' inflated estimates of their self-importance) and random errors; however, we do not require that subjective reports be unbiased to assess whether the derived values (a_{11}, a_{22},...,a_{NN}) correspond to the group members' subjective experiences. If we can show that there is a notable association between the estimated susceptibilities for actors and their subjective reports of influenceability, then the construct validity of the derived estimates will be importantly supported.

Finally, we will assess whether there is an association between the predicted efficiency with which an equilibrium is produced and the observed time taken by a group to reach a decision. The model stipulates that actors simultaneously revise their opinions and continue to do so until an equilibrium is reached. This simplifying process assumption is certainly flawed because interpersonal influences often occur in complex sequences. Moreover, group members may shortcircuit an influence process before equilibrium is attained and achieve a group decision that is based on a decision scheme (e.g., majority vote). Hence, there may not be any reliable association between the predicted and observed efficiency of the social influence process. It is important for us to ascertain whether the simplifying assumptions of the model are grossly misleading with respect to the actual efficiency with which groups attain consensus. An association between the observed and predicted efficiency of the social influence process would sup-

Table 1.   Three Experiments

Experiments	Groups	Issues	Trials
Tetrads	50	5	250
Triads	32	3	96
Dyads	36	2	72

port the construct validity of the *function*, equation (1) with equation (5), that describes the *process* of interpersonal influence.

METHODS AND PROCEDURES

Three Experiments

Table 1 presents an overview of the experiments drawn upon in this article. The form of these experiments was the same: (1) Each member of a group privately recorded their initial opinion on an issue. (2) The members of the group discussed the issue over a telephone network in which all or only some pairs of members were allowed to communicate. (3) After some prespecified time or upon reaching group consensus or upon reaching a deadlock, the group members privately recorded their final opinions on the issue and provided estimates of the relative interpersonal influences of the other group members upon their final opinions.

These experiments provided data on three of the four theoretical constructs involved in the influence model described by equation (7): actors' initial opinions ($y^{(1)}$), final opinions ($y^{(\infty)}$), and relative interpersonal influences (C) on an issue. Given these data, the fourth construct, actors' susceptibilities to interpersonal influence (A), were estimated with the method described in the Appendix.

Tetrads Experiment

This experiment involved 50 groups of college students whose members were asked to attempt to resolve their initial differences of opinion on various issues they had been asked to consider. The subjects were randomly assigned to positions within one of five different networks of interpersonal communication.[6] During the experiment neither the structure of the communication network nor individuals' positions in the network were altered.

Each group member occupied a private room and was given an issue to consider in isolation from the other three group members. Each person was asked to form and record an initial opinion on the issue under consideration. The group members then discussed their opinions with one another by means of a telephone system; each of the telephones displayed the names of persons with whom direct communication was possible and had buttons that opened lines of communication to these persons. Hence, only dyadic communication was permitted and (depending on the network structure) only certain communication channels could be activated by each subject. For example, in the "slash" network, members B and D could not converse with each other, but both could converse with network members A and C. Group members were instructed that they might communicate with other members of the group as frequently as they liked but that they must communicate at least once with each person whose name was listed on their telephones.

Group members were given up to twenty minutes to discuss an issue. Each group was instructed that attaining consensus was desirable and that most groups we had encountered had been able to reach consensus:

> Your goal is to reach consensus. If it seems difficult to reach consensus, remember that most groups are able to come to some decision if those who disagree will restate their reasons and if the problem is reread carefully.

Upon reaching group consensus or upon reaching a deadlock, the group members were asked to record their final opinions on the issue.

Each group dealt with five discussion issues in sequence. To eliminate crossover effects, the order of the discussion issues was systematically varied among groups. We took three discussion issues from the "risky shift" literature: Sports, Surgery, and School (see below). Two other issues were developed that involved a judgment about appropriate monetary reward: Asbestos and Disaster (see below). We selected these issues because individuals' opinions could be represented by real numbers—subjective probabilities on the "risky shift" issues or dollars on the monetary issues.[7]

Triads Experiment

This experiment involved 32 groups of college students. Each group dealt with the three "risky shift" discussion issues (Sports, Surgery, and School) in the context of either a complete or chain communication network (see note 6). One half of the triads operated under a "high" pressure condition and one half operated under a "low" pressure condition. In the "high" pressure condition, subjects were instructed that attaining consensus was desirable and that most groups we had encountered had been able to reach consensus:

> We would like you to reach an agreement. If at the end of twenty minutes there are remaining differences that you believe might be reconciled, you may have an additional ten minutes for discussion. You may terminate the session at any time if you believe that the remaining differences of opinion cannot be reconciled. However, it has been our experience that most discussion groups are able to reach an agreement within the twenty (plus optional ten) minute time frame.

In the "low" pressure condition subjects were instructed that any outcome was alright:

When the buzzer sounds a second time it is the signal for you to begin telephone communication with the other person. Now is the time to reconsider your choice. Discuss the situation with the other person. The conversation that you will have may or may not lead you to alter your first opinion, and you may or may not come to an agreement. Any of these outcomes are OK with us. You will have twenty minutes in which to discuss the issue. You may have an additional ten minutes if you want them.

Dyads Experiment

This experiment involved 36 groups of college students. Dyads were given up to 30 minutes to discuss an issue. Each dyad dealt sequentially with two of the "risky shift" issues—Surgery and School—that were involved in the other experiments. Eighteen of the dyads were placed under the "high" pressure condition and 18 dyads were placed under the "low" pressure condition which were described above in the triads experiment.

Discussion Issues

We took three discussion issues from the "risky shift" literature (Cartwright 1971):

You are asked to choose one of two alternatives. One alternative involves greater risk than the other, while also offering a greater potential reward. Consider the alternatives. Then indicate what probability of success would be necessary for you to choose the alternative which is potentially more rewarding, but which also carries a greater degree of risk.

Sports

You are a captain of a college team. You are playing in the crucial contest against your team's traditional rival. The game has been an intense struggle and now, in the final seconds of the game, your team is slightly behind. Fortunately, you are in a good position to successfully complete a play that will almost certainly produce a tie score. You are also in a position to attempt a play that is much riskier. If successful, it would result in a victory for your team; if unsuccessful, your team's defeat.

School

You are a college senior planning to go on for a Ph.D. For the Ph.D., you may enter Quality University. Because of Quality's rigorous standards, only a fraction of the graduate students manage to receive the Ph.D. you desire. You may also make a different choice and, to enter O.K. University. O.K. has a much poorer reputation than Quality. At O.K. almost every student receives a Ph.D.

Surgery

You have just completed a visit to your family doctor and then to a cardiac specialist. You have been told that you have a severe heart ailment. Due to your heart disease, you must drastically

curtail your customary way of life. There is an alternative. There is a medical operation available that has the potential to bring about a complete cure of your heart ailment. However, the
operation could prove fatal.

The responses (opinions) of the subjects were restricted to one of twenty probability values: .05, .10, .15, ..., 1. Previous research indicated that subjects have heterogeneous initial opinions on these issues and take them seriously.

Two questions were developed concerning an issue of monetary reward.

Asbestos

The Elmwood Unified School District has some older buildings with asbestos ceiling tiles
which must be removed. The job is dirty and tedious. Unskilled labor might be hired at the
minimum wage of $5.50 per hour; however some members of the school board believe that
the job calls for greater remuneration than $5.50 per hour in view of the potential hazards
in dealing with asbestos. How much ought the personnel who are going to do this work be
paid on an hourly basis?

Disaster

The 37th District Federal Court is hearing a case where plaintiffs in India have filed a class
action suit against the Consolidated Chemical Company of Hunnicutt, Maryland. One hun-
dred employees suffered irreversible lung damage as a consequence of an accident at company's plant in India and are no longer able to work at their former jobs at the plant. The
average income for these workers was US $375 per year (in a country where the average
per capita annual income in 1977 was US $150). Lawyers for the injured workers are seek-
ing two million dollars per plaintiff for the lost wages they would have earned and for puni-
tive damages. Lawyers for the company argue that if the company is forced to pay $200
million, it could not afford to maintain the plant, which has been marginally profitable. And
while the 100 plaintiffs may gain in wealth, the remaining 3,500 workers who depend on
the plant for their livelihood will find themselves out of a job. The lawyers for the company emphasize that while the company was not at fault in the accident, it is willing to
work out some reasonable form of compensation. What is the dollar amount that would be
just compensation for each of the plaintiffs?

Measure of Relative Interpersonal Influence

To operationalize the model, a measure is required of the relative interpersonal influence of each actor on another. This measure is employed in the
matrix $\mathbf{C} = [c_{ij}]$ that enters into equation (4). This is an $N \times N$ matrix with zeros
on the main diagonal in which $0 \leq c_{ij} \leq 1$ and $\Sigma_j^N \ c_{ij} = 1$. The construct c_{ij} is the
relative direct influence of the opinion of actor j on actor i.

In other work (Friedkin 1998), an approach has been developed to $\mathbf{C}$ that
derives a measure from features of structure of the communication network in
which two actors are situated. Friedkin's approach assumes that the communication network structure has *evolved* to reflect actors' power bases (French and
Raven 1959). In experimental settings this same approach could be taken if it

were based on observational data on the frequency and nature of the communications that occur in a small group. However, we have adopted a cruder, but serviceable, approach that relies on subjects' assessments of the relative influence of other subjects in forming their final opinion on an issue (Hunter 1953; Laumann and Pappi 1976, chap. 5; Merton 1968, chap. 12; Tannenbaum 1974).

The present approach to the matrix of relative interpersonal influences (i.e., C) has strengths and weaknesses. A strength is that power bases can only translate into direct interpersonal influence if they are *perceived*. Thus, for example, French and Raven's (1959) exegesis of power bases emphasizes the *perceptual* mediation of interpersonal influence. However, there are obvious difficulties, involving bias and random error, with relying on subjective reports. A key concern is the occurrence of bias; for example, actors may underestimate the influence of other actors and inflate their own importance. We mitigate the effects of such bias by drawing only on the *relative* values of the subjective reports for a measure of the relative influence of other actors. Another concern is whether actors can accurately disentangle the relative influences of multiple actors on them, especially where there is not a dominant actor whose influence is evident.[8] To the extent that this task is prone to error, the measure of C will be flawed, and errors will be introduced into some of our predictions.

To solicit information on relative interpersonal influences, we asked our subjects (after recording their final opinions on an issue) to estimate the extent to which each other group member influenced their final opinion:

> You have been given a total of 20 poker chips. Each chip represents influence upon your final opinion. Divide the chips into two piles, *Pile A* and *Pile B*. *Pile A* will represent the extent to which the conversations you had with the other persons influenced your final opinion. *Pile B* will represent the extent to which the conversations you had with the other persons did not influence your final opinion.
>
> Now place *Pile B* to the side and focus only on *Pile A*. Consider the extent to which you feel each member of the group influenced your own final opinion. Distribute the chips in *Pile A* into piles for each of the other members of the group according to how much they influenced your final opinion.

Based on these data, the measure of relative interpersonal influence, c_{ij}, is the number of "chips" that actor i accords to actor j divided by the total number of "chips" that actor i accorded to all other members of the group (i.e., the number of chips in *Pile A*).

A potential weakness of this measurement of the influence network in a group is that it is based on information subjects provide *after* they have completed their discussion of an issue. However, the influence network that is formed in a group on an issue is significantly associated with the opinion outcomes of the group on the next issue resolution trial (these results are available upon request). These results are consistent with a degree of stability in the influence network of a group across issues and lend support to our measure of the influence network. We rely on the posterior subjective assessments of subjects for the specification of their interpersonal influences because such assessments are most likely to take into account the specific influences among them on each issue under discussion.

A Subjective Measure of Actor's Susceptibility to Interpersonal Influence

Note that as part of the task described above, subjects were asked to assess the extent to which the conversations they had with the other persons did not influence their final opinion (i.e., the relative size of *Pile B*). These data correspond to an actor's *self-weight* ($w_{ii} = 1 - a_{ii}$) but were not employed to operationalize the model. Thus, we are able to inquire whether the parameter values for actors' susceptibilities to interpersonal influence (i.e., the a_{ii} which have been derived analytically) correspond to the *perceived* extent to which an actor has been influenced by other actors.

This measure, a subject's report on extent with which other actors have *not* influenced his or her opinion, is likely to be heavily biased by subjects' tendency to inflate their own importance. Such bias will be reflected in the intercept of the regression of a_{ii} on s_{ii}

$$a_{ii} = b_0 + b_1 s_{ii} + e_i, \qquad (21)$$

where s_{ii} is one minus the relative size of *Pile B*. Hence, we may rely on a test of the significance of b_1 (or more simply the correlation coefficient) to assess this association.

RESULTS

Table 2 reports the results of regressing the mean equilibrium opinion of the members of a group on the predicted mean opinion for the group. When a group has achieved consensus, the mean equilibrium opinion is simply that consensus. For each size group—dyad, triad, and tetrad—we report the results for groups that reached consensus (panel a) and groups that did not reach consensus (panel b). The model predicts group outcomes (in the case of consensus) and mean opinions (in the case of disagreement in a group) with a high degree of accuracy. The prediction is modestly less accurate for dyads than for triads and tetrads. The 90 percent confidence intervals are consistent with parameter values of zero (0) for the intercepts and one (1) for the slopes. In other analyses, which are not reported, this pattern of confidence intervals and high R-squares is maintained with two exceptions in samples that are divided according to issue (i.e., instead of the occurrence of consensus). One exception occurs in tetrads dealing with the disaster issue where the 95 percent confidence interval for the slope is [.673, .988], and the other exception occurs in dyads dealing with the surgery issue where the 95 percent

Table 2.   Unstandardized OLS Coefficients from the Regression of Observed
Mean Final Opinion of Group Members on Their Predicted
Mean Final Opinion in Different Size Groups

(a) Groups that did not form a consensus

	Tetrads	Triads	Dyads
Predicted Group Mean	.997***	.999***	1.031***
	(.004)	(.014)	(.050)
Constant	−2.903	.400	−2.149
	(1.636)	(.926)	(3.346)
R-square	.999	.991	.940
Number of cases	40	45	29

(b) Groups that reached consensus

	Tetrads	Triads	Dyads
Predicted Group Mean	.999***	1.019***	.949***
	(.012)	(.021)	(.096)
Constant	−8.996	−1.379	3.993
	(5.684)	(1.282)	(6.224)
R-square	.986	.979	.703
Number of cases	210	51	43

Notes: $* < .05 ** < .01 *** < .001$.
Standard errors are in parentheses.

confidence intervals for the intercept and slope are [1.936, 22.321] and [.706, .988] respectively.

Social psychological investigations of interpersonal influence have been split between psychological investigations that have tended to assume that pressures toward accommodation result in a movement toward the mean of initial opinions and sociological investigations that have tended to assume that such pressures result in a structure of stratification or domination. Both compromise and domination (inequality) are evident in the outcomes of small groups and, hence, a general model of social influence should allow for both.

Table 3 describes a simple typology of group outcomes: (a) consensus versus disagreement outcomes, (b) in the case of consensus, whether the agreement is a new compromise position or one of the existing initial opinions of a group member, and (c) in the case of a consensus on one of the members' initial opinions, whether the initial opinion is one of the two most extreme opinions or not. If the

Table 3. A Typology of Group Outcomes

	Dyads	Triads	Tetrads
Consensus			
Consensus on an extreme initial opinion	17	18	31
Consensus on an internal initial opinion	0	13	73
Consensus on a new opinion	26	20	106
Disagreement	29	45	40
Total Number of Cases	72	96	250

Table 4. Pearson Product-Moment Correlations of Actors' Subjective Experience of Interpersonal Influence and the Derived Coefficient of Actor's Susceptibility to Such Influence

	Tetrads	Triads	Dyads
Surgery	.460***	.695***	.518***
	(200)	(96)	(71)
School	.389***	.769***	.609***
	(200)	(96)	(72)
Sports	.314***	.685***	
	(200)	(96)	
Asbestos	.439***		
	(200)		
Disaster	.562***		
	(200)		

Notes: ***$p < .001$ (1-tailed).
              Number of cases in parentheses.

consensus involves a settlement on one of the two most extreme opinions in a group, the case is described as an instance of "consensus on an extreme initial opinion." If the consensus involves a settlement on an initial opinion that is *not* one of the two most extreme opinions in a group, the case is described as an instance of "consensus on an internal initial opinion." Finally, if the consensus involves a settlement upon an opinion that is not one of the group members' initial opinions, the case is described as an instance of "consensus on a new opinion."

The distribution of cases shows that group outcomes take a variety of forms and that no particular form is dominant. Obviously, it cannot be assumed that groups always reach consensus. Moreover, it cannot be assumed that groups strongly tend to form a consensus on compromise positions that are not held by any member or on one of the alternative existing initial opinions; they do both with substantial frequency. Finally, only a structure of unequal influence is consistent with

Table 5.   Correlations of Time to Reach Settlement
(Agreement or Stalemate) and the Predicted
Inefficiency of the Influence Process

	Tetrads	Triads	Dyads
All Groups	.161**	.208*	.088
	(250)	(96)	(72)
Groups with no consensus			
Groups with no breach of initial opinions	.097	.049	−.065
	(39)	(44)	(24)
Groups with breach of initial opinions	——	——	.106
	(1)	(1)	(5)
Groups with consensus			
Groups with no breach of initial opinions	.259***	.339**	.310*
	(210)	(51)	(34)
Groups with breach of initial opinions	——	——	−.709*
	(0)	(0)	(9)

Note: Time and inefficiency measures are transformed into their natural logarithms.
      * $p < .05$ ** $p < .01$ *** $p < .001$ (1-tailed).
      Number of cases are in parentheses.

a settlement of opinion on an extreme opinion and such settlements occur with a substantial frequency.

Table 4 shows that the derived coefficient of an actor's susceptibility to interpersonal influence (a_{ii}) is correlated with the actor's subjective assessment of the extent to which the other actor(s) influenced his or her opinion on an issue. In triads and tetrads, the coefficient is equivalent to the aggregate relative weight of the interpersonal influences upon the actor. In a dyad, since there is only one other actor, the coefficient is equivalent to the relative weight of the other actor. All of the associations are statistically significant.

Table 5 reports the correlations between the observed and predicted rapidity with which a settled agreement or stalemate is reached in a group. The observed rapidity is reported as the natural logarithm of the time taken by a group to reach a conclusion. The predicted rapidity is reported as the natural logarithm of number of iterations for the process described by equation (1) to reach an equilibrium, where an equilibrium is defined as the attainment of $\max_i (\, | y_i^{(t)} - y_i^{(t-1)} | \,) < \varepsilon$, where $\varepsilon = 10^{-10}$, a small change in opinions from one time period to the next. Separate correlations are reported for groups that reached consensus and those that did not. The correlations are not significant in groups that did not reach consensus. Among the groups that reached consensus, the correlations are significant in tetrads and triads, but not in dyads. However, the expected association between observed and predicted efficiency appears in dyads upon further analysis.

In dyads there are a substantial number of groups (14 in 72 trials) in which the final opinions of one or more members are outside the range of the group members' initial opinions. Such cases are anomalous because the model predicts that all opinions must lie within the range of group members' initial opinions. These anomalies rarely occurred in triads and tetrads. In triads, a breach of the range of initial opinions occurred in one group in 96 trials and in tetrads such a breach occurred in one group in 250 trials. The association between the observed and predicted inefficiency of the social influence process is *negative* (i.e., inconsistent with our theoretical expectation) in the dyads with the anomaly and *positive* (i.e., consistent with our theoretical expectation) in groups without the anomaly.

Finally, we confirm the prediction for dyads concerning the efficiency of consensus formation: the production of consensus is more rapid in the 17 cases where it involves a settlement on an initial opinion (4.7 minutes) than in the 17 cases where it involves a settlement on a compromise opinion (8.4 minutes).[9] In three of the former cases, there was an initial consensus of opinion; when these three cases are excluded the difference is in the expected direction (5.0 minutes versus 8.4 minutes) but dampened ($t = 1.63$, d.f.$=22$, $p = .059$).

CONCLUSIONS

We have described the process of opinion change in a group as an interpersonal accommodation in which each member of a group of actors weighs his or her own and other members' opinions on an issue, and repetitively modifies his or her opinion until a settled opinion on the issue is formed. When an equilibrium is achieved, the result of this process is either consensus or disagreement.

The theory encompasses various classical situations in which interpersonal influence has been studied—conformity and minority influence situations, status orders, and factionalism. The distinguishing features of these situations are the structures of influence and distributions of initial opinion that they involve. We suggest that a single process of interpersonal influence is involved in each situation and different outcomes arise as a result of this process unfolding in a particular structural context.

This theoretical integration also brings together the psychologists' viewpoint on interpersonal influence as a strain toward the mean of actors' initial opinions and the sociologists' viewpoint on such influence as a source of inequality and domination. These outcomes—convergence on the mean of initial opinions and convergence on the initial opinion of a particular actor or subgroup—are special cases of our theory. Because the social structure of groups vary, the outcomes of groups can take a variety of forms. Opinions may settle on the mean of group members' initial opinions; they may settle on a compromise opinion that is different from the mean of initial opinions; they may settle on an initial opinion of a group member; and they may settle on more or less altered opinions that do not from a consensus. Because all of these types of outcomes are frequent, a general model of social influence must encompass them all. The applicability of the present theory to these situations is part of its appeal.

We also report evidence from three experiments on issue-resolution episodes in dyads, triads, and tetrads. We have shown that the model predicts the mean final opinion of group members with a high degree of accuracy. We have supported the construct validity of the model in two respects. First, we have shown that the analytically derived value for the parameter that indicates actors' susceptibility to interpersonal influence is associated with actors' subjective experiences of interpersonal influence in an issue-resolution episode. Second, we have shown that the predicted efficiency of settlements is associated with the observed time to reach a settlement.

The surprise in these data was the occurrence of a substantial number of final opinions in dyads that were outside the range of group members' initial opinions. The mechanism of social influence that we have postulated is not consistent with movements of opinion outside the range of a group's initial opinions. Because the settled opinions of actors are weighted averages of their group members' initial opinions, all of the actors' settled opinions are expected to be in the range of the group's initial opinions on the issue. For a dyad, this means that

$$y_1^{(1)} \leq \left\{ y_1^{(\infty)}, y_2^{(\infty)} \right\} \leq y_2^{(1)} \tag{22}$$

when $y_1^{(1)} \leq y_2^{(1)}$. Violations of this mechanism are infrequent, but they do occur and our theory does not explain them.

The research on group polarization comes closest to suggesting that there may be an internal strain in groups to breach the range of initial opinions. The strain, which stems from the interpersonal interactions of group members, takes the form of an escalation or reinforcement of an initial inclination of the group toward one pole of an opinion continuum. Clearly, given sufficient escalation, groups members' settled opinions might all lie on one or more positions that are more extreme than any of the positions originally entertained by the group members. Group polarization is properly viewed as a main effect on opinions that is theoretically distinct from the accommodation process.[10] However, group polarization does not provide an adequate explanation of the frequent occurrence of breaching opinions in dyads. If such polarization were at work, then there should have been more frequent breaches in the triads and tetrads, but there were not. Perhaps, polarization is inhibited by the presence of third parties (Simmel 1950).

Our current speculation is that in the intimate context of a dyad, members reported *initial* opinions that may not have been entirely fixed. It has been shown that subjects will modify a reported opinion, in the absence of any interpersonal influences, when they are asked to think about the initial opinion again (Tesser 1978; Tesser, Martin, and Mendolia 1995). We suspect that subjects involved in isolated dyads are more likely to reevaluate the grounds on which they formulated their initial opinion than are subjects in larger groups ($N \geq 3$), in which such reevaluation is inhibited by the more complex and pressing interpersonal environment in which the subject is placed. This is a testable hypothesis that predicts that the frequency of breaching opinions should be reduced in dyads if subjects are asked to report, rethink and rereport their initial opinion before group interaction.

We see two main tasks for future work. First, work on the measurement of influence structures should be pursued. The early work of Simon (1953) and March (1955, 1956) has not resulted in a program of research that attempts to develop quantitative measures of the direct (unmediated) interpersonal influence of one actor on another. Subjective data have been employed in the present study; elsewhere, a structural approach has been developed (Friedkin 1998). The task is to fill an $N \times N$ matrix with scores that accurately reflect the unmediated influence of actor j on actor i for all pairs of actors.

Second, the process implications of the theory must be explored. Simplifying process assumptions have been made to make our model mathematically tractable; hence, it is axiomatic that this model of social influence will be imperfect at some level. For instance, it is obvious that interpersonal influences do not occur in the simultaneous way that is assumed by the present model and that there are more or less complex sequences of interpersonal influences in a group. Moreover, it also is clear that there may be short-circuits in the process of interpersonal influence, that is, groups may jump to a resolution (through a social choice mechanism) before all possible opinion changes have been exhausted on an issue. Thus, the task is to assess the domain of behavior that the model may reliably address and to weigh the relative advantages of improving the detailed accuracy of the model against a potential decrease in its general applicability.

APPENDIX

There are various approaches for making the social influence theory described by equation (1) operational, which depend on the availability of measures for the theoretical constructs. We have developed the following approach for estimating actors' susceptibilities to interpersonal influence $\mathbf{A}$ when data is available on actors' initial opinions, final opinions, and relative interpersonal influences; that is, $\mathbf{y}^{(1)}$, $\mathbf{y}^{(\infty)}$ and $\mathbf{C}$ respectively.

Assuming equilibrium, the scalar equation of the reduced-form, equation (7), is

$$y_i^{(\infty)} = a_{ii}(1 - a_{ii})y_i^{(\infty)} + a_{ii}^2 \sum_{j \neq i} c_{ij}y_j^{(\infty)} - (1 - a_{ii})y_i^{(1)} \qquad (A1)$$

from which it follows that

$$y_i^{(\infty)} - y_i^{(1)} = a_{ii}(y_i^{(\infty)} - y_i^{(1)}) + a_{ii}^2(\bar{y}_i^{(\infty)} - y_i^{(\infty)}) \qquad (A2)$$

and

$$(1 - a_{ii})(y_i^{(\infty)} - y_i^{(1)}) = a_{ii}^2(\bar{y}_i^{(\infty)} - y_i^{(\infty)}) \qquad (A3)$$

where

$$\bar{y}_i^{(\infty)} = \sum_{j \neq i} c_{ij} y_j^{(\infty)} \qquad (A4)$$

is a weighted average of the others' settled opinions.

Hence, for $\bar{y}_i^{(\infty)} - y_i^{(\infty)} \neq 0$

$$\frac{a_{ii}^2}{1 - a_{ii}} = \frac{y_i^{(\infty)} - y_i^{(1)}}{\bar{y}_i^{(\infty)} - y_i^{(\infty)}} \equiv \Delta_i \qquad (A5)$$

and

$$a_{ii} = \frac{-\Delta_i \pm \sqrt{\Delta_i^2 + 4\Delta_i}}{2} \qquad (A6)$$

The a_{ii} computed from equation (A6) is a complex number for $-4 < \Delta_i < 0$, greater than one for $\Delta_i \leq -4$, and less than one for $0 \leq \Delta_i$:

	$a_{ii} = \dfrac{-\Delta_i + \sqrt{\Delta_i^2 + 4\Delta_i}}{2}$	$a_{ii} = \dfrac{-\Delta_i - \sqrt{\Delta_i^2 + 4\Delta_i}}{2}$
$\Delta_i \leq -4$	$a_{ii} \geq 2$	$1 < a_{ii} \leq 2$
$-4 < \Delta_i < 0$	complex number	complex number
$\Delta_i \geq 0$	$0 \leq a_{ii} < 1$	$a_{ii} \leq 0$

But assumptions $w_{ii} = 1 - a_{ii}$ and $0 \leq w_{ii} \leq 1$ imply that $0 \leq a_{ii} \leq 1$. Hence, for each real valued Δ_i the estimate of a_{ii} is selected to be the real number in the legitimate range $[0,1]$, which is numerically the closer (in the complex plane) to either of the a_{ii} computed from equation (A6). The resulting solution set for $\bar{y}_i^{(\infty)} - y_i^{(\infty)} \neq 0$ is:

(a) $\Delta_i \leq -2 \Rightarrow a_{ii} = 1$

(b) $-2 < \Delta_i < 0 \Rightarrow a_{ii} = \dfrac{-\Delta_i}{2}$,

(c) $\Delta_i \geq 0 \Rightarrow a_{ii} = \dfrac{-\Delta_i + \sqrt{\Delta_i^2 + 4\Delta_i}}{2}$

Note that this solution assumes $\bar{y}_i^{(\infty)} - y_i^{(\infty)} \neq 0$, which will be violated when there is an equilibrium consensus or, in the absence of such consensus, when actor i has an equilibrium opinion that is the weighted average, $\bar{y}_i^{(\infty)}$, of the others' equilibrium opinions.

When $\bar{y}_i^{(\infty)} - y_i^{(\infty)} = 0$ and $y_i^{(\infty)} - y_i^{(1)} \neq 0$, then $a_{ii} = 1$; this implication follows from equation (A3). When $\bar{y}_i^{(\infty)} - y_i^{(\infty)} = 0$ and $y_i^{(\infty)} - y_i^{(1)} = 0$, then a_{ii} might be any value. Actor i's opinion has not changed either because actor i was not susceptible to interpersonal influence or because he or she was susceptible to such influence but remained in the same position as a result of exactly balancing cross-pressures. The former situation (which corresponds to $a_{ii} = 0$) is more likely than the latter. Therefore, it is assumed that $a_{ii} = 0$ with the understanding that this assumption is a potential source of error in the model.

ACKNOWLEDGMENTS

This article is based on work supported by the National Science Foundation under Grants No. SES85-10450 and SES85-11117. Earlier results from this work were presented at the Jacob Marschak Colloquium on Mathematics in the Behavioral Sciences, Anderson Graduate School of Management, University of California, Los Angeles, March 1989, and at the Annual Meetings of the American Sociological Association, San Francisco, August 1989, and Miami, Florida, August 1993. We gratefully acknowledge the contributions of Karen Cook, Shawn Donnelly, and Joseph Whitmeyer to the collection of some of the data on which this article draws. Direct correspondence to Professor Noah E. Friedkin, Department of Sociology, University of California, Santa Barbara, CA 93106.

NOTES

1. Consensus production is a ubiquitous outcome of group interactions, but so are disagreements that cannot be reconciled except by social choice mechanisms. The theory focuses on the social process that leads either to consensus or to a disagreement that cannot be reduced by opinion changes (because the opinion change process has been played out). Horowitz (1962, p. 182) has commented that "any serious theory of agreements and decisions must at the same time be a theory of disagreements and the conditions under which decisions cannot be reached." This theory satisfies Horowitz's criterion; compre with Abelson (1964).

2. This weighted averaging mechanism is consistent with Festinger's (1953) viewpoint on interpersonal influence as a finite distributed quantity. He argued as follows: "When a person or a group attempts to influence someone, does that person or group produce a totally new force acting on the person, one which had not been present prior to the attempted influence? Our answer is No—an attempted influence does not produce any new motivation or force. Rather, what an influence attempt involves is the redirection of psychological forces which already exist" (p. 237). Extensive empirical support for the assumption of a weighted averaging mechanism appears in work related to Anderson's information integration theory (Anderson 1981, 1991, 1996).

3. An even distribution of relative interpersonal influences for actor i, that is, $c_{ij} = 1/(N-1)$ for all j, is assigned in the special case when actor i is not influenced by any other actor. For such an actor, $a_{ii} = 0$, $w_{ii} = 1$ and, therefore, the interpersonal influences on that actor are zero.

4. Expectation states theory assumes the same rank ordering of influences; hence, our definition of a status order is a stricter form of such consistency. A general formal definition of a stratified influence network represented by W is one in which the columns of W can be arranged such that $\text{col}_{j_1}(W) < \text{col}_{j_2}(W) \leq \cdots \leq \text{col}_{j_N}(W)$, that is, entry-by-entry inequalities.

5. This extreme situation of equality of interpersonal influence may be rarely observed because of the greater influence of the opinion that is expressed first in a conversation and other effects that foster unequal interpersonal influences. However, even with such effects, two actors may be approximately equal in their influences on one another and slow to reach a consensus in dyads. See our later analysis of the data on dyads.

6. These networks are the star {A-C, B-C, D-C}, kite {A-B, A-C, B-C, C-D}, circle {A-B, B-C, C-D, D-A}, slash {A-B, B-C, C-D, D-A, A-C}, and complete {A-B, B-C, C-D, D-A, A-C, B-D} networks. Along with a chain {A-B-C-D}, these networks include all the nonisomorphic connected structures (connected graphs) that might occur in a group of four persons.

7. Further details about the design and experimental procedures (including the wording of the issues, instructions to subjects, and forms the subjects used to record their opinions) are available from the first author on request.

8. An actor may or may not perceive the direct influence of another actor. For instance, an actor may distort or forget the origins of his or her modified opinion on an issue. An actor's opinion may move toward the opinion of another actor who has a negligible total influence on this movement; conversely, his or her opinion may not move toward, and it may even more away from, the opinion of another actor who has had a substantial direct influence. Furthermore, the direct effect of one actor on another and the total effect of that actor may not correspond: the total effect of j on i may be large, so that i's opinion substantially reflects the initial opinion of j, and the direct effect of j on i may be slight; conversely, the total effect of j on i may be slight, and the direct effect of j on i may be large. The absence of congruence between direct effect and total effect is a potential source of instability in the structure and legitimacy of an influence network (Ridgeway and Walker 1995). We believe that the stability that is often achieved in small groups implies a congruence between these two effects. We hope to address this issue in future research.

9. These cases involve the 34 dyads in which there was a consensus and no breach of the range of initial opinions (see Table 5). The standard errors of these means are 1.9175 and .7111. Assuming independent samples and unequal variances, t = 1.812 (d.f. = 20) and p = .042 (1-tailed).

10. Hence, Friedkin and Johnsen (1990) modeled this effect by including an additional coefficient, δ, that is independent of the interpersonal influences, $\mathbf{y}^{(\infty)} = \delta \mathbf{V} \mathbf{y}^{(1)}$. Compare this with equation (10).

REFERENCES

Abelson, R.P. 1964. "Mathematical Models of the Distribution of Attitudes under Controversy."
    Pp. 142-160 in *Contributions to Mathematical Psychology*, edited by N. Frederiksen and
    H. Gulliksen. New York: Holt, Rinehart & Winston.
Anderson, N.H. 1981. *Foundations of Information Integration Theory*. New York: Academic Press.
Anderson, N.H., ed. 1991. *Contributions to Information Integration Theory*, 2 vols. Hillsdale, NJ:
    Lawrence Erlbaum.
Anderson, N.H. 1996. *A Functional Theory of Cognition*. Mahwah, NJ: Lawrence Erlbaum.
Arrow, K.J. 1951. *Social Choice and Individual Values*. New York: Wiley.
Asch, S.E. 1951. "Effects of Group Pressure upon the Modification and Distortion of Judge-
    ment." Pp. 117-190 in *Groups, Leadership and Men*, edited by M.H. Guetzkow. Pitts-
    burgh, PA: Carnegie Press.
Burt, R.S. 1982. *Toward a Structural Theory of Action*. New York: Academic Press.
Cartwright, D. 1971. "Risk Taking by Individuals and Groups: an Assessment of Research Employing
    Choice Dilemmas." *Journal of Personality and Social Psychology* 20: 361-378.
DeGroot, M.H. 1974. "Reaching a Consensus." *Journal of the American Statistical Association*
    69: 118-121.
Doreian, P. 1981. "Estimating Linear models with Spatially Distributed Data." Pp. 359-388 in *Socio-
    logical Methodology*, edited by S. Leinhardt. San Francisco: Jossey-Bass.
Erbring, L., and A.A. Yound. 1979. "Individuals and Social Structure: Contextual Effects as Endoge-
    nous Feedback." *Sociological Methods & Research* 7: 396-430.
Festinger, L. 1953. "An Analysis of Compliant Behavior." Pp. 232-256 in *Group Relations at the
    Crossroads*, edited by M. Sherif and M.O. Wilson. New York: Harper.
French, J.R.P. Jr. 1956. "A Formal Theory of Social Power." *Psychological Review* 63: 181-194.
French, J.R.P. Jr., and B. Raven. 1959. "The Bases of Social Power." Pp. 150-167 in *Studies of Social
    Power*, edited by D. Cartwright. Ann Arbor, MI: Institute for Social Research.
Friedkin, N.E. 1986. "A Formal Theory of Social Power." *Journal of Mathematical Sociology*
    12: 103-126.
Friedkin, N.E. 1990. "Social Networks in Structural Equation Models." *Social Psychology Quarterly*
    53: 316-328.
Friedkin, N.E. 1998. *A Structural Theory of Social Influence*. New York: Cambridge University Press.
Friedkin, N.E., and K.S. Cook. 1990. "Peer Group Influence." *Sociological Methods & Research* 19:
    122-143.
Friedkin, N.E., and E.C. Johnsen. 1990. "Social Influence and Opinions." *Journal of Mathematical
    Sociology*15: 193-206.
Goldberg, S.C. 1954. "Three Situational Determinants of Conformity to Social Norms." *Journal of
    Abnormal and Social Psychology* 49: 325-329.
Harary, F. 1959. "A Criterion for Unanimity in French's Theory of Social Power." Pp. 168-182 in
    Studies in Social Power, edited by D. Cartwright. Ann Arbor, MI: Institute for Social
    Research.
Horowitz, I.L. 1962. "Consensus, Conflict and Cooperation: A Sociological Inventory." *Social Forces*
    41: 177-188.

Hunter, F. 1953. *Community Power Structure*. Durham, N.C.: University of North Carolina.

Isenberg, D.J. 1986. "Group Polarization: A Critical Review and Meta-Analysis." *Journal of Personality and Social Psychology* 50: 1141-1151.

Janowitz, M. 1975. "Sociological Theory and Social Control." *American Journal of Sociology* 81: 82-108.

Lamm, H., and D.G. Myers. 1978. "Group-Induced Polarization of Attitudes and Behavior." *Advances in Experimental Social Psychology* 11: 145-195.

Latane, B. 1981. "The Psychology of Social Impact." *American Psychologist* 36: 343-356.

Laumann, E.O., and F.U. Pappi. 1976. *Networks of Collective Action: A Perspective on Community Influence Systems*. New York: Academic Press.

March, J.G. 1955. "An Introduction to the Theory and Measurement of Influence." *American Political Science Review* 49: 431-451.

March, J.G. 1956. "Influence measurement in Experimental and Semi-Experimental Groups." *Sociometry* 19: 260-271.

Marsden, P.V., and N.E. Friedkin. 1993. "Network Studies of Social Influence." *Sociological Methods & Research* 22: 127-151.

McGarty, C., J.C. Turner, M.A. Hogg, B. David, and M.S. Wetherell. 1992. "Group Polarization as Conformity to the Prototypical Group Member." *British Journal of Social Psychology* 31: 1-20.

Merton, R.K. 1968. *Social Theory and Social Structure*. New York: Free Press.

Moscovici, S. 1976. *Social Influence and Social Change*. London: Academic Press.

Moscovici, S. 1985. Social Influence and Conformity." Pp. 347-412 in *Handbook of Social Psychology*, edited by G. Lindzey and E. Aronson. New York: Random House.

Ridgeway, C.L., and H.A. Walker. 1995. "Status Structures." In *Sociological Perspectives on Social Psychology*, edited by K.S. Cook, G.A. Fine, and J.S. House. Boston: Allyn and Bacon.

Sherif, M. 1936. *The Psychology of Social Norms*. New York: Harper.

Simmel, G. 1950. *The Sociology of Georg Simmel*. New York: Free Press.

Simon, H.A. 1953. "Notes on the Observation and Measurement of Political Power." *Journal of Politics* 15: 500-516.

Stasser, G., N.L. Kerr, and J.H. Davis, 1989. "Influence Processes and Consensus Models in Decision-Making Groups." Pp. 279-326 in *Psychology of Group Influence*, edited by P.B. Paulus. Hillsdale, NJ: Lawrence Erlbaum.

Tannenbaum, A.S. 1974. *Hierarchy in Organizations*. San Francisco: Jossey-Bass.

Tesser, A. 1978. "Self-Generated Attitude Change." Pp. 289-338 in *Advances in Experimental Social Psychology*, edited by J. Berkowitz. New York: Academic Press.

Tesser, A., L. Martin, and M. Mendolia. 1995. "The Impact of Thought on Attitude Extremity and Attitude-Behavior Consistency." Pp. 73-92 in *Attitude Strength: Antecedents and Consequences*, edited by R.E. Petty and J.A. Krosnick. Mahwah, NJ: Lawrence Erlbaum.

Turner, J.C., and P.J. Oakes. 1989. "Self-Categorization Theory and Social Influence." Pp. 233-275 in *Psychology of Group Influence*, edited by P.B. Paulus. Hillsdale, NJ: Lawrence Erlbaum.

UNDERSTANDING NETWORK EXCHANGE THEORY

Michael J. Lovaglia

ABSTRACT

Although Network Exchange Theory (NET) has been successful at predicting exchange behavior, it can benefit from a nontechnical explanation. Formal theories, because of their terseness and rigor, can be misunderstood or
ignored even by researchers in related subfields. An informal explanation that
stays true to the formal theory contributes to the field by increasing the number of researchers who understand the theory. Here, the foundations of NET
are laid out in an accessible way. In the theory, power is an exchange advantage produced by the structure of the network. NET predictions about which
positions will have power derive from the fundamental view that social actors
prefer more profit to less and some profit to none at all. If the structure of a
network allows a position to exclude others from profitable exchange, then
that position has power. How NET predicts where exchange processes will
break networks apart is explained, as well as how it predicts subtle power
differences among positions in networks. Nontechnical explanations can be
valuable aids to theoretical development by opening theories to the ideas of a
wider audience.

Advances in Group Processes, Volume 16, pages 31-59.
Copyright © 1999 by JAI Press Inc.
All rights of reproduction in any form reserved.
ISBN: 0-7623-0452-9

Network Exchange Theory (NET) guides one of the most successful research programs in sociology at one of the most difficult tasks in social science: predicting human behavior. It has also weathered attacks from those who dispute its claim to explain exchange processes in social networks.[1] The theory, however, faces a bigger challenge. As Network Exchange Theory has become more successful at predicting human behavior, it has become more complex and difficult to use. Many people interested in social exchange are daunted by the theory's technical language, mathematics, and computer programs. This need not be the case. The beauty, logic, and usefulness of the theory can be appreciated in a general way using plain language. Here, then, is Network Exchange Theory for those who wish to understand it, but who may not need the technical expertise used to predict behavior.

Many social relations involve exchange (Homans 1961; Blau 1964). Economic transactions are an obvious example. At work, we exchange our labor for money, and then we exchange the money for food, clothing, and a place to live. Exchange also occurs in more subtle ways. Suppose I go to a senior colleague for help with a problem at work. She will likely share her knowledge without expecting me to pay her for it. Nonetheless, an exchange takes place. Those who share their expertise gain prestige and social status in organizations. When I use the knowledge she provided to solve my problem, I acknowledge her competence and my dependence on it. She has exchanged knowledge for prestige.[2]

EXCHANGE IN NETWORKS

An individual who occupies a network position with rich exchange opportunities can profit from that position at the expense of others who have relatively poor exchange opportunities. In Network Exchange Theory, the advantage conferred by an individual's position in an exchange network is called *power*.

The bureaucratic hierarchy of an organization is one way to structure exchange relations in a network. For example, a junior analyst may not have direct access to experts in other departments of her company but may have to channel requests for information through her supervisor. Her supervisor, because of his position in the hierarchy, has the power to restrict access to information the junior analyst needs. More generally, social networks create patterns that constrain exchange relations. Some positions in a social network may have more opportunities to exchange than do others. Also, some positions may have access to exchange relations that are more profitable than are others.

Network Exchange Theory sets out to explain and predict the power of different positions in an exchange network. For example, consider a network with two kinds of positions, employers and workers. Employers have power over workers when unemployment is high. Employers can keep wages low because workers cannot find comparable sources of income elsewhere. Employers, then, are in a position of power over workers in the network. Those who occupy high power

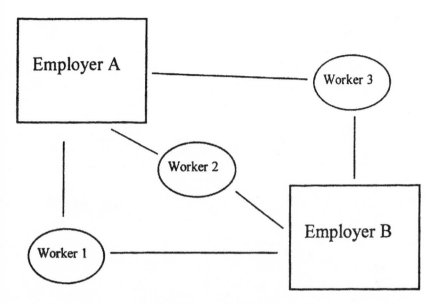

Figure 1A.   Labor Market:
All Potential Workers Are Equally Available to All Prospective Employerss

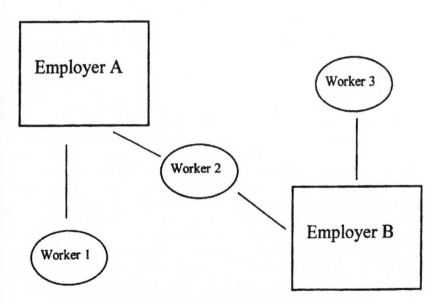

Figure 1B.   Exchange Network:
Network Position Determines Availability of
Potential Workers to Prospective Employers

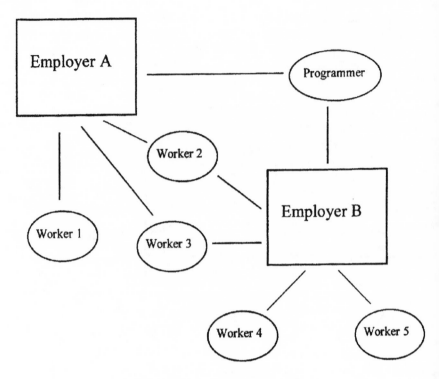

Figure 2. Exchange Network:
Terms of Exchange Give Some Positions an Advantage

positions in an exchange network benefit more than do those who occupy low power positions. When unemployment is high, employers can exchange a little of their money for a large amount of a worker's labor.

In some ways, the Network Exchange Theory view of social exchange is similar to that used by economists. Economists see social exchange as the product of two forces: supply and demand. They look at the network of employers and workers as a labor market. When unemployment goes up, the supply of labor increases, overmatching employers' demand for labor. The relative lack of demand for labor allows employers to keep wages down. With wages low enough, fewer workers offer to supply their labor. Supply and demand come back into balance. Both the market approach and the network approach share the same basic premise: Social actors prefer more profit to less profit and a little profit to none at all.

The network exchange approach differs from the market approach by identifying the structure of relationships among those who exchange (Wasserman and Faust 1994). The labor market approach assumes that all workers are equally available to all potential employers, as is shown in Figure 1A. However, employers and workers may not just form a labor market where all employers bid for all workers' services. Employers and workers may be networked in a particular pattern as showin in Figure 1B. For example, Figure 1B could represent geographical restrictions that prevent some workers from applying for jobs at both employers. More generally, some employers require certain types of workers. Some workers do not qualify to perform certain jobs or are not located where the jobs are. And nearly all workers qualify for several different kinds of jobs that may or may not be offered by different employers. Various constraints shape networks of employers and workers.[3]

The market approach assumes a large number of employers and workers, so that no one employer or worker has a large impact on the outcome of negotiations. Within a larger labor market, then, there can exist a network that gives some workers relative power over the employers with whom they exchange, even though the market is characterized by high unemployment. For example, computer programmers adept at the latest hot programming language may be able to choose among several competing job offers and command premium pay, even in the midst of a national recession. Those competing offers result from the programmer's position in an exchange network, as illustrated in Figure 2.

Suppose that Employers A and B in Figure 2 both have two jobs to fill. Each employer needs a programmer to fill one job and a less specialized worker to fill the other job. Less specialized workers face a tough labor market. They must compete with a number of workers like themselves who qualify for the two available nonprogramming jobs. Thus, some workers face unemployment. However, employers have more job openings than there are qualified programmers to fill them. A qualified programmer, then, is in a network position that has more exchange opportunities than it needs. Such positions have power.

You can see from Figure 2 that a programmer will be able to pick between the offers of Employers A and B. Thus, the programmer is in a position of power. Meanwhile, less specialized workers must compete against each other for the two positions available to them. Employers are in a position of power over the less specialized workers.

Network Exchange Theory explains how the pattern of relations in an exchange network determines the amount of resources acquired in exchange by different individuals in the network. Researchers interested in exchange networks would like to predict, for example, how much extra pay a sought-after computer programmer will acquire as a result of her position in the network of employers and workers to which she has access.

Network Exchange Theory and Research

Naturally occurring exchange networks can be extremely complicated. People and organizations are connected to each other in a variety of overlapping ways that can change unexpectedly. For example, events outside the workplace can pro-

Table 1. Terms Used In Network Exchange Theory

Term	Definition
Actor	Occupant of a network position which may be an individual, a team, or a corporation.
Exchange	A trade of one commodity for another that benefits both trading partners. Because exchange produces profit, in research settings exchange partners may simply divide a profit pool.
Network	A pattern of potential exchange relations among positions where all are connected by an exchange relation to at least one other position.
Position	The specific pattern of potential exchange relations connecting an actor to others in the network.
Power	An advantage in network position that allows an actor to acquire more than half of the profit pool when exchanging with a partner.
Profit	The resources acquired by an actor as the result of exchange.
Profit Pool	The total profit available to be divided by two actors as the result of exchange during a round.
Round	A period where actors may attempt to exchange—that is, to negotiate the division of a profit pool.
Structure	The shape of a network or part of a network, where the pattern of exchange relations gives some positions exchange advantages over others.

foundly affect the relationship between a boss and worker. A worker might inherit a large sum of money. Or, a boss might go through a divorce and start struggling to raise three children on her own. The effects of these kinds of changes on the exchange relationship between a boss and worker would be difficult to predict, even if researchers were aware of them. One strategy for studying networks is to start with a controlled set of simplified conditions.

Network exchange researchers study social exchange in simple settings, gradually increasing the complexity as their knowledge increases. For example, exchange involves at least two distinct commodities (using the word in a very broad way). Work might be exchanged for money, or security for affection. The value people place on different commodities varies for a lot of reasons. But because an exchange by definition always results in benefit for both parties to it (Homans 1961), exchange researchers often view exchange as the division of a profit pool. Some total amount of profit results when an exchange occurs. Power is indicated when one exchange partner can repeatedly get more than half of the available profit. Exchange researchers can pinpoint network structure as the cause of unequal profit because they have ruled out other factors by tightly controlling the conditions of exchange (see Table 1 for definitions of terms commonly used in Network Exchange Theory).

The standard network exchange setting contains a single type of exchange relation between individuals who negotiate the division of a profit pool. When two individuals exchange one valued commodity for another, they both profit from the exchange to some degree. An exchange by definition benefits both parties to it. Thus, their total profit from the exchange can be seen as a profit pool that they have agreed to divide. In network exchange research, exchange relations are simplified to the point where all individuals do is divide the profit pool that would have resulted had they exchanged two commodities. The size of that pool is usually set by the researcher. Most experiments consist of a series of periods in which individuals negotiate the division of a profit pool. Each negotiation period is called a *round* of exchange, and the profit pool between any two connected individuals starts fresh with each round. If individuals fail to reach agreement on the division of the profit pool by the end of a round, then they get nothing from that profit pool in that round.

In Network Exchange Theory, individual participants who occupy positions in an exchange network are often called *actors* because exchange partners can be persons or teams or corporations. When actors agree on the division of a profit pool, each actor receives the portion of the pool specified in the agreement. Actors who do not agree to exchange realize no profit.

Cook and Emerson (1978) created an experimental setting that has become the prototype for current network exchange research. They used a pool of 24 profit points between connected pairs of actors in the network. Each profit point might be worth about 5 cents to a participant in an experiment. So if two people agree on a 12-12 division of their profit pool, each would earn 60 cents for that round of bargaining. When two actors divide the profit pool equally, neither has demonstrated power over the other. If they agreed to divide the pool, giving 10 points to actor **A** and 14 points to actor **B**, then **A** would get 50 cents and **B** would get 70 cents. Actors attempt to negotiate exchange in a series of rounds. A 24-point profit pool exists between related actors at the beginning of each round of bargaining. Actors who fail to reach agreement on how to divide the pool receive no profit for that round. To explain how power develops in exchange networks, it is useful to think about network actors exchanging in this simplified setting.

Power in Exchange Networks

The term *power* has many meanings. Network exchange researchers investigate power as the advantage an actor may have in bargaining due to her position in the structure of an exchange network. Network exchange researchers control differences between actors to isolate the effects of network position on the profit that actors acquire. Power, then, is an actor's ability to acquire more valued resources than a partner when the two exchange.[4] If an actor can get 16 points when dividing a 24-point profit pool with a partner who gets the remaining 8 points, then the actor has demonstrated power over her exchange partner. Although this is a narrow definition of power, it has the potential to encompass important phenomena.

It is easy to see how, in a general way, social structures confer an enormous amount of power on individuals who hold certain positions in them. President Clinton, for example, occupies a position in the political structure of the United States. Although the political structure is much more complicated than a simple

$$A_1\text{---}B_1\text{---}C\text{---}B_2\text{---}A_2$$

Figure 3. Five-Line Network

exchange network, we can see that President Clinton's power comes almost entirely from his position as President of the United States. Although certainly talented and competent, Bill Clinton's capabilities as a person are not dramatically different from many more ordinary citizens. When he leaves office, his power will be reduced drastically because he will occupy a less powerful position. A look at the careers of U.S. Presidents after they leave office demonstrates the power of position. Recent Presidents Richard Nixon, Gerald Ford, Jimmy Carter, and Ronald Reagan have had little impact on public policy since they left office. The opinions of past presidents are rarely sought on current policy problems, and their attempts to help—for example, Jimmy Carter's diplomatic missions—may be taken less than seriously. As this is being written, former President George Bush has made headlines as the first past president to skydive, not for any contribution he has made to public policy. In society, power conferred by network position overshadows that created by individual talents and abilities.

ANALYZING NETWORK STRUCTURE

To analyze the power conferred by position in an exchange network, Network Exchange Theory starts with simple structures. Exchange networks can be drawn as diagrams with letters for positions, and lines connecting positions where a potential exchange relation exists. For example, consider the network in Figure 3, a five-actor network connected in a line.

Each distinct position has a letter. Mirror image positions share the same letter but different subscripts. For our purposes, one end of the five-line network is the same as the other. For example, A_1 and A_2 occupy structurally equivalent positions on opposite ends of the network. Lines between positions indicate exchange relations. A_1 can exchange with B_1 and no one else. B_1 can exchange with either A_1 or C, and so on. Recall the example of a network of employers who compete with each other to hire a few available computer programmers. B_1 and B_2 might represent programmers. Suppose that because B_1 wishes to work in a particular region of the country, she has applied for a job with companies A_1 and C. Meanwhile, B_2 has applied for a job with C and A_2. No other qualified applicants are available for the programming positions at the three companies. The result is the five-line network depicted in Figure 3. The primary goal of Network Exchange Theory is to explain the exchange process in a way that allows us to determine how much profit each position in the network will acquire over a series of

$$A_1 - B_1 - A_2$$

Figure 4. Three-Line Network

exchanges. Will programmers be able to command premium pay from employers as the result of their position in this exchange network?

Even in the relatively simple five-line network, the answer is not obvious. Suppose actors can only exchange once in a round of bargaining—for example, an employee may be able to work for only one company at a time. A good case had been made that C, being the most central, would have a power advantage. But Cook and colleagues (1983) showed that, in fact, the B positions obtained much more profit than not only the A positions but C as well. Despite its centrality, the C position was about as weak as a social actor can be in an exchange network. The B positions have a strong power advantage over the other positions in the five-line network. Computer programmers would command considerable extra pay in this simplified network. As the number of positions and exchange relations in a network increases, the difficulty of determining which positions have power increases exponentially. Further, we would like to know not only who will have power in the network but the exact strength of each position relative to its exchange partners.

Identifying Strong Power Differences and Determining Network Structure

The structure of the five-line network produced the strong power differences discovered by Cook and colleagues (1983). Network Exchange Theory determines whether such strong power differences exist in a network. How it locates strong power differences can be shown with two even simpler line networks. Network Exchange Theory offers the fascinating insight that all exchange networks can be seen as collections of simpler line structures leading away from a particular position (Willer and Patton 1987). If we know how exchange processes produce power in simple line networks, then we can use them to understand more complex networks. We can figure out the contributions made to a position's power by all the simpler line networks that lead away from it in the exchange network. And while more complex networks exhibit increasingly subtle variations in power among positions, decomposing complex networks into simpler components has proven to be a powerful analytic strategy (Lovaglia et al. 1995a, 1996).

The three-line network illustrated in Figure 4 is the simplest exchange network whose structure produces power differences among positions. Suppose that actors can only exchange once in a round of bargaining. For the three-line network, then, only one exchange can occur in each round. B exchanges with either A_1 or A_2 but not both in every round. One of the A positions will be left out in every round, but

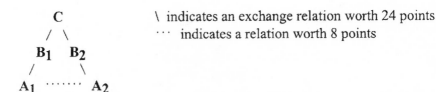

Figure 5. A Network with Differently Valued Exchange Relations

B need never be excluded from exchange. Over several rounds of bargaining, exchange might proceed as follows. A_1 might divide the 24-point profit pool 12-12 with **B**. Then, A_2 (who had been excluded and earned nothing in round one) might offer **B** a little more, thinking a little profit is better than none. A_2 and **B** might divide the pool at 10-14. Now A_1 who was excluded in round two might offer **B** more to get back into the bargaining. A_1 and **B** might exchange at 6-18 in round 3. This pattern might well continue over a number of rounds until **B** was getting almost all the profit, 23 of the 24 points available in each round. The structure of the network induces the **A** positions to bid for the single available exchange opportunity with **B**. Network structure gives **B** the opportunity to earn more profit than the **A** positions. **B**, then, has power over them.

Why does **B** have power over her partners in the three-line network? Network Exchange Theory explains that networks can produce power differences when the number of actors vying for exchange exceeds the number of available exchanges (Willer 1981, 1984). That is, if there are more actors than available exchange opportunities, some will be excluded from profitable exchange. Excluded actors, wishing to avoid another round of zero profit, accept less profit on subsequent rounds. Thus, if a position's location in the network allows it to control whether its partners are excluded from exchange, that position has a strong power advantage. In our example of the computer programmer, more companies required her rare programming skills than there were trained programmers available. The relative lack of available programmers forced employers to bid up their salary offers. By accepting a job offer with one employer, the programmer would effectively exclude other employers from the programming expertise they require. The programmer has power over the employers who wish to hire her.

The first derivation of Network Exchange Theory, then, is based on the premise that actors prefer more profit to less and a little profit to none at all:

> Strong power differences between positions in a network are induced by a structure that allows an actor to control whether its partners are *excluded* from profitable exchange.

It is important to emphasize that it is not simply exclusion from exchange that creates power but exclusion from *profitable exchange*. That is, power can be created when an actor is excluded from a high-profit exchange and forced to accept a low-profit alternative exchange. For example, suppose that as a result of cutbacks in defense spending, an engineer cannot find a job in her profession. Because there are more engineers than available engineering jobs, the engineer has been excluded from profitable employment. She then might accept a job as a teacher, earning about half as much as an engineer. She has been included in a low-profit exchange relation, but she has also been excluded from a high-profit exchange. We would say that she has been excluded from profitable exchange to the extent that the value of the two alternative exchange relations differ.

Cook and colleagues (1983) landmark study of the five-line network showed how power develops when exchange relations have different values. They tied the ends of the five-line network together in a low-profit alternative exchange relation as illustrated in Figure 5. The exchange relation between A_1 and A_2 was worth only 8 points as indicated by the dotted line connecting the two. That is, A_1 and A_2 divided a profit pool of 8 points when they exchanged. All other exchange relations were worth 24 points. Nonetheless, the high power, **B** positions had strong power advantages. Further, power reached its limit close to the difference in value of high-profit and low-profit relations. **B** actors could get approximately 17 points when exchanging with either **C** or one of the **A** actors, and probably would have gotten more had the experiment continued. The theoretical maximum is 20 because A_1 and A_2 would each get 4 points if they exchanged equally with each other. Thus a **B** actor would have to offer an **A** actor at least 4 to compete, leaving 20 for **B**.

Network Exchange Theory begins the analysis of power in networks by identifying strong power differences. Analysis of more subtle power differences can then be conducted on those networks that do not display strong power differences between positions. Networks are analyzed in stages—first strong power differences then weak power differences—because strong power differences can break networks apart. The next section describes the process by which strong power differences produce produce breaks between positions in some networks. Only after network breaks have been determined can further analysis yield accurate predictions of subtle power differences.

In analyzing strong power differences, Network Exchange Theory does not specify how actors process information about being excluded from exchange. It simply states that being excluded from exchange causes actors to lower their demands in bargaining. They might learn from experience, getting a feel for whether they will be excluded based on whether they have been excluded in the past. This would be a behaviorist view, or what Macy (1990) called a backward-looking actor. Or, they might search their environment for clues to their relative strength in the bargaining to come. This would be a rational or cognitive perspective, or what Macy (1990) called a forward-looking actor. Later, to make accurate predictions of the amount of profit actors will receive when power differences are small, the theory brings in assumptions about both mechanisms. Net-

$$A_1—B_1—B_2—A_2$$

Figure 6.   Four-Line Network

work Exchange Theory actors can look both backward and forward—at least a little, given the limited information usually available to them. But before analyzing weak power differences, Network Exchange Theory identifies strong power differences between positions and determines the location of network breaks.

PATHS OF POWER

Power develops along the paths of exchange relations in a network and changes when those paths change. We have seen how strong power differences developed between positions in the three-line network. One way to better understand strong power differences is to learn to create a network without them. By adding an actor to the end of the three-line, we make the four-line network shown in Figure 6. It turns out that changing the network structure in this way has drastic effects on how power develops in the network.

We now have four actors, all of whom can be included in the two exchanges that can occur in any round, A_1 with B_1 and B_2 with A_2. Because no position need necessarily be excluded from exchange, we would not expect strong power differences to develop.

The four-line is still simple enough for us to step through the exchange process just as we did with the three-line. Suppose in the first round of exchange, A_1 and B_1 agree to divide the pool 12-12. An even split seems reasonable. B_2 and A_2 might do the same. This stable pattern could continue with no power developing at all. But what if B_1 and B_2 agree to exchange on a particular round? Both A actors will be excluded and earn nothing. Because they prefer some profit to none, A actors might offer B actors more than an even split of profit on the next round. Perhaps A_1 divides the pool 11-13 with B_1, and A_2 divides the pool 10-14 with B_2. However, the strong power development that occurred in the three-line network—in which B ended up taking almost all available profit—is not likely in the four-line network. As long as A actors offer even slightly more than an even split to the B's, B actors have no incentive to exchange with each other and a stable equilibrium results.

Remember that Network Exchange Theory actors always prefer more profit to less, even slightly less, and even if taking a small loss now would result in a bigger gain later. Very intelligent B actors in the four-line might get together to increase their advantage over A actors. If B actors exchange with each other every so often at 12-12, foregoing the slightly higher offers of the A actors, then A

actors would increase their offers substantially. Network Exchange Theory actors are not that smart. They will always take an immediate small profit even if delaying gratification would result in much larger rewards later.[5] We might expect slight power differences to occur among positions in the four-line network, but no strong power differences should emerge.

Willer and Patton (1987) explained why strong power differences emerge in the three-line but not in the four-line network. In the three-line network, **A** actors have no alternative to exchange with **B** but **B** can exchange with either **A**. Thus, **B** has the structural capacity to exclude from profitable exchange one **A** actor in each round. In fact, **B** is required to do so by the structure of the network. **B** need not attempt to use power or even recognize its existence. **B**'s power derives from the structure of the network and the assumption that actors prefer more profit to less. When **B** accepts an attractive offer from an exchange partner, the other partner is inevitably excluded from exchange (Willer and Skvoretz 1997). In response, **A** actors bid against each other driving up **B**'s profit. In the three-line network, **B** has an alternative exchange partner while the **A** actors do not. However, if an actor is added to the end of a three-line network, one of **B**'s alternative partners now has an alternative. **B** can no longer exclude either partner from a profitable exchange. One of them can exchange with someone else. In general, having an exchange partner adds to a position's power. But if the partner has an alternative partner of her own, that power is reduced (Willer and Patton 1987).

Networks of dating partners are good examples of exchange networks that develop power differences. On a date, two people may exchange a variety of valued resources, for example, gifts, affection, intimacy, jokes, and laughter if the date goes well. People also may date more than one person over a period of time, so a network forms of people connected to each other through their interest in dating various other members of the network. The structural conditions that produce power are also present. A date generally consists of only two people. Others may have been excluded. For example, suppose that you are attracted to Kelly. If Kelly is also attracted to you, then the two of you can get together and both benefit. But suppose that Toby becomes attracted to Kelly. You are now on the end of a three-line network with Kelly in the middle between you and Toby. If Kelly goes out with Toby, then you will be excluded. You spend the evening alone. If Kelly goes out with you, then Toby will be excluded. Thus, Kelly has power over you and Toby. On subsequent dates, you may offer Kelly more than you otherwise would. To reduce the possibility that you will be excluded from a date, you might spend more money and wait more patiently if Kelly is late. You might go to a basketball game because Kelly is a fan when you would rather have gone to the ballet.

Power in the dating network changes dramatically if Toby has an alternative to dating Kelly. (We can probably add one more person to the network and still keep the names straight.) Suppose Lee arrives and becomes interested in Toby, creating the four-line network illustrated in Figure 7. Lee increases Toby's power because now Toby has an alternative date. Toby can go out with Lee if Kelly is not inter-

You — Kelly — Toby — Lee

Figure 7.   Four-Line Dating Network

ested. But Lee's interest in Toby affects more than just Toby's power. A more subtle and interesting implication is that Lee's interest in Toby reduces Kelly's power over *you*. Kelly no longer has the power to play you and Toby against each other. Your relationship with Kelly will be much more equal. Perhaps on the next date you can go to the ballet if you want. You may not even know Lee and be only vaguely aware of Toby, but their interests and behavior influence your relationship with Kelly. Changes in a network that occur quite a distance from a position can affect the power of that position (Marsden 1987).

The changes in power development produced by adding an actor to the end of a three-line network proved to be the key to the initial analysis of power in exchange networks. Power can be seen as rippling along the lines of exchange relations leading away from a network position. The first problem in analyzing an exchange network is to determine whether a position is high power, low power, or equal power with respect to its partners in the network. Markovsky and colleagues (1988) developed a general method for determining whether any positions would have a strong power advantage, such as **B** does in the three-line network, and if so, which ones. They saw the lines of exchange relations in a network as paths leading away from individual positions. For example, in the three-line network, A_1 is two exchange relations from A_2. The path leading away from A_1 goes through **B** then on to A_2. That is, A_2 is A_1's partner's partner. We know that a position's power is reduced when its partner has a partner. Thus, a path of two network relations leading away from a position takes power away.

On the other hand, adding a partner to a position adds power to that position. In the three-line network, **B** has a strong power advantage because she has two partners who do not have partners of their own. That is, **B** has two partners one exchange relation away. Thus a path one exchange relation in length adds power. The same can be said for all odd-length paths. Remember the dating network in Figure 7. Your exchange relation with Kelly gave you resources. You and Kelly shared power equally. That path to Kelly, one relation in length, gave you power. Then Toby arrived. You were connected to Toby by a path two exchange relations in length, from you through Kelly to Toby. That even-length path took your power away, giving Kelly power over you. But then Lee arrived, reducing Kelly's power over you and bringing your relationship back close to equality. You were connected to Lee by a path three exchange relations long, from you to Kelly, then from Kelly to Toby, and then from Toby to Lee. Odd-length paths leading away from a position add to its power.

Table 2. GPI values in Simple Networks

	Number of Paths of Different Lengths			
	1-paths(+1)	2-paths (−1)	3-paths (+1)	GPI value
Network and Position				
Three-line (Figure 4)				
A	1	1		+1 − 1 = 0
B	2	0		+2 − 0 = 2
Four-line (Figure 6)				
A	1	1	1	+1 − 1 + 1 = 1
B	2	1	0	+2 − 1 + 0 = 1

Just as odd-length paths add to a position's power, even-length paths rob a position of power. Adding another actor onto the end of the four-line network gives the five-line network shown in Figure 3. Recall that Cook and colleagues (1983) showed that actors on the end of the five-line network were at a strong disadvantage in power. At one end of the five-line network, A_1 is connected to A_2 (on the other end) by a path that is four exchange relations long. The even-length path robs A_1 of its power. In the same way, the even-length path between A_1 and A_2 in the three-line network that is two exchange relations long robs A_1 of its power.

The Graph-theoretic Power Index (GPI) is simply a method for counting up paths of various lengths leading away from a position (Markovsky et al. 1988). The result is an estimate of whether a position will have an extreme power advantage over its partners in the network. A position with a preponderance of odd-length paths will have a strong power advantage over a partner who has a larger proportion of even-length paths.

The GPI method is easy to grasp. In the three-line method, for example, A_1 has a path one relation long to **B** and a path two relations long through **B** to A_2. GPI gives odd-length paths a value of +1 and even-length paths a value of −1. GPI then adds these path values together. A_1's GPI value is $1 + -1 = 0$. **B**, on the other hand, has two paths leading away from it, one to each of the **A** actors. Both paths are one exchange relation in length. **B**'s GPI value is $1 + 1 = 2$. Because **B**'s GPI value is greater than A_1's, we can tell that **B** has a strong power advantage over A_1 when they exchange. Table 2 shows how paths are counted to produce GPI index values for the three-line and four-line networks. GPI analysis predicts strong power differences in the three-line network because the **B** position has a higher GPI value than either **A** position has. In contrast, GPI predicts no strong power differences in the four-line network because all positions have equal GPI values. Although GPI calculations are simple for some networks, they can be quite elaborate for others. (For details of the method and its application to complex networks, see Markovsky et al. 1988; Lovaglia et al. 1995a, 1996.)

NETWORK BREAKS

Determining whether a strong power advantage exists in a network is important because such relations can split networks apart. Network exchange actors always prefer more profit to less. If some partners always offer more than others, exchanges will never occur with the potential partners who offer less. Exchange relations that are never used cannot be included in a meaningful analysis of power development. For example, if a position has a strong power advantage, it soon is offered nearly all the available profit on each round. But suppose it is also connected to another position with a strong power advantage? The two advantaged positions will never exchange because they will not offer each other the large amounts of profit that their disadvantaged partners will. In effect, the network will break apart at that point. It is important, then, to determine whether such strong power advantages exist before analyzing the network further. Accurate prediction of profit in exchange networks requires first knowing the underlying structure of the network being analyzed. Then, further application of analytic tools such as the GPI can be used to correctly determine the relative power of network positions (Markovsky et al. 1988).

In general, when strong power differences exist in a network, the network will stay together if all positions are either high or low in strong power. Otherwise the network will break into subnetworks. That is, distinct, stable networks form when connected positions all have either strong power advantages or strong power disadvantages (Lovaglia et al. 1995a). Networks are also stable when no actor has a strong power advantage. Network breaks occur when an actor with a strong power advantage has a partner with an attractive alternative. That partner need not bid for the fewer and fewer resources offered by the strong power actor. The attractive, that is, less demanding, alternative will always offer more in exchange than will a very strong partner. Predicting where breaks will occur in a network, then, also follows from the assumption that actors prefer more profit to less:

> Exchange breaks down between very strong positions and partners who have less demanding alternatives. This breakdown produces independent subnetworks.

The discovery that power differences can break networks apart has broad implications for sociology. It shows how formal theory development not only illuminates a narrow theoretical problem but also produces unexpected insights into the nature of society. For example, it would be interesting to explain how actors might alter network structure to acquire a strong power advantage. Network Exchange Theory suggests that actors can acquire a strong power advantage in just two ways: colonization and monopolization (Lovaglia et al. 1995a). The analysis of network breaks implies that adding relations between an actor and others in the network will never produce a strong power difference. An added relation between two actors who both have a strong power advantage over others will not

Figure 8. Five-T Network

be used. Neither will a relation between a strongly advantaged actor and one who has an attractive alternative to the strongly advantaged position. And, adding relations between two disadvantaged actors allows them to share equally in available resources without giving them the power to dominate others. However, going outside the network to establish relations with isolated actors who have no alternatives will produce a strong power structure. This is the familiar strategy of colonization that nations have long pursued. The other way for an actor to acquire a strong power advantage is to eliminate any alternative exchange relations that potential exchange partners might have. This is a strategy of monopolization. For example, business organizations may adopt cutthroat pricing strategies to drive their competitors out of business. Or, a corporation may try to buy up all competing firms in a market niche. If successful, these strategies would produce a strong power advantage for the corporation. After eliminating alternative sources of supply, the corporation could increase prices to its customers virtually at will. Union busting is also a monopolization strategy. By breaking the relations among workers, employers can exloit each worker as an isolated exchange partner in a strong power network.

In the simpler realm of formal theory, the Five-T network illustrated in Figure 8 shows clearly how network structure produces breaks in exchange networks. Notice that A_1-B-A_2 forms a strong power three-line network with **B** high in power. The **A** positions must bid for exchange with **B** or be excluded. But **C** need not bid for exchange with **B**. **C** has a willing partner in **D** who has no alternative. **C**, then, is not willing to offer **B** enough to satisfy **B**'s demands because **D** will demand less of **C** than **B** will. The network breaks between **B** and **C**. The logic is simple and compelling. Further, Markovsky and colleagues (1988) demonstrated that the Five-T network does break between **B** and **C** as predicted.

However, you may have noticed that the analysis of the Five-T network is too simple. In even simple five-position networks like the Five-T, the problem for analysis is knowing where to start. Yes, A_1-B-A_2 forms a strong power three-line network, but how do we know that unless we already know that a break will occur between **B** and **C**? Why don't we begin by assuming that **B-C-D** form a strong power three-line network for example? GPI is such a powerful tool in network

Table 3. GPI values in the 5-T Network

	Number of Paths of Different Lengths			
	1-paths(+1)	2-paths (–1)	3-paths (+1)	GPI value
Initial Analysis				
A	1	1	1	+1 – 1 + 1 = 1
B	3	1	0	+3 – 1 + 0 = 2
C	2	1	0	+2 – 1 + 0 = 1
D	1	1	1	+1 – 1 + 1 = 1

Note that **C** appears to have two two-paths, one through **B** to A_1 and another through **B** to A_2. (See Figure 8.) However, the paths are partially redundant as both go through **B**. GPI analysis only counts those paths of each length that are *nonintersecting*, having no other position in common. Thus only one of **C**'s two-paths is counted. Given **C**'s GPI of 1, **C** will not exchange with **B** because **C** has an alternative in **D**, who has a lower GPI than **B** does. Thus, the network breaks between **B** and **C**. GPI analysis is then performed on the resulting subnetworks.

Final Analysis

Subnetwork A_1–B–A_2

A	1	1		+1 – 1 = 0
B	2	0		+2 – 0 = 2

Subnetwork **C-D**

C	1			1
D	1			1

analysis because it identifies strong power substructures within networks, allowing it to predict where breaks in exchange networks will occur.

Table 3 gives the GPI analysis for the Five-T network shown in Figure 8. Because the Five-T network breaks, a complete GPI analysis requires two stages. In the first stage of the analysis, **B** receives a GPI score of two while all other positions receive a GPI score of one. Thus, **B** has power over its exchange partners as indicated by its higher GPI score. However, Network Exchange Theory assumes that actors prefer to exchange with those partners who have the lowest GPI. The idea is that stronger partners, those with high GPI scores, will demand more profit from an exchange. For the Five-T network, Table 3 shows that **C** will prefer exchange with **D** who has a GPI of one over exchange with **B** who has a GPI of two. The network breaks between **B** and **C** because **C** will exchange exclusively with **D**. Stage two applies GPI analysis to the resulting subnetworks. A_1-B-A_2 is the familiar strong power three-line network. **B** has a GPI of two while the GPI of both **A** actors is zero. **C** and **D** form a dyad where GPI for both actors is one.

Table 4. Power Differences among Positions in
Strong Power and Weak Power Networks

	Strong Power	Weak Power
High	Progressive advantage: Comes to command nearly all available profit	Limited advantage: Can acquire 51% to 75% of available profit depending on network structures
Low	Progressive disadvantage: Eventually gives up nearly all available profit	Limited disadvantage: Can acquire 25% to 49% of available profit depending on network structures

GPI successfully predicts the distribution of power in the strong power structures it identifies (Markovsky et al. 1988; Skvoretz and Willer 1993). High-power positions eventually garner nearly all the available profit when exchanging with their low-power partners. However, if no strong power differences between positions exist in a network, then all positions might be equal in power (such as **C** and **D** in the dyad that breaks off from the Five-T Network in Figure 8). Or, as in the four-line network in Figure 6, relatively weak power differences might occur between positions. After GPI has ruled out strong power in a network, another tool is needed to determine the extent of any weak power differences between network positions. Weak power analysis was developed to determine which positions have a weak power advantage over others in networks where no strong power differences exist (Markovsky et al. 1993).

Identifying Weak Power Differences between Network Positions

The idea of weak power complicates the picture of exchange in networks. Being clear about the terminology of Network Exchange Theory will avoid confusion. Two kinds of power differences are found in exchange networks: strong power differences and weak power differences (see Table 4.) When strong power differences occur, advantaged actors need never be excluded from exchange but at least one disadvantaged actor is excluded on every round. The strong power structure prevents disadvantaged actors from exchanging with each other. Disadvantaged actors, then, bid against each other for the relatively few exchange opportunities with advantaged actors. An advantaged actor in a strong power structure is said to be high strong power. A disadvantaged actor in a strong power structure is said to be low strong power. As exchange proceeds over a series of rounds, strong power differences increase until high strong power positions command nearly all the available profit from exchange. Low strong power positions eventually get almost nothing.

Figure 9.   Kite Network

When weak power differences occur, a position has a power advantage over another. However, unlike strong power differences, weak power differences are relatively small and self-limiting. A position with such a small advantage is said to be high weak power, while a position with a small disadvantage is said to be low weak power (as shown in Table 4). Recall the example of the four-line network in Figure 6. A weak power difference exists in the four-line network because the **A** actors need only offer a little more than an even split of the profit pool to entice **B** actors into an exchange. In weak power structures, either no position need ever be excluded as in the four-line network, or all positions are liable to exclusion as in the Kite network. (See Figure 9.) For example, if **D** exchanges with E_1 in the Kite, then E_2 is excluded. **D** can also be excluded if the **E** actors exchange with each other. If **D** becomes too demanding, then **E** actors will find each other to be willing partners. Power in the Kite remains very close to equal for all positions, although **D** has a detectable weak power advantage (Markovsky et al. 1993). **D** is a high weak power position, while the **E** positions are low weak power.

In both strong power and weak power structures, power develops when actors prefer more profit to less and some actors are more liable to be excluded from profitable exchange than others. However, while low weak power positions face a greater likelihood of exclusion than high weak power positions, that likelihood can be eliminated by offering more profit to a partner. In contrast, low strong power actors face the certainty of periodic exclusion from exchange no matter what strategy they employ. By continuing to offer more and more profit to a high strong power partner, a low strong power actor can at best delay but not prevent eventual exclusion.

Weak power analysis operates on the premise that actors who are frequently excluded from exchange will offer more to their partners than will actors seldom excluded from exchange. This follows from our original assumption that Network Exchange Theory actors always prefer more profit to less and a small amount of profit to none at all. Actors excluded from exchange earn nothing. They are likely to offer more profit to their partners in subsequent rounds. They will earn less in each round but will be included in exchange more often.

It turns out that network structure alters the likelihood that a network position will be excluded from exchange. Consider the **C-D** dyad that broke away from the Five-T network in Figure 8. Each position has one partner. Neither is likely to be excluded from exchange. No power differences between **C** and **D** are expected to occur. However, we saw that the structure of the 4-line has quite different effects on the likelihood that different positions will be excluded. The **B** positions in the 4-line can maintain a weak power advantage over the **A** positions.

The four-line network is simple enough that the structure's effect on how likely a position is to be excluded can be readily seen. Suppose that all positions start out equally likely to reach an agreement with any potential partner. That is, we assume that no extraneous reasons make one partner preferable other than the amount of resources being offered. For example, family ties are not a factor. The structure of the four-line network tells us that the **A** positions will more often be excluded than the **B** positions. **B** positions need never be excluded. If **B** actors cannot exchange with each other, they will find an **A** actor who is willing. The **A** actors do not have an alternative and risk being excluded. If **B** actors are equally likely to choose each other or an **A** for exchange, then they will both decide to pick each other 25 percent of the time, excluding both A actors. Other things being equal, then, **A** actors will be excluded 25 percent of the time.[6]

In network structures where no strong power differences exist, weak power analysis concludes that actors less likely to be excluded from exchange have a small to moderate power advantage over partners who are more likely to be excluded. Network Exchange Theory can then rank positions in terms of the likelihood that they will be excluded from exchange. Those positions ranked higher are predicted to have a weak power advantage when they exchange with those ranked lower (Markovsky et al. 1993). Experimental studies in diverse settings have consistently supported the predictions of weak power analysis.[7]

As Table 4 shows, high weak power actors can command 51 to 75 percent of the available profit. Low weak power actors can command 25 to 49 percent of available profit (Lovaglia et al. 1995b). The next section describes how Network Exchange Theory predicts the exact amount of profit earned by actors in weak power networks.

Bargaining Resistance and the Magnitude of Subtle Power Differences

Strong power analysis showed that high strong-power actors can eventually acquire the maximum amount of profit possible from exchange. Weak power analysis ranks the power of positions in weak power networks but does not predict the exact amount of profit each actor will earn. For example, in the four-line network, **A** positions are prone to exclusion 25 percent more than **B** positions. But how much profit is **B**'s advantage worth? That is the fundamental problem Network Exchange Theory sets out to solve, and the one with which we began this paper. It is a simplified version of the question, How much extra money can that sought-after computer programmer earn as a result of her position in the network of employers and workers?

To predict how much an actor will acquire from exchange, we have to explain how network structure impacts the bargaining decisions of actors. How does network structure motivate actors to accept or resist the offers of their partners? The answer requires some assumptions about how actors process the information they have.

Network Exchange Theory assumes that actors who are frequently excluded from exchange will accept less profit when they agree to exchange. In contrast, actors seldom excluded from exchange will resist agreement until they get a favorable offer from a partner. Weak power analysis quantifies a position's structural liability to be excluded from exchange. However, for structural liability to have an effect on actors' bargaining decisions, actors must have some idea about how liable their position is to being excluded from exchange. A sense of how liable they are can come from experience, the frequency of being excluded in previous rounds of exchange (Friedkin 1992). Unfortunately, it is not possible to know in advance the frequency and timing of a position being excluded during exchange. If we did, we would be a long way toward predicting how much profit a position would acquire. The problem is more difficult. Network Exchange Theory must use only the information provided by the initial conditions of exchange and network structure to predict the profit each position will earn. We need some aspect of network structure that we can use to indicate the frequency and timing of exchange. It seems reasonable to assume that a position's structural liability to be excluded will determine, in part, the timing and frequency of exclusion during exchange. So, Network Exchange Theory uses a position's likelihood of being excluded—calculated during weak power analysis—to estimate the frequency and timing of exclusion. That is, a position's structural liability of being excluded is used to as an indicator of an actor's motivation to accept or resist the offers of her partners (Lovaglia et al. 1995b).

Actors may also estimate their liability to being excluded directly from their knowledge of network structure.[8] But knowledge of network structure is limited in various ways in different exchange settings. For example, when you buy a new car, you do not know the total amount of profit the dealer will make if you agree to a particular price. Similarly, the sought-after computer programmer does not know how much an employer can afford to pay for her services. In fact, the employer may not know. However, in most exchange networks, actors at least know the number of potential partners they have. You may have shopped at four car dealers, for example, and the computer programmer may have answered help-wanted ads from five companies looking for her particular skills. If the programmer had found a page of want ads for jobs requiring her skills, then she may feel she is in a strong bargaining position and will hold out for a good salary. However, if she had found only a single ad, then she might be quick to accept a job that offers less. In a wide variety of exchange settings, then, the number of potential partners an actor has can be used to estimate her motivation to accept or resist the offers of her partners.

In sum, network exchange theory uses two factors to estimate the relative motivation actors have to resist agreement with their partners: (1) weak power analysis of a position's liability to be excluded and (2) the number of partners a position has.

Given two connected network positions with different likelihoods of being excluded, we want to predict how much of the profit pool each will get when they exchange. Now that we have a way (although imperfect) to estimate an actor's relative motivation to resist the offers of her partners, we need some formula to determine the exact amount of profit produced for actors with different levels of resistance.

The resistance formula predicts the power of positions in exchange networks using actors' two exchange motives: hope for high profit and fear of being excluded from profit.

It seems likely that actors in exchange networks weigh competing motives in deciding how tough to bargain. Napolean I in his *Maxims* identified two motives that determine human behavior, hope for gain and fear of loss. Similarly, Willer (1981, 1984, 1987) proposed that actors' hopes of high profit and fear of being excluded from profit determine their resistance to exchange. Hope for high profit and fear of being excluded are motives one might expect of Network Exchange Theory actors who prefer more profit to less and even a small profit to none. For example, an actor frequently excluded from exchange may expect that pattern to continue, diminishing her hopes for future profit, and decreasing her resistance to exchanging with a partner. Further, an actor with many potential exchange partners may feel it unlikely that she will be excluded, increasing her resistance to exchange. Resistance analysis produces a mathematical formula that weighs these competing motives and predicts the amount of profit a position will acquire in exchange with a partner. All that is needed is some estimate of an actors' motives. Network Exchange Theory assumes these motives are directly related to an actor's likelihood of being excluded from exchange and the number of exchange partners available (Lovaglia et al. 1995b).

Resistance analysis produces an exact prediction of the number of profit points that a position will acquire in exchange with a partner.

By using weak power analysis and the number of available partners to estimate actors' motivation to exchange, the resistance formula produces highly accurate predictions of the profit acquired by positions during exchange (Lovaglia et al. 1995b).

While we are currently limited to simplified exchange situations with only one type of exchange relation, Network Exchange Theory has answered the question that prompted its development: How much profit does the structure of a network produce for an actor in it? The answer is beautiful in that it blends a few basic principles to tackle a complicated problem. At the same time, a complicated series of calculations is required to estimate profits in very simple exchange networks. Those calculations need not interfere with our appreciation of Network Exchange Theory's form.

An Outline of Network Exchange Theory

Network Exchange Theory explains how power in exchange networks comes from basic principles about how actors handle profit and how network structure alters the profit potential of different positions in it. The explanation has three main parts:

I. Identifying strong power differences and network structure

    A. The foundational premise of Network Exchange Theory is common to many other theories: Actors prefer more profit to less profit, and some profit to none at all.

    B. Network structure can require some positions to exclude others from profitable exchange. Excluded actors, preferring some profit to none, bid against each other to avoid future exclusion. Thus, systematic exclusion produces strong power differences in exchange networks.

    C. When multiple partners compete for exchange with a position, at least one must be excluded. That is, partners one exchange relation away from a position add to its power. However, if those partners have partners, then the position cannot systematically exclude them. That is, positions two exchange relations away from a position detract from its power. In general, odd-length exchange paths leading away from a position add power, while even-length paths take power away.

    D. When networks are seen as combinations of simpler advantageous and disadvantageous paths leading away from network positions, it is possible to locate strong power differences between positions in networks.

    E. Strong power differences can produce breaks in networks which, when identified, allow further analysis.

II. Identifying weak power differences

A. Having identified the true structure of the network including any substructures that result from strong power differences, weak power differences can be identified between positions where no strong power differences exist. Weak power analysis is based on the same fundamental premise: Actors prefer some profit to none.

B. Actors frequently excluded from exchange receive less profit than do those excluded less often. Network structure makes some positions more liable to exclusion than others.

C. Relative weak power differences are indicated by the likelihood that a position can be excluded from exchange.

III. Predicting the magnitude of subtle differences in power

A. To predict the amount of profit an actor will agree to accept requires an understanding of the actor's motivation to agree or resist agreement with a partner's offer. The analysis, as in the previous two sections, begins with the fundamental premise that actors prefer more profit to less and some profit to none.

B. Because excluded actors gain nothing from exchange, they are motivated to offer more profit to their partners in subsequent rounds. Offering more profit reduces an actor's likelihood of being excluded. Actors resist exchange and demand more from partners to the extent that they perceive it unlikely they will be excluded.

C. Two sources provide actors information about the apparent ease with which they can be excluded: the past frequency of being excluded and the number of potential exchange partners available. Network exchange theory uses the structural likelihood of being excluded as an indicator of the actor's perception of past exclusion.

D. The resistance formula calculates actors' resistance to exchange as a balance between two essential motives: their hope for high profit and their fear of being excluded. Network exchange theory assumes both motives are a joint function of the structural likelihood of being excluded and number of potential exchange partners.

E. Using the likelihood of being excluded and number of partners to estimate the actor's motivation, the resistance formula calculates accurate predictions of the amount of profit produced by exchange for network positions.

Network structure creates power for positions by making some positions more liable to exclusion from profit than others. If actors prefer more profit to less, they will reduce their demands and offer more to their partners when threatened with being excluded. Because network structure allows and in some cases requires positions to exclude others from exchange, some positions have the power to acquire resources at others' expense. Using these basic principles and focusing on the process by which exchange produces power in networks, Network Exchange Theory not only explains power differences in exchange networks but makes accurate predictions of the profit each position will acquire.[9]

FUTURE DIRECTIONS

Network Exchange Theory's success has spurred research in the field. Several researchers have developed competing models in recent years (Bienenstock and Bonacich 1993; Friedkin 1995; Bonacich 1996; Burke 1996; Yamaguchi 1996). In general, successful models agree on the fundamental principles of network exchange. Different approaches, however, model the exchange process in novel ways. For example, Burke's (1996) identity model views social exchange actors as striving to maintain an identity standard. When actors perceive that outcomes contradict their identity, they change their behavior in an attempt to reestablish that identity. The process of network exchange becomes a self-regulating feedback loop, like the thermostatic control of a home heating system. Using Burke's identity model, if actors' are assumed to have an identity which prefers more profit to less, predictions are very close to the observed profit acquired by various positions in exchange experiments—comparable to the predictions of Network Exchange Theory.

Work continues as well on simplifying and refining Network Exchange Theory. The fundamentals of network exchange have been worked out using a handful of network structures with five or fewer positions. However, the complexity of exchange processes goes up dramatically when networks have as few as six or seven positions. Simplified methods of analysis are advisable even with the aid of computers. A new method of identifying strong power differences and locating network breaks is being developed. It combines the process focus of Network Exchange Theory with the elegance of game theory solutions (Willer, Simpson, and Pennell 1997; Bonacich 1996).

Computer-aided analysis is perhaps the most promising area for rapid expansion of Network Exchange Theory, as it is in many disciplines. With successful competing theories available, computer programs are being developed to compare predictions of competing theories for ever more complex networks (Lovaglia et al. 1996). Those networks for which competing theories disagree can be culled for further analysis and tests using human actors. The potential exists for analysis of more complex networks than has previously been thought possible. A prediction of the profit that sought-after computer programmer can expect from her position in the network of employers and workers may not be far off.

ACKNOWLEDGMENT

Support from the National Science Foundation Grant SBR-9515364 aided the preparation of this article. Correspondence should be addressed to Michael Lovaglia, Department of Sociology, University of Iowa, Iowa City, IA 52242. E-mail: michael-lovaglia@uiowa.edu.

NOTES

1. References to technical articles and evidence are included where appropriate for those interested in further study. Everyone else may safely ignore them. The major innovations in Network Exchange Theory and much supporting evidence can be found in two books and four articles (Willer and Anderson 1981; Willer 1987; Markovsky, Willer, and Patton 1988; Markovsky et al. 1993; Skvoretz and Willer 1993; Lovaglia et al. 1995b). Willer and Szmatka (1993) provide supporting evidence from a cross-national comparison. Criticism, comments, and rejoinders in the debate over Network Exchange Theory can be found in Cook, Gillmore, and Yamagishi (1986), Willer (1986), Yamagishi and Cook (1990), Markovsky, Willer, and Patton (1990); Cook and Yamagishi (1992); Yamaguchi (1996); Markovsky et al. 1997; Bienenstock and Bonacich (1997); and Markovsky (1997).

2. Exchanges may be either explicitly negotiated or nonnegotiated. Network Exchange Theory has focused on negotiated exchanges. Other researchers have focused on non-negotiated exchange. See, for example, Molm (1990, 1997a, 1997b).

3. One way the labor market approach handles this is to specify a labor market as only those employers and employees that can exchange. Employee-employer relationships in society at large could then be specified by properly aggregating all the local labor markets. For more on markets and networks, see Berkowitz (1988) as well as Coleman's (1990) treatment of subsytems of exchange. A network approach would specify the pattern in which local labor markets are related, affecting labor relations in each market.

4. While an actor's position may enable her to acquire more resources than a partner, she might not use that power. One of the problems for Network Exchange Theory to solve is the extent to which actors use their power in different situations. See Willer, Lovaglia, and Markovsky (1997) for a more complete discussion of various conceptions of power.

5. See Erger (1997) for a model of exchange that presumes more intelligent actors. However, in designing network exchange experiments using university students, problems most often occur in getting students to recognize and make use of all the power that is available to them. Nearsighted, strictly rational actors in simulations can often do better than human negotiators. Testing a model of intelligent, gratification-delaying actors could be a problem because of the implicit assumption that human participants in experiments would outperform near-sighted, strictly rational actors. Theoretical and methodological development in this area could make a substantial contribution to the field.

6. See Markovsky et al. (1993) and Lovaglia et al. (1995b) for the details of weak power analysis. Predicting actual exclusion rates and frequency of exchange between connected positions may require consideration of factors other than the structurally determined likelihood of a position's being excluded. See Skvoretz and Lovaglia (1995) for one method.

7. Markovsky et al. (1993); Bienenstock and Bonacich (1993); Skvoretz and Willer (1993); Lovaglia et al. (1995b); and Thye, Lovaglia, and Markovsky (1997).

8. Network Exchange Theory here brings in the idea that actors are at least a little forward looking. Thus the theory assumes that actors make decisions based on a combination of learning

from experience and rational calculation. In most experiments with human actors some combination of the two seems likely.

9. Empirical studies focused on the exchange process include Skvoretz and Zhang (1996) and Thye, Lovaglia, and Markovsky (1997).

REFERENCES

Berkowitz, S.D. 1988. "Markets and Market Areas: Some Preliminary Formulations." Pp. 261-303 in *Social Structures: A Network Approach*, edited by B. Wellman and S.D. Berkowitz. Cambridge: Cambridge University Press.

Bienenstock, E.J., and P. Bonacich. 1993. "Game Theory Models for Exchange Networks: Experimental Results." *Sociological Perspectives* 36: 117-135.

Bienenstock, E.J., and P. Bonacich. 1997. "Network Exchange as a Cooperative Game." *Rationality and Society* 9: 36-65.

Blau, P.M. 1964. *Exchange and Power in Social Life*. New York: Wiley.

Bonacich, P. 1996. "A Psychological Basis for a Structural Theory of Power in Exchange Networks." Presented to the Annual Meeting of the American Sociological Association, August, New York.

Burke, P.J. 1996. "An Identity Model of Network Exchange." *American Sociological Review* 62: 134-150.

Coleman, J.S. 1990. *Foundations of Social Theory*. Cambridge, MA: Belknap.

Cook, K.S., and R.M. Emerson. 1978. "Power, Equity and Commitment in Exchange Networks." *American Sociological Review* 43: 721-739.

Cook, K.S., and T. Yamagishi. 1992. "Power in Exchange Networks: A Power-Dependence Formulation." *Social Networks* 14: 245-265.

Cook, K.S., R.M. Emerson, M.R. Gillmore, and T. Yamagishi. 1983. "The Distribution of Power in Exchange Networks: Theory and Experimental Results." *American Journal of Sociology* 89: 275-305.

Cook, K.S., M.R. Gillmore, and T. Yamagishi. 1986. "Point and Line Vulnerability as Bases for Predicting the Distribution of Power in Exchange Networks: Reply to Willer." *American Journal of Sociology* 92: 445-448.

Erger, J.S. 1997. The Emergence of Cooperation in Exchange Networks. Ph.D. dissertation. University of Iowa.

Friedkin, N.E. 1992. "An Expected Value Model of Social Power: Predictions for Selected Exchange Networks." *Social Networks* 14: 213-229.

Friedkin, N.E. 1995. "The Incidence of Exchange Networks." *Social Psychology Quarterly* 58: 213-221.

Homans, G.C. 1961. *Social Behavior: Its Elementary Forms*. New York: Harcourt Brace Jovanovich.

Lovaglia, M.J., J. Skvoretz, B. Markovsky, and D. Willer. 1995a. "Assessing Fundamental Power Differences in Exchange Networks: Iterative GPI." *Current Research in Social Psychology* 1:8-15 <http://www.uiowa.edu/~grpproc>.

Lovaglia, M.J., J. Skvoretz, D. Willer, and B. Markovsky. 1995b. "Negotiated Exchanges in Social Networks." *Social Forces* 74: 123-155.

Lovaglia, M.J., J. Skvoretz, B. Markovsky, and D. Willer. 1996. "Automated Theoretical Analysis of Exchange Networks." *Connections* 19: 38-52.

Macy, M.W. 1990. "Learning Theory and the Logic of Critical Mass." *American Sociological Review* 55: 809-826.

Markovsky, B. 1997. "Network Games." *Rationality and Society* 9:67-90.

Markovsky, B., J. Skvoretz, D. Willer, M.J. Lovaglia, and J. Erger. 1993. "The Seeds of Weak Power: an Extension of Network Exchange Theory." *American Sociological Review* 58: 197-209.

Markovsky, B., D. Willer, and T. Patton. 1988. "Power Relations in Exchange Networks." *American Sociological Review* 53: 220-236.

Markovsky, B., D. Willer, and T. Patton. 1990. "Theory, Evidence and Intuition." (Reply to Yamagishi and Cook.) *American Sociological Review* 55: 300-305.

Markovsky, B., D. Willer, B. Simpson, and M.J. Lovaglia. 1997. "Power in Exchange Networks: Critique of a New Theory." *American Sociological Review* 62: 833-837.

Marsden, P.V. 1987. "Elements of Interactor Dependence." Pp. 130-148 in *Social Exchange Theory*, edited by Karen S. Cook. Newbury Park, CA: Sage.

Molm, L.D. 1990. "Structure, Action and Outcomes: The Dynamics of Power in Exchange Relations." *American Sociological Review* 55: 427-447.

Molm, L.D. 1997a. "Risk and Power Use: Constraints on the Use of Coercion in Exchange." *American Sociological Review* 62: 113-133.

Molm, L.D. 1997b. *Coercive Power in Social Exchange*. Cambridge: Cambridge University Press.

Skvoretz, J., and M.J. Lovaglia. 1995. "Who Exchanges with Whom: Structural Determinants of Exchange Frequency in Negotiated Exchange Networks." *Social Psychology Quarterly* 58: 163-177.

Skvoretz, J., and D. Willer. 1993. "Exclusion and Power: A Test of Four Theories of Power in Exchange Networks." *American Sociological Review* 58: 801-818.

Skvoretz, J., and P. Zhang. 1997. "Actors' Responses to Outcomes in Exchange Networks: The Process of Power Development." *Sociological Perspectives* 40: 183-197.

Thye, S., M.J. Lovaglia, and B. Markovsky. 1997. "Responses to Social Exchange and Social Exclusion in Networks." *Social Forces* 75: 571-603.

Wasserman, S., and K. Faust. 1994. *Social Network Analysis: Methods and Applications*. Cambridge: Cambridge University Press.

Willer, D. 1981. "Quantity and Network Structure." Pp. 109-127 in *Networks, Exchange and Coercion*, edited by David Willer and Bo Anderson. New York: Elsevier/Greenwood.

Willer, D. 1984. "Analysis and Composition as Theoretic Procedures." *Journal of Mathematical Sociology* 10: 241-270.

Willer, D. 1986. "Vulnerability and the Location of Power Positions: Comment on Cook, Emerson, Gillmore, and Yamagishi." *American Journal of Sociology* 92: 441-444.

Willer, D. 1987. *Theory and the Experimental Investigation of Social Structures*. New York: Gordon and Breach.

Willer, D., and B. Anderson, eds. 1981. *Networks, Exchange and Coercion*. New York: Elsevier/Greenwood.

Willer, D., and T. Patton. 1987. "The Development of Network Exchange Theory." Pp. 199-242 in *Advances in Group Processes*, Vol. 4, edited by E.J. Lawler and B. Markovsky. Greenwich, CT: JAI Press.

Willer, D., and J. Skvoretz. 1997. "Games and Structures." *Rationality and Society* 9: 5-35.

Willer, D., and J. Szmatka. 1993. "Cross-National Experimental Investigations of Elementary Theory: Implications for the Generality of the Theory and the Autonomy of Social Structure." Pp. 37-82 in *Advances in Group Processes*, Vol 10, edited by E.J. Lawler, B. Markovsky, K. Heimer, and J. O'Brien. Greenwich, CT: JAI Press.

Willer, D., M.J. Lovaglia, and B. Markovsky. 1997. "Power and Influence: A Theoretical Bridge." *Social Forces* 76: 571-603.

Willer, D., B, Simpson, and K, Pennell. 1997. "Breaking Networks and Finding Power Structures." Presented to the Annual Meeting of the American Sociological Association, August, Toronto.

Yamagishi, T., and K.S. Cook. 1990. "Power Relations in Exchange Networks: A Comment on 'Network Exchange Theory.'" *American Sociological Review* 55: 297-300.

Yamaguchi, K. 1996. "Power in Networks of Substitutable and Complementary Exchange Relations: A Rational-Choice Model and an Analysis of Power Centralization." *American Sociological Review* 61: 308.

ALTRUISM VERSUS SELF-INTEREST IN SOCIAL SUPPORT
COMPUTER SIMULATIONS OF COOPERATION AND PARTNER SELECTION IN SUPPORT NETWORKS

Andreas Flache and Rainer Hegselmann

ABSTRACT

The stronger altruistic feelings are among group members, the higher the level of group solidarity. This "altruism hypothesis" is intuitively appealing. However, the invisible hand paradigm suggests that instrumental reciprocity between self-interested actors may suffice to attain solidarity. Our analysis argues that the altruism hypothesis and the invisible hand paradigm are partly consistent for a central realm of solidary behavior, social support. We model social support networks in which individuals vary in neediness and are free to change partners. Computer simulations show nonlinear effects of altruism on social support. Consistently with the invisible hand hypothesis, a

Advances in Group Processes, Volume 16, pages 61-97.

dense support network may arise on the basis of reciprocity between pure egoists. However, as predicted by the altruism hypothesis, higher levels of altruism may foster social support in weakly altruistic groups. Finally, our analysis refutes the altruism hypothesis for strongly altruistic groups. In these groups, altruism may actually reduce solidarity in social support. Strong altruistic motivations drive overly compassionate weak members into mutual help, excluding stronger partners from support relations, at the expense of an efficient allocation of collective resources for social support.

INTRODUCTION

Traditional sociology predicts higher levels of solidarity for groups that mobilize positive fellow feelings among their members. For example, Durkheim (1912) believed that in primitive groups religious rituals bind individuals together as if they were blood relations, even if they are not (cf. Morrison 1995, p. 194). As a consequence, Durkheim points out that members are willing to comply with obligations of prosocial behavior, such as mutual help. Durkheim's analysis reflects earlier work of moral philosophers that suggests that sentiments, such as love, pity, or compassion, may be the driving force of solidary behavior. Classical authors, such as Hutcheson, Hume, and Smith, stressed the existence of benevolence, compassion, pity, empathy, sympathy, and altruism. More precisely, these authors claim an acquired or inherent individual motivation to take into account others' fortune. In his *Theory of Moral Sentiments* (TMS), Smith opens with the following statement:

> How selfish soever man may be supposed, there are evidently some principle in his nature, which interest him in the fortune of others, and render their happiness necessary to him, though he derives nothing from it except the pleasure of feeling it. Of this kind is pity or compassion, the emotion we feel for the misery of others, the emotion when we either see it, or are made to conceive it in a very lively manner" (Smith 1759 [1982], p. 9).

More recently, Smith's claim was supported by a review of research into such altruistic behavior as blood donation, saving refugees, or voluntary contribution to community activities (Piliavin and Charng 1990). The study concludes that "theory and data now being advanced are more compatible with the view that true altruism—acting with the goal of benefiting another—does exist and is part of human nature" (p. 27). To summarize, Durkheim's discussion of religion, classical moral philosophy, and recent empirical evidence suggest a proposition that we call the "altruism hypothesis": The stronger the altruistic feelings that groups evoke between members, the higher the level of group solidarity.

The altruism hypothesis is intuitively appealing. However, the well-known invisible hand paradigm suggests that solidarity may thrive without altruism. Mandeville and again Smith are classical representatives of the paradigm. They emphasize the predominance of egoistic motives. These authors then argue that individuals' pursuit of self-interest may suffice to bring about collectively desirable outcomes. In *Wealth of Nations* (WN), Smith writes:

> He...neither intends to promote the public interest, nor knows how much he is promoting it...he intends only his own gain, and he is in this, as in many other cases, led by an invisible hand to promote an end which was no part of his intention" (Smith 1776 [1981], Vol. 1, p. 456).

Ever since Smith there has been an intensive discussion whether or how Smith's arguments are or can be shown to be consistent. Generally, discussions of solidarity in moral philosophy integrated Smith$_{TMS}$ (the author of TMS), while those in economics followed Smith$_{WN}$ (the author of WN). In the latter tradition, positive fellow feeling has no place in explanations of solidarity. Instead, research in economics and rational choice sociology argues that solidarity may result from the behavior of purely self-interested individuals. More precisely, solidary behavior is seen as instrumental reciprocity in exchanges involving contributions to others' welfare. Rather than positive fellow feeling, the conditions that sustain reciprocity explain solidarity. Hechter (1987), for example, focuses on individuals' dependence on group resources. Axelrod (1984) emphasizes that a sufficient "shadow of the future" may stabilize cooperative behavior in ongoing exchanges.[1] These studies suggest an "invisible hand hypothesis": groups may attain considerable levels of group solidarity without mobilization of altruistic sentiments among members.

This article argues that the altruism hypothesis and the invisible hand hypothesis may be partly consistent for the realm of social support. Certainly, to help others in need is one of the central elements of solidary behavior.[2] We propose a model of social support that identifies conditions for both positive and negative effects of individual altruism on supportive behavior. Our approach combines the notions of social support networks (Hall and Wellman 1985) and social exchange (Emerson 1972). We assume that solidary behavior is embedded in networks of help exchanges. In these networks, actors vary in their need for help and are to some degree free to change partners. To model individual behavior, we then integrate purposive action and altruistic motivations. More precisely, we follow Smith$_{WN}$ and assume that purposive actors aim to find exchange partners that are maximally attractive from their point of view. At the same time, we apply Durkheim and Smith$_{TMS}$ and assume that groups may evoke a certain level of altruism that modifies actors' selfish preferences. Computer simulations reveal nonlinear effects of altruism on exchange outcomes. Consistently with the invisible hand hypothesis, instrumental reciprocity in exchanges of support suffices to generate dense support networks. However, consistent with the altruism hypothesis, positive fellow feelings may foster social support in egoistic or moderately altruistic groups. In these groups, prosocial sentiments lead "strong" group members to neglect returns on investment and to form exchange relations with "weaker" partners. Finally, our results refute the altruism hypothesis for groups that are already strongly altruistic. Social support may suffer when the strength of altruistic motivations exceeds a critical threshold. In a strongly altruistic group, mutual support of overly compassionate weak actors may exclude strong members from exchange relations, at the expense of an efficient allocation of the group's resources for social support.

The remainder of the paper presents the argument in detail. In the next section, we develop the analytical point of departure, a game theoretical analysis of the effects of altruism on dyadic support relations. Then, we extend the model in by including partner selection. This is followed by the presentation of simulation results. The last section discusses results and puts forward conclusions.

ALTRUISM IN DYADIC SUPPORT RELATIONS

The dyadic exchange relation between two individuals, say Ego and Alter, is the basic building block of support networks. In our analysis, the exchange outcomes that actors expect to arise from the dyadic relationship shape their perception of the attractiveness of potential partners. Accordingly, the analysis of exchange behavior in the dyad is the first step in modeling the partner selection process in the network. In this section we therefore ignore for the moment the assumption that actors are free to change partners. We focus exclusively on ongoing exchanges in an isolated dyad. It turns out that our model of altruism in the dyad is consistent with the invisible hand hypothesis, because it predicts successful support exchange between purely selfish actors that face a future together that is sufficiently long. At the same time, we find support for the altruism hypothesis. Our analysis shows that the stronger individuals' altruistic motivations are, the more easily successful support exchanges may be attained. In particular, altruistic motivations facilitate those exchanges that benefit only the weaker partner in terms of pure self-interest. Moreover, our results show that the attractiveness of weak exchange partners consistently increases with the strength of altruistic motivations. However, we will later demonstrate that exactly this property of altruism may change the effect of altruistic sentiments on solidarity as soon as partner selection is feasible.

The following presents the model of altruism in the dyad. The exchange dyad is modeled as a repeated support game. The first subsection describes individual neediness and support actions in the game, while the second specifies the incentive structure participants face. Finally, the game theoretical analysis of both individual exchange behavior and partner attractiveness in the support game is presented.

Individual Neediness and Support Actions

We assume that the participants in the exchange between Ego and Alter are fully characterized by a specific level of neediness. Neediness reflects both an actor's capability to provide help and the need for help. More precisely, we assume that the capability to provide help and the need for help are inversely related. The more help Ego needs in a certain period of time, the less help he can give to Alter in the same period.[3] We feel that this assumption often is plausible for social support. For example, consider the effects of variation in hunting skills on the individual neediness for food donation in a hunter-gatherer group. Skillful members may both have more food to share with others and less need for food support themselves as compared to weaker members. Similarly, in a rural village only some members may be wealthy enough to afford expensive farming machinery. These farmers do not need to borrow others' machines, but they might lend their machinery to less wealthy members. Technically, we model individual neediness i, n_i, as a number between zero and one ($0 \leq n_i \leq 1$). Conversely, i's capability to provide help is $1 - n_i$. An actor who is maximally needy ($n_i = 1$), needs help "all the time" but he is not capable of supporting his partner. By contrast, an actor who is minimally needy himself ($n_i = 0$) never needs support, but he is capable of providing a full unit of help.

We model the ongoing exchange between Ego and Alter as a repeated support game that consists of consecutive iterations of a constituent game. For simplicity, both actors have only two decision options in the constituent game, to provide help (Cooperate), and to not provide help (Defect). To further simplify, we assume that participants make these decisions simultaneously and independently.[4] The effects of cooperation and defection depend on actors' neediness levels. The smaller the neediness of Ego, n_i, and the larger the neediness of Alter, n_j, the larger the amount of help that Ego gives (and Alter receives), when Ego decides to support Alter (C). Technically, we assume that Ego's cooperation gives $n_j(1 - n_i)$ units of help to Alter in the corresponding iteration. However, when Ego fails to support Alter, Ego provides zero units of help. Conversely, Ego receives (and Alter gives) $n_i (1 - n_j)$ units of help if Alter supports Ego (C). At the same time, Ego receives zero units of help when Alter gives no support (D). Finally, we assume that actors always face some uncertainty about whether the relationship will continue. More precisely, we model this uncertainty with a continuation probability α. The repeated support game may end after each iteration with a probability of $(1 - \alpha)$, whereas the game continues with probability α. Clearly, the larger the probability of continuation, the longer the shadow of the future. In the section on exchange behavior below, we show how this shadow of the future shapes actors' exchange behavior.

Table 1.   Payoffs in the Constituent Support Game

	C		D	
C	$R_{ij} = G_{ij} - L_{ij}$ $R_{ji} = G_{ji} - L_{ji}$		$S_{ij} = -L_{ij}$ $T_{ji} = G_{ji}$	
D	$T_{ij} = G_{ij}$ $S_{ji} = -L_{ji}$		$P_{ij} = 0$ $P_{ji} = 0$	

The Incentive Structure

The incentive structure actors face in the support game reflects the preferences of partly altruistic actors. More precisely, we assume that the exchange decisions generate payoffs that express costs and benefits of the exchange from the point of view of purely self-interested individuals. However, the utility Ego effectively derives from an exchange outcome may depend on both payoffs for Ego himself and payoffs for Alter, weighed by the degree of Ego's altruism.

To model payoffs, we use mutual defection, DD, as the baseline outcome that yields a payoff of zero to both participants. In the outcome DD, actors neither receive help nor provide support. Self-interested actors gain from being supported, as compared to the baseline. At the same time, actors incur some loss if they provide help themselves. More precisely, the larger the amount of help Ego receives, the larger his gain is. Conversely, the more help Ego provides, the larger his loss. Technically, we model i's gain from receiving help from j, G_{ij}, and i's loss as a result of giving help to j, L_{ij}, as follows:

$$G_{ij} = n_i(1 - n_j)B$$
$$L_{ij} = (1 - n_i)n_jE \qquad (1)$$

The parameters B and E are positive constants that weigh the benefit, B, of receiving one unit of help against the effort costs, E, of providing the unit. It is a central assumption in our analysis that self-interested individuals may in principle benefit from mutual support. To ensure this, we assume that Ego's benefits of receiving a unit of help exceed Ego's costs of "producing" a unit, hence $B > E$. Table 1 illustrates the incentive structure that ensues for the constituent support game. For consistency with the literature, we use the standard notation for the Prisoner's Dilemma game (PD) to denote outcomes and payoffs. However, notice that the support game is not necessarily a PD. We discuss the conditions under which the support game constitutes a PD further below. We denote the payoffs corresponding with the outcomes CC, DC, CD and DD as reward (R), temptation (T), sucker's payoff (S) and punishment (P), respectively. The subindices i and j indicate that payoffs vary for different combination of neediness levels. For example, R_{ij} denotes the payoff that an actor of neediness level i attains from mutual cooperation with a partner of neediness level j. Notice that the game is not necessarily symmetrical. Players derive different payoffs for corresponding outcomes, unless they are equally needy.

Table 2. Utilities in the Constituent Support Game

	C	D
C	$R'_{ij} = (1 - \sigma)R_{ij} + \sigma R_{ji}$ $R'_{ji} = (1 - \sigma)R_{ji} + \sigma R_{ij}$	$S'_{ij} = (1 - \sigma)S_{ij} + \sigma T_{ji}$ $T'_{ji} = (1 - \sigma)T_{ji} + \sigma S_{ij}$
D	$T'_{ij} = (1 - \sigma)T_{ij} + \sigma S_{ji}$ $S'_{ji} = (1 - \sigma)S_{ji} + \sigma T_{ij}$	$P'_{ij} = (1 - \sigma)P_{ij} + \sigma P_{ji} = 0$ $P'_{ji} = (1 - \sigma)P_{ji} + \sigma P_{ij} = 0$

Table 1 shows that cooperation in the support game may conflict with actors' self-interest. Nothing guarantees reciprocation within one iteration. Particularly in short-term relationships, self-interested actors might be tempted to withhold support. More precisely, not to help is always a dominant strategy in the constituent game, because $T_{ij} > R_{ij}$ and $P_{ij} > S_{ij}$. Exploiting a partner who provides help is the most profitable outcome for a selfish actor and to be exploited by a partner who fails to help is least attractive, regardless how needy the players are. Clearly, the support game may face self-interested actors with a PD structure. However, the game is not necessarily a PD. In a PD, both players prefer mutual cooperation (CC) to mutual defection (DD) despite incentives to defect unilaterally. In the support game, however, it is possible that only the weaker player may be interested in mutual support.[5] More precisely, when Alter is too weak in comparison with Ego, then Ego may not receive enough help from a weak Alter to compensate the investment in support of Alter ($G_{ij} < L_{ij}$). As a consequence, Ego may prefer mutual defection to mutual support ($P_{ij} > R_{ij}$).

Table 1 is not the game that partly altruistic actors really play. We assume that partly altruistic actors aim to maximize the utility of exchange outcomes, rather than payoffs. Only for purely egoistic players payoffs represent utilities. To introduce altruism, we model Ego's utility as a weighed mean of Ego's payoff and Alter's payoff (cf. Taylor 1987, chapter 5). The more sympathy, σ, Ego feels for Alter, the more Ego's utility depends on Alter's payoff.[6] More precisely, we assume Ego places weight σ on Alter's payoff and weight $1 - \sigma$ on his own payoff, with σ ranging between 0 and 1. Hence, a sympathy value of $\sigma = 0$ indicates that Ego is a "pure egoist," whereas $\sigma = 1$ expresses that Ego is a "pure altruist" who exclusively maximizes Alter's payoff. Moreover, to focus on between-group effects of altruism, we assume that the group is homogeneous in the sympathy parameter σ. Table 2 shows the ensuing constituent support game. The symbols $T', R', P',$ and S' denote utilities of the outcomes DC, CC, DD, and CD, respectively.

Clearly, with pure self-interest ($\sigma = 0$) the game of Table 2 is equivalent to Table 1. It seems intuitively clear that altruism ($\sigma > 0$) may mitigate or even resolve the cooperation problems that self-interested actors face in the game of Table 1. To test this intuition, the next section provides a game theoretical analysis.

Exchange Behavior and Partner Attractiveness: The Game Theoretical Analysis

Our analysis of individual behavior in the exchange dyad combines the notion of purposive behavior ($Smith_{WN}$) with the assumption of partly altruistic preferences ($Smith_{TMS}$). To model purposive behavior we employ economics' model of rational choice. The core of this model is the assumption that actors choose the course of action that maximizes utility. Alternative models of "goal-driven" behavior in social exchange have been proposed, particularly models that draw on social learning theory (Homans 1974; Macy 1991a). We use rational choice rather than social learning, because invisible hand theorizing has most prominently been elaborated in neoclassical economics and sociological rational choice theory (Coleman 1990). Accordingly, with $\sigma = 0$, our analysis is consistent with previous invisible hand theorizing, whereas we include altruistic preferences with $\sigma > 0$.

To analyze rational decision making in the exchange process, we use game theory. This theory addresses rational decision making, taking into account the interdependence of rational actors in the exchange process. Game theoretical analysis has revealed an intuitively appealing solution for the cooperation problem that self-interested actors face in the support game. Broadly, the solution is conditional cooperation in repeated interaction (cf. Friedman 1986; Taylor 1987). In repeated interaction, self-interested actors may be motivated to give support if they expect that their partner applies a help strategy based on reciprocity. Rational egoists may then refrain from exploitation of their partner in the present, because they anticipate that the consequence is to lose the partner's support in the future. However, there are two prerequisites for conditional cooperation between rational egoists. First, actors need to face a "shadow of the future" that is sufficiently long to deter defection. Second, mutual cooperation needs to be profitable from both players' point of view, that is, the support game is a Prisoner's Dilemma. To specify these prerequisites more precisely, we apply the game theoretical solution concept of the Nash-equilibrium.

In a Nash-equilibrium, none of the players faces an incentive to unilaterally change strategy as long as all other players also follow their respective equilibrium strategy (for a formal definition and a detailed discussion, see, e.g., Kreps 1990, pp. 402-410). Game theorists widely agree that rational players' decisions necessarily entail a Nash-equilibrium. Friedman (1971) applied the concept to indefinitely repeated games like our support game. To identify prerequisites for conditional cooperation, he considered a class of extreme strategies that are easy to analyze, so-called trigger strategies. A player following a trigger strategy always supports his partner in the first iteration of the game, but in subsequent iterations support is only given on the condition that the partner gave support in all preceding iterations. Hence, eternal punishment follows any deviation from cooperative behavior. Mutual conditional helping on the basis of trigger strategies constitutes a Nash-equilibrium when the probability α for continuing the relation in the next period is not lower than a certain threshold value α'. In that case, the loss that a defector faces from his opponent's retaliation in the future is not compensated by the short-term gain in the present iteration. For trigger strategies, the corresponding threshold continuation probability can be easily computed on the basis of the payoffs of the constituent Prisoner's Dilemma game (cf. Friedman 1986, pp. 77-89). Applied to the support game, Friedman's result yields the following theorem.

Theorem 1. The Cooperation Condition. Mutual conditional cooperation on the basis of trigger strategies is an equilibrium[7] of the repeated support game when the continuation probability α is larger than or equal to both α'_{ij} and α'_{ji}, where:

$$\alpha'_{ij} = \frac{T'_{ij} - R'_{ij}}{T'_{ij} - P'_{ij}} = \frac{((1-\sigma)E - \sigma B)(1 - n_i)n_j}{((1-\sigma)B - \sigma E)(1 - n_j)n_i} \text{ and}$$

$$\alpha'_{ji} = \frac{T'_{ji} - R'_{ji}}{T'_{ji} - P'_{ji}} = \frac{((1-\sigma)E - \sigma B)(1 - n_j)n_i}{((1-\sigma)B - \sigma E)(1 - n_i)n_j}. \tag{2}$$

Proof: Friedman 1986, pp. 77-89.

Figure 1 visualizes the effect of sympathy, σ, on the cooperation condition. To compute the figure, we assumed that the benefit of receiving a unit of help, B, is four times as large as the effort required to produce the unit, E;: more concretely, $B = 4$ and $E = 1$. The figures chart the largest of the threshold continuation probabilities a'_{ij} and a'_{ji}, as a function of the combination of neediness levels n_i and n_j. Between figures, we gradually increase the sympathy level starting with pure egoism ($\sigma = 0$). The white space in the figures indicates the range of (n_i, n_j) combinations where the support game is not a Prisoner's Dilemma. Equation (2) shows that in this region at least one of the probabilitities a'_{ij} and a'_{ji} exceeds 1. Hence, there is no valid continuation probability for which conditional cooperation is rational behavior if the support game is not a PD.

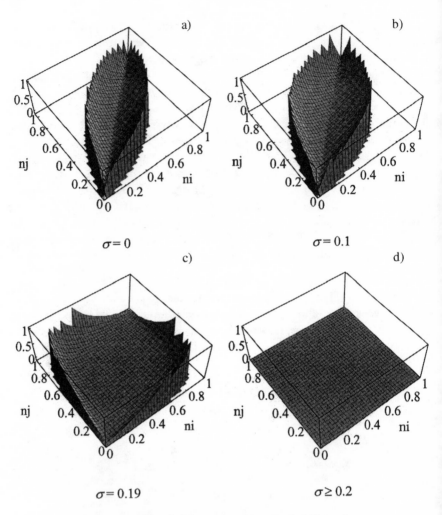

Figure 1. Threshold Continuation Probability α' as a
Function of Combination of Neediness Levels (n_i, n_j)
for Four Different Levels of Sympathy, σ.

Figure 1A shows the cooperation condition for purely self-interested actors
$(\sigma = 0)$. Clearly, the more different the neediness levels of the actors involved
are, the larger the continuation probability, α, that is required for conditional
cooperation. However, for a considerable range of pairings of neediness levels, cooperation is feasible without altruistic sentiments. The cooperation condition for $\sigma = 0$ reflects the cost-benefit considerations of the less needy
player. The less help he receives in comparison with the help he gives, the

longer the expected duration of the exchange relationship required to deter the player from defection. The white range in Figure 1A indicates that sufficient stability is no longer attainable, as players' neediness levels are too dissimilar. Figures 1B, 1C, and 1D demonstrate how increasing sympathy affects cooperation. Figure 1D represents the limiting case. When sympathy exceeds a critical level of $\sigma = 0.2$, cooperation problems are entirely resolved. More precisely, in Figure 1D, the threshold continuation probability universally drops to $\alpha' = 0$. As a consequence, cooperation becomes the only rational behavior in all pairings of neediness levels, regardless of the shadow of the future.[8] Between the two extremes of pure egoism ($\sigma = 0$) and altruism sufficient for universal cooperation ($\sigma \geq 0.2$), increasing sympathy gradually mitigates the cooperation problem actors face. Comparison of Figures 1B and 1C with Figure 1A shows two main differences. The first difference is that the range of pairings for which cooperation is in principle attainable becomes broader as sympathy increases.[9] On closer inspection, it shows that the combination of neediness levels for which the condition $\alpha' \leq 1$ is met in Figure 1A is a subset of the combinations that meet the condition in Figure 1B. This set, in turn, is a subset of the corresponding combinations in Figure 1C. The second difference between pure egoism ($\sigma = 0$) and "moderate altruism" ($0 < \sigma < 0.2$) is that the stability required for conditional cooperation declines, as sympathy gets larger. This is indicated by the smaller height of the surface in Figure 1C as compared with Figures 1A and 1B, respectively. The surfaces attain the same height of $\alpha' \approx 1$ only at the "edge," where pairings are so dissimilar in neediness that almost infinite duration of the game is required for cooperation. However, the greater the sympathy, the further this edge moves to the extremes, that is, the more dissimilar are the neediness pairings at the edge.

Our analysis of the prerequisites for conditional cooperation is consistent with the invisible hand hypothesis in the prediction that social support is feasible between egoistic individuals. At the same time, our results partly confirm the altruism hypothesis. The model implies that the more sympathy actors feel for the other, the less restrictive the conditions are under which rational actors may attain mutual support. However, while this result shows that sympathy makes cooperation easier to attain, the analysis does not reveal how sympathy shapes the attractiveness of support partners. To address partner attractiveness, we compute the utility actor i may expect to derive per iteration from a support relation with a potential partner j. For simplicity's sake, we assume that the shadow of the future, α, is common knowledge and equal for all actors. This implies that a rational actor i uses the cooperation condition to predict whether cooperation can be attained with a particular partner j. Actor i expects to attain the reward of support exchange with j, R'_{ij}, if the cooperation condition is satisfied for the pairing (ij). At the same time, i expects zero utility for a partner with whom cooperation is unattainable. Figure 2 charts partner attractiveness from the point of view of i, as a function of the combination of neediness levels n_i and n_j. To show how the restriction of the

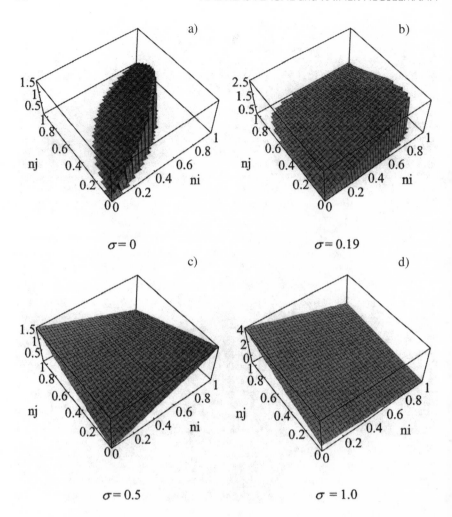

Figure 2. Partner Attractiveness from i's Point of View
as a Function of Combination of Neediness Levels
(n_i, n_j) for Four Different Levels of Sympathy, σ.

cooperation condition affects partner attractiveness, we assumed $\alpha = 0.75$.
Between figures, we gradually increase the sympathy level starting with pure egoism ($\sigma = 0$). The white space in the figures indicates the range of (n_i, n_j) combinations where cooperation cannot be attained with $\alpha = 0.75$.

Figure 2A represents partner attractiveness under conditions of pure self-interest ($\sigma = 0$). Comparison with Figure 1A shows that the white space is somewhat larger in Figure 2A than in Figure 1A. This indicates that with $\alpha = 0.75$ mutual support is rational only for a subset of the pairings that play a PD. To illustrate partner attractiveness, we discuss the effect of Alter's neediness, n_j on Alter's attractiveness for Ego's neediness fixed at $n_i = 0.5$. Broadly, Figure 2A shows that the smaller Alter's need for support, the more attractive Alter is from Ego's perspective. More precisely, the figure demonstrates that potential partners of Ego have zero attractiveness, as soon as their neediness falls below $n_j = 0.25$ or it exceeds $n_j = 0.75$. This illustrates why cooperation may fail to arise between Ego and Alter. Ego may be too needy relative to Alter's neediness ($n_j < 0.25$), so that a shadow of the future of $\alpha = 0.75$ is not large enough to deter Alter's defection. Conversely, Alter may be too needy relative to Ego's neediness ($n_j > 0.75$) so that Ego fails to resist the temptation. Between these extremes, Figure 2A reveals a negative slope for the effect of Alter's neediness, n_j, on Alter's attractiveness. For $n_i = 0.5$, Alter's attractiveness declines from $R' = 1.375$ at $n_j = 0.25$ to $R' = 0.125$ at $n_j = 0.75$. The figure shows that this effect obtains regardless of Ego's level of neediness.

Figures 2B, 2C, and 2D demonstrate that higher levels of sympathy gradually shift the qualitative pattern of partner attractiveness. Figure 2B shows the case of "moderate altruism" ($0 < \sigma < 0.2$). With $\sigma = 0.19$, the range of pairings that succeed to cooperate with a shadow of the future of $\alpha = 0.75$ is considerably larger as compared to pure self-interest ($\sigma = 0$). At the same time, the qualitative pattern of partner attractiveness within the range of feasible pairings remains unchanged. Like pure egoists, moderately altruistic actors find cooperative partners the more attractive, the less needy the partner. However, comparison of the slope in Figure 2A and Figure 2B also indicates that moderate altruism mitigates the quantitative effect of Alter's neediness on Alter's attractiveness for Ego. Assuming a neediness of Ego of $n_i = 0.5$, we find that the attractiveness of a cooperative Alter declines from $R = 1.5$ at $n_j = 0.02$ to $R = 0.01$ at $n_j = 0.98$, a reduction of 1.55 per unit of neediness, as compared to the reduction of 2.5 per unit of neediness that we found for purely self-interested actors.

The qualitative pattern of partner attractiveness no longer resembles the case of pure self-interest, as soon as sympathy is large enough to entirely resolve cooperation problems ($\sigma \geq 2$). In particular, with "balanced altruism" ($\sigma = 0.5$), Ego cares equally for his own payoff and for Alter's payoff. As a consequence, for Ego finding a partner that maximizes Ego's utility R'_{ij} is equivalent to finding a partner that maximizes the joint payoff of the dyad, $R_{ij} + R_{ji}$. Figure 2C shows how this results in distinct partner preferences for strong actors ($n_i < 0.5$) as opposed to weak actors ($n_i > 0.5$). The graph shows that the joint payoff is maximized when the number of units of help exchanged in the dyad per iteration is as large as possible. For strong actors this entails finding partners that are maximally needy. At the same time, weak actors maximize joint payoff if they attain a partner who needs as little support as possible.

Figure 2D, finally, demonstrates that "strong altruism" ($\sigma = 1.0$) entirely alters actors' partner preferences. For fixed neediness of Ego, the surface of the figure increases only in the direction of higher neediness of Alter, n_j. At this level of sympathy, Ego is exclusively interested in maximizing Alter's payoff and vice versa. As a consequence, Ego strives to find a partner that is as needy as possible. Ego increases his own utility of the exchange outcome with every unit of support that Ego gives to Alter.

To summarize, the game theoretical analysis of altruism in the dyad confirms the invisible hand hypothesis. Self-interested actors may attain cooperation in social support, but only with partners who are sufficiently similar in neediness. Moreover, within the range of cooperative partners, self-interested actors prefer stronger members to weaker ones. Consistent with the altruism hypothesis, however, higher sympathy reduces both the similarity of neediness levels and the shadow of the future required to sustain conditional cooperation. As a consequence, beyond a critical sympathy level, increasing sympathy broadens the range of actors that are compassionate enough to find help exchanges with weak partners more attractive than help exchanges with strong partners. In the following, we analyze how these effects of sympathy on partner attractiveness shape the outcomes of the partner selection process in a support network.

A MODEL OF ALTRUISM IN SUPPORT NETWORKS

The Cellular Automata Framework

To model partner selection, we employ a *cellular automata* (CA) framework (cf. Hegselmann and Flache 1998). In this framework, the support network is embedded in a *two-dimensional cellular grid*. The neighbor cells of a particular location constitute the occupant's neighborhood. We assume that actors simultaneously play support games with all neighbors in their neighborhood. However, not all sites on the grid are occupied. This allows the modeling of partner selection in terms of migration. More precisely, we assume that actors attain a migration chance from time to time. A migration chance is the opportunity for an actor to leave his present location and to move to a free location in a neighborhood with more attractive partners. Finally, we use computer simulation to derive from actors' repeated migration decisions the structure of the emergent support network.

We employ the CA framework because we feel that it provides a easy to handle tool to capture three characteristic features of support networks: locality, overlapping neighborhoods, and interdependence of numerous individual partner choices (cf. Hegselmann and Flache 1998).

Support networks are characterized by *locality*, because actors' outcomes are primarily affected by the small fraction of network members that are directly related to a focal individual. Moreover, partner selection may be locally restricted to a certain degree, because both accessibility of information and costs of migration may increase with actors' distance from a potential new position in the network. At the same time, local neighborhoods in support networks may often *overlap*, because actors may be directly or indirectly related to the same exchange partners. Finally, support networks may face actors with *interdependence of numerous individual partner choices*. For example, relationships with strong members may be a scarce good in support networks, because the number of actors competing for these relationships may exceed the number of partners that strong actors are willing to support. As a consequence, an actor occupying a "slot" in the personal network of a strong member may restrict the partner choices of numerous others and vice versa. Although the CA framework allows a straightforward model of locality, neighborhood overlap and interdependence of individual choices in a support network, the framework also imposes a number of potentially restrictive simplifications. For example, our model assumes homogeneity in the maximal number of neighbors of an individual actor. We discuss in the concluding section how simplifications like this one may affect our analysis. The remainder of this section describes how the CA framework is used to model support networks. Assumptions about interaction structure and migration options are described and the model of migration behavior is specified.

Interaction Structure, Migration Options, and Migration Behavior

Interaction Structure

In the cellular world, actors "live" at the surface of a *torus* so that their world can be represented as a checkerboard without borders. Individuals simultaneously and independently participate in a repeated support game with every member of the *interaction window* of their present cell. Figure 3 illustrates the interaction window. The interaction window is modeled as a von Neumann neighborhood, that is, neighbors are the adjacent cells in the west, north, east, and south of the focal cell. However, cells in the interaction window are not necessarily occupied with individuals. To model migration opportunities, we assume that there are less group members than are locations on the checkerboard. Accordingly, the "game" Ego played with an empty cell always yields a utility of zero per iteration. To compute the overall utility Ego attains per iteration, we simply sum up the utilities Ego obtains in all support games he participates in.

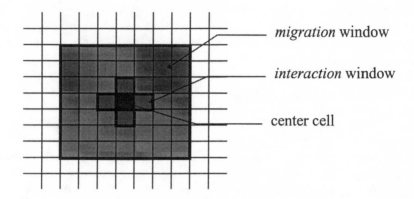

Figure 3.   Basic Windows in the Cellular World

Migration Options

From time to time individuals get the chance to migrate to a new neighborhood. More precisely, the simulation consists of a number of consecutive periods. In every period, every individual receives a migration option with an *exogenous migration probability m*. Migration options are evaluated and/or used in *sequential* order according to the results of the lottery. Individuals who not receive a migration option play one iteration of all their support games in the corresponding period. Individuals who have the chance to migrate may move to a new location and then immediately play the first iteration of the support games with their new neighbors. However, individuals may also decide to not make use of the migration option and just continue the support games with their present neighbors. To model locality and scarcity of partners, we assume that migration can only occur within a certain *migration window* and *only to vacant destination cells*. Moreover, the information that actors have about location and neediness levels of other members is restricted to the migration window. As Figure 3 shows, an individual who received a migration option is located in the center of its migration window. For simplicity, we assume that the window is a square of an odd size that is equal for all individuals.

Migration Behavior

Broadly, our model of individual migration behavior applies the simple rule "move to the network position that maximizes utility in the *present* network structure." As simple as this rule is, closer inspection reveals that the rule is a "boundedly rational" (Simon 1955) heuristic rather than a perfectly rational solution to the problem of finding a optimal migration strategy. To explain, two problems arise in the analysis of the consequences of a particular migration decision. First, to perfectly assess the attractiveness of a particular position, actors need to take into account the effects of their own and others' *future* migration on the network structure. Second, migration behavior and exchange behavior in support relations are interdependent. Actors' decision to migrate to a particular neighborhood depends on their expectations about their own and others' behavior in support exchanges both in the present neighborhood and in the potential new location. Future behavior in support exchanges, in turn, is shaped by the length of the shadow of the future actors expect to face in a particular relation. However, actors' estimate of the shadow of the future needs to take into account future migration decisions of both themselves and their exchange partners. At the moment we are not capable of solving the problem of how to model fully rational migration strategies that in turn would presuppose a model of actors' fully rational anticipation of others' migration behavior. Instead, our analysis explores the implications of the simple and plausible migration heuristic described below.

Our migration heuristic assumes that actors do not anticipate their own and their neighbors' migration behavior when they assess the shadow of the future in support games. Instead, actors use the pessimistic (and wrong) assumption that they and their neighbors will use every option to leave. In addition, the probability of getting migration options, m, is common knowledge. With these assumptions all actors face the same subjective continuation probability in every support game. This is the probability that both Ego and Alter get no chance to migrate in the next iteration, hence $\alpha = (1 - m)(1 - m)$. Every player i then checks whether the cooperation condition is satisfied with respect to a particular neighbor j. If the cooperation condition is satisfied for the combination of neediness levels (n_i, n_j), the neighbors will support each other and expect to be supported in the next iteration. Otherwise, both players will defect and expect each other to defect.

We assume that actors use the pessimistic guess of α to anticipate whether potential new neighbors will cooperate in future support relationships. More precisely, in our analysis every actor knows instantly and perfectly *all individuals' positions in the world and the neediness levels of all (real or potential) neighbors.* Moreover, actors are aware of the payoffs and utilities of the support game both from their own and their partners' point of view. In our migration heuristic actors make use of this knowledge to predict and compare exchange outcomes at their present location and potential future positions in the network.

Finally, the migration heuristic models actors' risk preferences in making the actual migration decision. To model risk preferences we assume that all individuals know that relative to their own neediness level they are in a *best social position* when they are surrounded by four individuals of the most attractive neediness level willing to exchange support with them. At the same time,

Table 3.   Assumptions of the Simulations

Basics:	
interaction window:	von Neumann neighborhood
migration window:	11×11 with the focal individual in the center.
world:	21×21 (torus)
Class structure:	35 individuals per neediness class $\Rightarrow$
	a total of 315 individuals/136 empty sites
	All individuals have the same sympathy level σ.
Payoffs:	$B = 4, E = 1 \Rightarrow \qquad benefit/effort = 4$
Minimum level:	50%
Probability for getting migration option:	$m = 0.05 \qquad \Rightarrow \qquad \alpha = 0.903$

actors know the *worst social position*. This is the position in which their neighborhood consists exclusively of members with the least attractive level of neediness, including empty cells. We assume that actors are risk seeking in the sense that they risk migration even to inferior positions when they are dissatisfied with their present location. An individual is satisfied with a position that offers at least the utility of the worst social position plus a certain fraction of the difference between the utility at the best and the worst social position. We refer to this fraction as minimum level. *Satisfied individuals* will migrate only if they can get a position that is at least as good as the position they have. *Dissatisfied individuals* will seize every migration option and accept even worse new locations in the hope to find a better position by future moves which might be accessible from the new location.

ALTRUISM IN SUPPORT NETWORKS: SIMULATION RESULTS

We employed computer simulation to assess the effects of individual altruism on support networks. For comparison, the simulations use a baseline scenario where purely egoistic actors ($\sigma = 0$) achieve an extended support network that is characterized by a relatively high degree of stability. For this scenario, we assume a migration probability of $m = 0.05$ per period.[10] Furthermore, in every simulation run all individuals initially are randomly distributed in the cellular grid. Finally, for simplicity we assume that the population of the group consists of only a small number of different *neediness* classes. All members within neediness class i have equal neediness, n_i. More concretely, the group comprises nine neediness classes with $n_1 = 0.1$, $n_2 = 0.2,...n_9 = 0.9$. Table 3 summarizes assumptions underpinning the simulations.

To demonstrate effects of sympathy, we proceed in two steps. First, we compare selected scenarios representing qualitatively different levels of altruism. Then we present an overview of the effects of sympathy. For this, we vary the sympathy parameter across the entire range of feasible values ($0 \leq \sigma \leq 1$).

Scenarios

The scenario of "pure egoism" ($\sigma = 0$) is compared with the three qualitatively different levels of altruism represented in Figure 2: "moderate altruism" ($\sigma = 0.19$), "balanced altruism" ($\sigma = 0.5$) and "pure altruism" ($\sigma = 1.0$), respectively. We evaluate networks in terms of the aggregated payoff, that is, individual payoffs per iteration summed across all dyads in the network. Aggregated payoff is an indicator of the central dependent variable of our analysis, the degree of solidarity in the group. To explain, with $B > E$ every unit of support exchanged in some dyad of the network increases aggregated payoff, because the benefit of the help exchange to the recipient exceeds the costs of the helper. Hence, the larger aggregated payoff, the more support group members receive on average from their peers. Accordingly, we compute in the following the aggregated payoff of a particular support network in terms of the *egoistic preferences* represented in Table 1, even when we assume that individuals' sympathy exceeds zero.

Figure 4 represents the pattern of a support network as it typically emerges under pure egoism ($\sigma = 0$) from the initial random configuration after 1000 simulation periods. For interpretation of Figures 4 to 8 notice the following:

- White cells are empty cells.
- Round cells are dissatisfied with their social position (i.e. attain less than the expected 50 percent of the difference between worst and best social position). Squared cells are satisfied actors.
- Short white lines connecting two actors indicate bilateral cooperation.
- Different gray levels represent different neediness classes, as described by the legend at the bottom of the figures. The neediness of Class 1 is $n_1 = 0.1$, neediness of Class 2 is $n_2 = 0.2$, and so on.

Pure Egoism ($\sigma = 0$)

Consistent with the invisible hand paradigm, Figure 4 demonstrates that pure egoism entails a *dense solidarity network*. The density of the support network is seen in that almost every member of the population has one or more support relationships with some other actor. In Figure 4, the average individual has 3.52 out of 4 possible support partners (mean value of 10 replications with a standard deviation of 0.06). In particular, even most of the "unattractive" actors

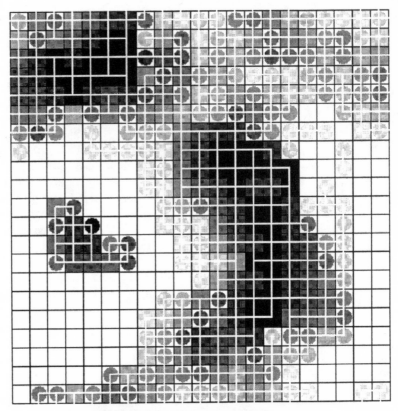

neediness classes:

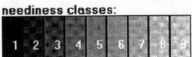

Figure 4. Support Network Under Pure Egoism
($\sigma = 0$) after Approximately 1000 Simulation Periods.
Aggregated Payoff $A = 611$.

with high neediness are embedded in support relations. On closer inspection, however, the network reveals a distinct *onion-like segregation pattern*. Clusters of members of the least needy Class 1 tend to form the core of the "onion," around which a "shell" has emerged that primarily consists of members of neediness Class 2. This shell, in turn, is surrounded by a further shell consisting of members of classes 3 and 4 and so forth. The further the distance from the core of the network, the larger the degree of neediness of the individuals located at this distance. At the periphery of the network, we almost exclusively find members of the highest neediness classes 8 and 9. The network structure reflects the pattern of partner attractiveness represented in Figure 2A. All classes strive to occupy neighborhoods with a maximal number of members of the least needy class with whom support exchange is attainable. With exception of the most attractive Class 1, however, the "target classes" are searching for better partners as well. Needy classes are satisfied with neighboring stronger classes, but it is just that which makes the stronger classes willing to move. Eventually, a stable configuration arises when members of Class 1 flock together in a cluster surrounded by members of the next attractive Class 2. Members of the core cluster then have no further incentive to move, because they already have the most attractive partners available. At the same time, members of the surrounding shell are not capable of invading the core cluster. As a consequence, they fail to find a better position than they already have. Similarly, the best what members of Class 3 can attain in this situation is a position close to the members of Class 2, and so on.

In terms of aggregated payoff, this patterns yields $A = 611$ per iteration of the support game. On average, an individual attains a payoff of approximately 0.48 per iteration and per neighboring cell in the network of Figure 4. For comparison, notice that a maximally needy player ($n = 1$) attains a payoff of 4 when he receives help from a player who is maximally capable to provide help ($n = 0$). However, a meaningful interpretation of aggregated payoffs requires an assessment of the best and the worst network structure from the group's point of view. The subsequent remark provides this assessment.

Remark: The collective optimum. Support networks formed by a benevolent dictator.

Clearly, the worst case in terms of aggregated payoff arises when there are no support relations at all in the cellular world. In this case, the aggregated payoff is $A = 0$. Conversely, in the collective optimum all neighbors necessarily mutually support each other. The underlying reason is our assumption that the gains for the recipient of a unit help exceed the costs the helper incurs ($B > E$). However, to assess the aggregated payoff in the best case, we also need to know how actors are optimally distributed in the cellular world. To approximate an optimal distribution, we simulated a benevolent dictator who gradually improves the network in order to maximize aggregated payoff. At the outset of our simulations, the dictator imposes mutual cooperation in all support relations, regardless of the combination of neediness levels. Starting from a random distribution, the dictator then randomly selects two individuals and calculates whether swapping their positions increases aggregated payoff. If this is the case, our Leviathan "orders" the individuals to exchange their positions and to continue cooperation with all new neighbors they encounter. This process continues until the dictator attains no more gains

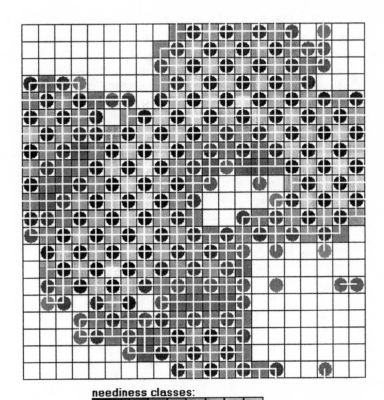

neediness classes:

Figure 5. Support Network Created by
"Benevolent Dictator". Aggregated Payoff $A = 1099$.

in aggregated payoff. Figure 5 shows a support network as it typically
arises from this procedure.

The network in Figure 5 maximizes the difference between the neediness levels
of solidarity partners. Almost all possible relations between members of classes 1
and 9 have been formed. Furthermore, the network contains a large number of
relations between classes 2 and 8, classes 3 and 7, and so forth. Figure 2C illustrates that this network structure maximizes aggregated payoff, because it maximizes the total amount of help that is provided in the group. The network matches
those actors who are most in need of help with those partners who are most capable of giving help. With $A = 1099$, the corresponding aggregated payoff exceeds
the worst case of $A = 0$ by almost twice the amount that was achieved by the invis-

ible hand operating on pure egoism ($A = 611$).[11] Moreover, as Figure 2C shows, the higher the gains a benevolent dictator can achieve, the larger the differences between neediness levels. This explains why in the support network of Figure 5, extreme pairings (1 and 9) tend to be in the core of the network. In the core of the network, the largest number of matches can be realized, because individuals have no empty neighbor cells. Accordingly, the dictator assigns those pairings to the core that yield the highest joint payoff.

Finally, the distribution of satisfied and dissatisfied actors in Figure 5 indicates how egoistic actors assess the collective optimum from their individual perspective. Members of the classes 1 to 4 are dissatisfied with their positions, that is, they attain less than 50 percent of the pay-

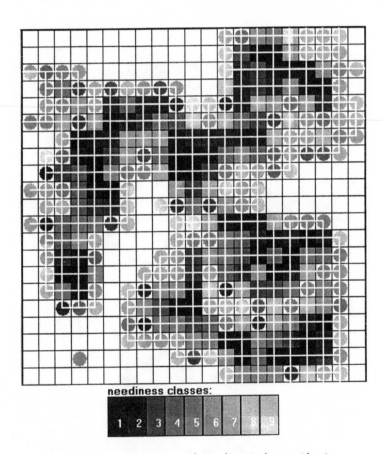

neediness classes:

| 1 | 2 | 3 | 4 | 5 | 6 | 7 | 8 | 9 |

Figure 6. Support Network Under Moderate Altruism ($\sigma = 0.19$) after Approximately 1000 Simulation Periods. Aggregated Payoff $A = 801$

off they could achieve in the best social position. At the same time members of classes 5 to 9 are satisfied. This suggests that under pure egoism the collectively optimal network is unstable in the absence of the dictator. We conducted explorative simulations that show the effects of removing the dictator from a world populated with purely egoistic individuals. In the simulations, members of classes 1 to 4 immediately "fled" from their positions and formed clusters with their own kind. As a consequence, the deserted members of classes 5 to 9 were driven to the margin of the network and after a short time the onion-like pattern of Figure 4 reemerged. In the following, we use the aggregated payoff of the collectively optimal network of Figure 5 to evaluate effects of gradually increasing altruism.

Moderate Altruism (σ = 0.19)

Figure 6 shows a network as it typically arises after approximately 1000 iterations from the behavior of moderately altruistic individuals. This networks shows an onion-like segregation pattern similar to the one of pure egoists (Figure 4). However, the pattern is less accentuated, because now matches arise that were not possible with $\sigma = 0$. For example, some support relations form between members of classes 1 and 4 or between classes 2 and 7. This reflects the effect of sympathy on the cooperation condition. The larger the sympathy the broader the range of pairings for which the cooperation condition is satisfied. Closer inspection of the network structures illustrates the effect. Under pure egoism, the average difference in neediness levels between solidarity partners is 0.08, whereas this difference increased to 0.18 under moderate altruism. As predicted by the altruism hypothesis, the changes in network structure result in a higher level of solidarity between moderate altruists as compared to pure egoists. More precisely, with $A = 801$ the network yields about 73 percent of the aggregated payoff in the approximate optimum, $A = 1099$, whereas only 56 percent were attained under pure altruism ($A = 611$).

The distribution of satisfied individuals in Figure 6 indicates that the support network of moderate altruists is relatively stable. The large majority of satisfied individuals ceased to migrate in this network, because they can attain no better positions than they already have. As a consequence, the overall structure of the network hardly changes any more, because dissatisfied actors mainly occur at the margins of the network. Like the benevolent dictator, moderate individual altruism improves aggregated payoffs as compared to pure egoism. In contrast to the dictator, however, moderately altruistic individuals attain this gain not at the cost of a network that is unstable in the absence of external coercion.

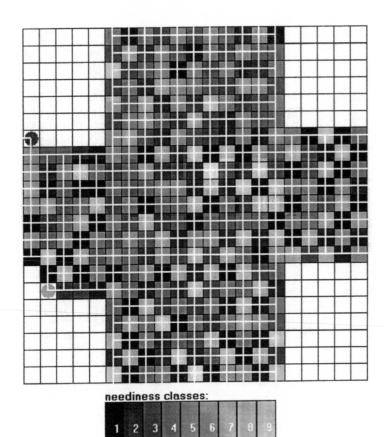

Figure 7. Support Network under Balanced Altruism ($\sigma = 0.5$)
after Approximately 1000 Simulation Periods. Aggregated Payoff $A = 1038$

Balanced Altruism ($\sigma = 0.5$)

Our simulations reveal that balanced altruism generates a network that is clearly superior in terms of aggregated payoff as compared to the scenario of moderate altruism. This clearly confirms the altruism hypothesis for the range of sympathy levels between zero and 0.5. Figure 7 shows the typical network resulting under balanced altruism after approximately 1000 iterations. The figure illustrates that with balanced altruism support relations arise between classes 1 and 9, classes 2 and 7, and so on. With $A = 1038$ the aggregated payoff is about twice as large as with pure egoism, and it comes close the approximate optimum of $A = 1099$.

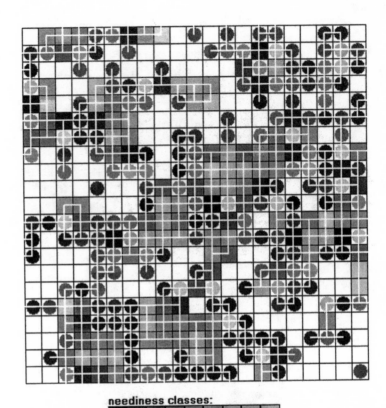

neediness classes:

| 1 | 2 | 3 | 4 | 5 | 6 | 7 | 8 | 9 |

Figure 8. Support Network under Pure Altruism ($\sigma = 1.0$)
after Approximately 1000 Simulation Periods. Aggregated Payoff $A = 708$

The high aggregated payoff attained under balanced altruism indicates that the network contains many relations with a large difference in neediness between exchange partners. Under balanced altruism, the average difference in neediness levels in a support relation is about 0.38, as compared to 0.18 for moderate altruism and 0.08 for purely egoistic actors (mean values based on 10 replications per condition). However, the network might still be improved from the group's point of view. For example, Figure 5 shows that almost all possible relations between members of classes 1 and 9 were formed in the network created by the benevolent dictator. By contrast, in the network of balanced altruists only about 25 percent of the relations of members of Class 1 are relations with members of Class 9. However, this discrepancy does not result from actors' altruistic preferences. Instead, the difference results from a coordination problem actors face. With balanced altruism ($\sigma = 0.5$), the altruism condition is satisfied and actors always cooperate with their neighbors. Accordingly, the problem to find a maximally attractive social position boils down to finding partners that maximize the joint payoff from mutual cooperation, $R_{ij} + R_{ji}$. As a consequence, "balanced altruists" strive to attain the same social positions that a benevolent social planner would assign to them. However, under balanced altruism migration decisions are "decentralized," as opposed to the "centralized" regime of the benevolent dictator. Individuals have no possibility to agree on swapping their positions with others. Instead, they can only move to free locations. Accordingly, individuals' migration decisions may entail stable networks that are collectively suboptimal. The reason is that a network stabilizes as soon as all individuals are satisfied with their social positions and cannot find better locations. In that case, the road to a superior configuration is "blocked," because no individual unilaterally leaves its location even when exchanging positions might still improve the aggregated payoff.

In terms of aggregated payoff, the network of balanced altruists is slightly inferior to the product of the benevolent dictator. However, the network comprises a extremely large proportion of satisfied actors. Figure 7 shows that almost every member of the population is satisfied with his social position. With $\sigma = 0.5$ almost all support relations in the emergent network come close to what actors wish to obtain. More precisely, as Figure 2C shows, actors with less than 50 percent neediness ($n_i < 0.5$) attain their satisfaction level already when they find a partner who has more than 50 percent neediness, and vice versa. This is true for almost all of the relations that formed in the network of Figure 7. As a consequence, the network not only generates a large aggregated payoff, but it also is considerably stable even without external control of a benevolent dictator.

Pure Altruism ($\sigma = 1.0$)

Pure altruism represents an extreme assumption. Under pure altruism, individuals exclusively aim to maximize others' payoff, regardless of the costs they incur themselves. Figure 8 shows that the resulting network approximates a reversed "pure egoism structure." More precisely, in the network of Figure 8 needy actors tend to form core clusters around which shells of individuals with lower neediness arise. At the same time members of classes 1 and 2 occur primarily at the margin of the network where they mostly are dissatisfied with their social position. However, this pattern is less accentuated as compared to its "egoistic counterpart" of Figure 4. The average difference in neediness between solidarity partners is 0.215, a value that clearly exceeds the corresponding difference of 0.08 that arose under pure egoism. At the same time, support partners are more similar than they are under balanced altruism, where the average difference in neediness was 0.38.

The effects of pure altruism partly contradict the altruism hypothesis. We find that the increase of sympathy from balanced altruism ($\sigma = 0.5$) to pure altruism ($\sigma = 1.0$) fails to foster group solidarity. More precisely, the aggregated payoff for pure altruists is $A = 708$. This payoff only slightly exceeds the level attained under pure egoism ($A = 611$), but it clearly falls below the result obtained with balanced altruism ($A = 1038$).

The partner preferences of purely altruistic individuals explain the network pattern of Figure 8. Figure 2D shows that under pure altruism, the most popular support partners are those who are maximally needy. As a consequence, clusters of individuals of the highest neediness classes tend to be stable once these clusters are formed. As in the case of pure egoism, members of the "core clusters" fail to find more attractive social positions than they already have. However, there is an important difference between pure egoism and pure altruism. Under pure egoism, the cooperation condition restricts the network to pairings that are relatively similar in their neediness levels. As a consequence, needy actors do not even try to enter neighborhoods populated by the least needy classes, because they anticipate that their potential neighbors are not willing to form support relations with them. Under pure altruism, by contrast, the possible range of pairings is not restricted, because with $\sigma = 1$ mutual cooperation is attainable for every combination of neediness levels. Accordingly, members of the least popular strong classes continuously try to invade clusters of needy actors. This destabilizes the clusters because it drives their members to leave their locations. This difference in behavior explains why the reversed onion in Figure 8 is less accentuated than its counterpart of Figure 4. It also explains the relatively large proportion of dissatisfied individuals in Figure 8. Particularly actors with low neediness fail to find their desired partners. As a consequence they make risky migration decisions which often leave them with positions yielding utilities below the satisfaction level.

The Effects of Sympathy: An Overview

To give an overview, we computed the effects of sympathy across the entire range between pure egoism and pure altruism. This allows to distinguish regions of the parameter space where the altruism hypothesis applies from regions where effects of sympathy conflict with the hypothesis. The analysis reveals that balanced altruism is a tipping point for the effects of sympathy. Altruism fosters group solidarity in weakly altruistic groups ($\sigma \leq 0.5$). At the same time, group solidarity suffers from still higher levels of altruism in strongly altruistic groups ($\sigma > 0.5$). Figures 9 to 11 illustrate the tipping point. To compute the figures, we varied sympathy, σ, between 0 and 1, in steps of 0.1. For every step we measured aggregated payoff in the networks emerging after 1000 iterations, based on mean values of 50 replications per condition.

Figure 9 shows effects of sympathy on aggregated payoffs. The graph demonstrates that groups attain the highest aggregated payoff with balanced altruism ($\sigma = 0.5$). Both lower and higher sympathy levels entail support networks

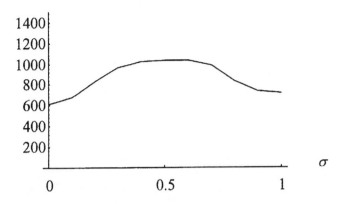

Figure 9. Aggregated Payoff as a Function of Sympathy σ

that are less efficient as compared to the results of balanced altruism. In both cases, networks tend to form in which support partners are relatively similar in their neediness levels. In weakly altruistic groups, the reason is that "popular" individuals of low neediness aim to build support relations with each other. This drives needy actors to the margin of the network where they find only partners from their own classes. As predicted by the altruism hypothesis, solidarity benefits from altruism in weakly altruistic groups. In these groups, higher sympathy both broadens the range of pairings that attain cooperation and increases the popularity of needy members as exchange partners. However, contrary to the altruism hypothesis, the reversed effect occurs in strongly altruistic groups. Needy actors cluster together and preclude strong individuals from support exchanges with weak partners. Higher levels of sympathy only exacerbate the problem, because needy actors become increasingly popular and strong actors are increasingly unpopular as exchange partners when sympathy rises. In both weakly and strongly altruistic groups, the collective capacities for providing help are suboptimally utilized as compared to balanced altruism. Help capacities are only optimally exploited when there are as many support relations as possible between partners who are maximally different in their neediness. Figure 9 illustrates that the closest approximation to such an optimal network is the pattern resulting from the behavior of individuals that put the same weight on their own payoffs as they put on the payoffs of others (balanced altruism).

The invisible hand paradigm predicts that self-interested actors attain a network that is collectively desirable in the sense of pareto efficiency. A network is pareto efficient, when at least some members of the population will be worse off after a change of the network structure. To assess pareto efficiency of the effects of sympathy, we measured aggregated payoffs separately for different neediness classes. Figure 10 shows how sympathy affects class specific aggregated payoffs. For this

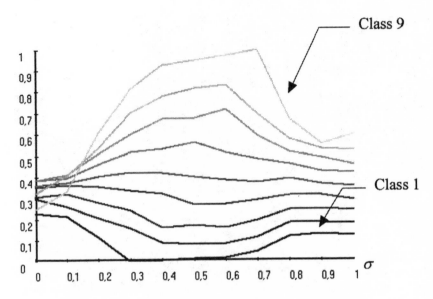

Figure 10.   Aggregated Payoffs, Computed Separately
for Different Neediness Classes as a Function of Sympathy, σ

figure, we normalized the class specific aggregated payoffs to the interval [0,1], where zero represents the lowest aggregated payoff ever attained by some neediness class and 1 is the highest level that occurs.

Figure 10 reveals that classes with middle neediness attain the highest payoffs in the baseline scenario of pure egoism ($\sigma = 0$). More precisely, the payoffs of the middle classes 4 to 7 exceed both the payoffs of very needy classes (8 and 9) and of classes of lower neediness (1, 2, and 3). This distribution reflects the interplay of two factors, the potential gain from receiving support and the degree to which this potential can be actually exploited. Potentially, the larger the neediness the higher the gains from being supported. For example, exchanging support with a member of Class 1 yields a payoff of $R_{11} = 0.27$ for another member of Class 1, whereas a member of Class 9 attains a payoff of $R_{91} = 3.23$ in this exchange. However, under pure egoism, members of weak classes fail to exploit the potential gains of support. To illustrate, under $\sigma = 0$, members of Class 1 attain on average about 95 percent of their optimal payoff of exchanging with another member of Class 1, R_{11}. At the same time, members of Class 9 achieve only approximately 8 percent of the corresponding optimal payoff of R_{91}.

Figure 10 illustrates that sympathy levels larger than zero fail to generate a pareto efficient redistribution of aggregated payoffs, as suggested by the invisible hand paradigm. More precisely, our simulations reveal two regions for the effects of sympathy on the relative positions of the neediness classes. We distinguish the region of *low sympathy* ($0 \leq \sigma \leq 0.5$) from the area of *high sympathy* ($0.5 < \sigma \leq 1.0$). Under low sympathy, Figure 10 shows, gains from increasing sympathy by and large accrue to the weak members of the group. However, under high sympathy the winners in terms of payoffs are the strong classes and weak members lose in comparison with balanced altruism. At the same time, the gain in overall aggregated payoff in the region of low sympathy (Figure 9) shows that pareto improvements are in principle attainable through redistribution of collective profits. Here, gains from higher sympathy are large enough to both compensate the classes of low neediness and leave some benefit for the classes of high neediness. Finally, Figure 10 reveals a paradoxical consequence of altruism. In the region of high sympathy, the shift in relative positions of classes conflicts with the "intentions" of the winning actors. With sympathy larger than 0.5, most members of the population wish to give as much help as possible, but only needy classes attain this goal in the corresponding networks. In terms of partly altruistic preferences, needy classes benefit from the effects of altruism in this region of the parameter space. At the same time, classes of low neediness incur a utility loss. However, in terms of the egoistic preferences represented in Figure 10, increasing exclusion from support relations benefits strong neediness classes, whereas increasing inclusion in support relations is to the disadvantage of needy actors.

DISCUSSION

Results and Conclusions

Traditional sociology and moral philosophy suggest an "altruism hypothesis." The stronger the altruistic feelings that groups evoke among members, the higher the level of group solidarity. However, in the wake of the invisible hand paradigm, economics and rational choice sociology propose that groups may often attain considerable levels of solidarity purely on the basis of members' pursuit of self-interest. Our analysis argues that both the altruism hypothesis and the invisible hand hypothesis are partly consistent with a plausible model of a central realm of solidary behavior, social support. We propose a model of social support networks that assumes members who vary in neediness and are free to change support partners. In this model, individuals aim to maximize attractiveness of their support partners. At the same time, a certain degree of altruism modifies individuals' selfish preferences. Computer simulations revealed nonlinear effects of altruism on social support. Consistently with the invisible hand hypothesis, dense support networks may arise on basis of reciprocity between pure egoists. However, as predicted by the altruism hypothesis, higher levels of altruism may foster social support in weakly altruistic groups. In these groups, altruism may prod strong members to exchange help with needy partners, a tendency that increases the amount of support provided in the group. Finally, our analysis refutes the altruism hypothesis for strongly altruistic groups. In these groups, altruism may actually reduce solidarity in social support. Strong altruistic motivations drive overly compassionate weak members into mutual help, excluding stronger partners from support relations at the expense of the efficiency of the utilization of collective resources for social support.

Our results put the invisible hand paradigm into perspective. Consistently with the paradigm, we show that pareto efficient allocations of social support may be attained even with purely self-interested preferences. At the same time, the simulations demonstrate that selfish groups may gain from higher levels of altruism, even in terms of egoistic preferences. However, to turn these gains into pareto improvements, a redistribution problem needs to be solved. We found that the strong and least needy individuals are those who lose due to altruism, because they have to give much more help than under egoistic preferences. Accordingly, strong actors shoulder the costs for increasing the aggregated payoff of the group. At the same time, collective gains from higher altruism are large enough to redistribute "altruism profits" such that those who lose are fully compensated. Of course, this requires the plausible assumption that the benefits for the recipient of a unit of help exceed the costs for its provider.

Our analysis also questions the intuitively appealing altruism hypothesis. Surprisingly, we showed that altruism may actually reduce solidarity in groups that are already strongly altruistic. This leads beyond previous analyses of unintended negative effects of prosocial behavior. Heckathorn (1990), for example, showed that overly effective social control may lead actors into a suboptimal outcome. In Heckathorn's analysis self-interested actors may develop "overcontrol" enforcing production of a collective good even when individuals' benefits from consumption of the good fall below their costs of contribution. In a similar vein, Macy's (1993) computer simulations of social control suggested that pressures to contribute a fair share in collective action may lead noncontributors to join in the collective effort at a point where their efforts are no longer needed due to diminishing returns on investment. Both Heckathorn and Macy identified the possibility of inefficient "overcooperation." Our analysis goes further and suggests that altruism may actually reduce cooperation even when higher levels of solidarity are efficient from the group's point of view. This effect can be attributed to the inclusion of an assumption that is plausible for the realm of social support: partner selection under scarcity of exchange partners. As a consequence, in our simulations the scramble of overly altruistic actors for needy partners may exclude strong members from exchanges. However, strong members are those who could provide help most efficiently from the group's perspective. This is a new form of Heckathorn's (1991) Altruist's Dilemma.

Limitations and Directions for Future Research

Our analysis employs simplifications that might limit generalizability of the conclusions. In particular, we assume that groups are homogenous in altruism, we model (boundedly) rational decision making and we embed partner selection in a two-dimensional regular cellular world. We discuss these potential limitations in turn and propose corresponding directions for future research.

To focus on between-group effects of altruism, we assumed that within a group all individuals have the same degree of sympathy with others. Clearly, this conflicts with intuitions about altruism. The pity and compassion Smith and others (including the common sense) have in mind is a compassion for those in misery. In future research, we shall explore effects of a negative correlation between altruism and neediness. Two lines of inquiry seem promising. In a first approach, we plan to employ the present model but add the assumption that individual altruism and individual neediness are randomly distributed with a negative correlation. We expect that this will mitigate but not suppress negative effects of altruism. Higher levels of average altruism may now drive weak (and selfish) actors into exchanges with strong altruists. As a consequence, help is efficiently distributed even in groups with sympathy larger than $\sigma = 0.5$. However, as average altruism approaches its maximum of "pure altruism," altruism spreads to the weaker classes as well. Hence, negative effects of sympathy reoccur for highly altruistic groups. The second approach aims to endogenize variation in altruism. We may assume that all individuals have the same interest in helping Alter, but the marginal increase in utility of helping Alter declines with Alter's wealth. For example, if Ego is poor, Ego may hurt himself greatly by providing a unit of support, but have little effect on the happiness of a rich Alter. With this assumption, altruism can be homogeneous, yet, needy agents will act as if they are more egoistic. In fact, were needy actors to obtain more resources, they would be just as altruistic as the resourceful agents.

We used the assumption of bounded rationality to model individual decision making. However, widespread criticism of the "psychological unrealism" of the rational actor model has prompted social dilemma researchers to employ alternative approaches, in particular social learning theory. These analyses suggested that outcomes of the analysis may often be sensitive to the underlying model of action (Macy 1991b; Flache 1996). This led us to explore in recent studies the effects of learning vs. rationality in support networks (Flache and Hegselmann 1999; Flache and Hegselmann 1998). The analysis showed that the approaches were similar in qualitative predictions. At the same time, there were considerable differences in quantitative results. This previous work focused on self-interested preferences. In the future we will use computer simulation to assess whether conclusions of the present study of altruism are robust against variation of the bounded rationality assumption. More particularly, we will combine the learning model of our previous work with the assumption of partly altruistic preferences.

Further explorations of alternative behavioral assumptions may draw on recent social psychological evidence about effects of neediness and exit possibilities on cooperation. In the present volume, Boone and Macy (1998) report experiments that use a card game ("Trump") to manipulate both actors' neediness for support from their partner (resource dependence) and possibilities for exit from the relationship (relational dependence). The authors found that subjects follow surprising behavioral heuristics. For example, subjects tended to ignore the possibility of defection when they needed help themselves. Boone and Macy characterize this as the rule "If you need your partner's help, offer yours." This and similar heuristics may be easily integrated in our framework and studied by means of computer simulations.

Finally, our analysis uses a cellular automata framework that is characterized by a two-dimensional social space, a von Neumann neighborhood structure and a regular cell grid. We believe that the number of dimensions of the CA has little effect on our results. The partner selection mechanism that in our study generates nonlinear effects of altruism is widely independent of the social space in which networks are embedded. The important assumption is the restriction of the number of partners of a single individual. With this restriction, exchanges that exclude less popular members tend to form as soon as most individuals have the same partner preferences. As a consequence, social support suffers both from low sympathy and from high sympathy, regardless of the social space in which actors move to find new partners. The assumption of a von Neumann neighborhood might be more critical for our results, because it precludes transitive exchange networks. If A is a neighbor of B and B is a neighbor of C, then in a von Neumann neighborhood A can never be a neighbor of C. However, in the present analysis we assumed independence of Ego's support exchanges with different Alters. Accordingly, the outcome of A's exchange with B is the same, whether A may also exchange with C or not. Clearly, the independence assumption may itself be regarded as implausible for exchanges of social support. Nevertheless, for the moment we plan to retain this assumption because it greatly facilitates the game theoretical analysis. Our next step in the analysis of framework effects will be to relax the assumption of a regular grid structure. We began to develop *irregular grids* that allow for cells with different numbers of next neighbors (cf. Hegselmann, Flache and Möller forthcoming). Irregular grids promise interesting new possibilities for modeling social support. For example, it seems plausible that network positions may vary in structural constraints on access to partners because of variation in population density between geographical areas. As a consequence, individuals may need more support per relation (and give more support per relation) in regions where only few potential partners are accessible. The effect of this structural constraint on social support networks can be easily addressed in an irregular CA.

While careful exploration of model extensions is required, we believe that our analysis revealed a new and interesting possibility for the effects of altruism on solidarity. High levels of altruism may impede solidarity, when opportunities to act solidary are scarce and individuals vary in their capability to efficiently provide help. In this situation, group solidarity may suffer from altruism, because overly compassionate weak members may get in the way of more capable strong members, at the expense of those who need help.

ACKNOWLEDGMENTS

We wish to thank an anonymous reviewer for helpful suggestions and inspiring criticism. This research has been conducted within a project on modeling the dynamics of social dilemma situations. It was financed by the German Science Foundation (Deutsche Forschungsgemeinschaft-DFG: Grant no. HE 1412/4-1).

NOTES

1. Axelrod's term "shadow of the future" refers to the expected duration of a future relationship from the point of view of the participants.

2. Lindenberg (1998) argues that solidarity is a pattern of behavior that is consistent across five distinct social-dilemma situations: helping others in need, contributing to a common good, resisting the temptation to breach agreements, taking not more than a fair share in sharing situations, and willingness to make up things in mishap situations. We do not claim that our analysis applies to this broad concept of solidarity. Instead, our focus on networks of help exchange imposes a scope condition of this study.

3. With this assumption, we focus on situations in which needy actors can reciprocate "help" only in terms of a comparable sort of help and not in terms of some *other* commodity valued by less needy partners. This precludes exchanges like that of care for affection (or reproduction chances) between parents and their children. Although this assumption limits the scope of our analysis, we argue that the assumption applies to a considerable range of social support situations.

4. With this assumption, the support game used here is different from the support game used in Hegselmann and Flache (1998). The main difference is that *bilateral* help is always possible in the game we use here, although the degree varies for different neediness class combinations. By contrast, the support game of Hegselmann and Flache (1998) allows in each period only *unilateral* help. As a consequence, that game imposes *imperfect* information that greatly complicates the game theoretical analysis. Obviously, there are different plausible approaches to model what in daily life is simply called *mutual help*.

5. More precisely, the support game always guarantees $R > P$ for the player who is less needy, regardless of the combination of neediness levels. To facilitate presentation, we do not present the mathematical proof. However, we have proven all results of the game theoretical analysis, and we will provide the proofs on request.

6. Note that this implies some form of interpersonal comparison of payoffs. This assumption is plausible when gains and losses represent quantities that are objectively measurable, such as the amount of food available to each member of a hunter-gatherer group.

7. More precisely, the equilibrium is a subgame perfect Nash equilibrium (spe). It is not necessarily a unique spe. That is, we assume that players solve the problem of equilibrium selection and coordinate on this spe.

8.   More precisely, we have proven that for every pairing of neediness levels (n_i, n_j), there is a critical sympathy level between zero and one of $\sigma^{CC} = E/(E+B)$, such that CC is the unique solution of the constituent support game, as soon as $\sigma > \sigma^{CC}$ (assuming $B > E$)

9.   We have proven for every pairing of neediness levels (n_i, n_j) and every level of sympathy, σ, that the larger one of the two threshold continuation probabilities always declines as σ increases.

10.   Flache and Hegselmann (1998) and Hegselmann (1998) studied the effects of the migration rate, m, on the pattern of support networks between pure egoists. These studies find that increasing migration rates reduce the density of support networks and, eventually, lead to the total collapse of support relations when the migration rate exceeds a critical level. In the present article we keep m constant because we focus on the effects of sympathy.

11.   The value of $A = 1099$ is only an approximation to the absolute optimum. However, we know that the approximation is fairly accurate. We showed analytically that the true optimum can never be larger than $A = 1197$. We attain this upper limit as follows. We represent collective utility as a linear function in which the independent variables in this function represent the number of support relations for every combination of neediness classes (ij). Standard numerical techniques then allow the maximation of the function under a number of constraints. These constraints are (1) that there are four support relations per individual and (2) that the support network is fully symmetric. The numerical result corresponds to the simulations of the benevolent dictator. In the optimum, only pairings of classes (1,9), (2,8), and so on, are formed. At the same time, we know that the related aggregated payoff is an upper limit for the true optimum because this optimal network cannot be embedded in the cellular world used in our simulations.

REFERENCES

Axelrod, R. 1984. *The Evolution of Cooperation*. New York: Basic Books.

Boone, T., and M.W. Macy 1998. "Dependence and Cooperation in the Game of Trump." Pp. 161-186 in *Advances in Group Processes*, 5, edited by E.J. Lawler. Greenwich, CT: JAI Press.

Coleman, J.S. 1990. *Foundations of Social Theory*. Cambridge: Harvard University Press.

Durkheim, E. 1912 (1965). *The Elementary Forms of Religious Life*. New York: Free Press.

Emerson, R.M. 1972. "Exchange Theory. Part II: Exchange Relations and Networks." Pp. 58-87 in *Sociological Theories in Progress*, Vol. 2, edited by J. Berger, M. Zelditch, and B. Anderson. Boston: Houghton Mifflin.

Flache, A. 1996. *The Double Edge of Networks*. Amsterdam: Thesis Publishers.

Flache, A., and R. Hegselmann. 1998. "Rational vs. Adaptive Egoism in Support Networks. How Different Micro Foundations Shape Different Macro Hypotheses." Pp. 261-275 in *Game Theory, Experience, Rationality. Foundations of Social Sciences, Economics and Ethics. In Honor of John C. Harsanyi* (Yearbook of the Institute Vienna Circle 5), edited by W. Leinfellner and E. Köhler. Dordrecht: Kluwer.

Flache, A., and R. Hegselmann. 1999. "Rationality vs. Learning in the Evolution of Solidarity Networks: A Theoretical Comparison." In *Computational and Mathematical Organization Theory* 5: 97-127

Flache, A., and M.W. Macy. 1996. "The Weakness of Strong Ties: Collective Action Failure in a Highly Cohesive Group." *Journal of Mathematical Sociology* 21: 3-28.

Friedman, J.W. 1971. "A Non-Cooperative Equilibrium for Supergames." *Review of Economic Studies* 38: 1-12.

Friedman, J.W. 1986. *Game Theory with Applications to Economics*. New York: Oxford University Press.

Hall, A., and B. Wellman. 1985. "Social Networks and Social Support." Pp. 23-41 in *Social Support and Health*, edited by S. Cohen and S.L. Syme. New York: Academic Press.

Hechter, M. 1987. *Principles of Group Solidarity*. Berkeley: University of California Press.

Heckathorn, D. 1990. "Collective Sanctions and Compliance Norms: A Formal Theory of Group-Mediated Social Control." *American Sociological Review* 55: 366-384.

Heckathorn, D. 1991. "Extensions of the Prisoner's Dilemma Paradigm: The Altruist's Dilemma and Group Solidarity." *Sociological Theory* 9: 34-52.

Hegselmann, R. 1998. "Experimental Ethics—A Computer Simulation of Classes, Cliques and Solidarity." Pp. 298-320 in *Preferences,* edited by C. Fehige and U. Wessels. Berlin: De Gruyter.

Hegselmann, R., A. Flache, and V. Möller. Forthcoming. "Cellular Automata Models of Solidarity and Opinion Formation: Sensitivity Analysis." in *Social Science Microsimulation: Tools for Modeling, Parameter Optimization and Sensitivity Analysis,* edited by R. Suleiman, K.G. Troitzsch, N. Gilbert, and U. Mueller. Heidelberg: Springer-Verlag.

Heglselmann, R., and A. Flache. 1998. "Understanding Complex Social Dynamics—A Plea for Cellular Automata Based Modelling." *Journal of Artificial Societies and Social Simulation* 3: http://www.soc.surrey.ac.uk/JASSS.

Homans, G.C. 1974. *Social Behavior. Its Elementary Forms.* New York: Harcourt Brace Jovanovich.

Kreps, D.M. 1990. *A Course in Microeconomic Theory.* New York: Harvester.

Lindenberg, S. 1998. "Solidarity: Its Microfoundations and Macro Dependence. A Framing Approach." Pp. 61-112 in *The Problem of Solidarity: Theories and Models,* edited by P. Doreian and T.J. Fararo. Newark, NJ: Gordon and Breach.

Macy, M.W. 1991a. "Learning to Cooperate: Stochastic and Tacit Collusion in Social Exchange." *American Journal of Sociology* 97: 808-843.

Macy, M.W. 1991b. "Chains of Cooperation: Threshold Effects in Collective Action." *American Sociological Review* 56: 730-747.

Macy, M.W. 1993. "Backward Looking Social Control." *American Sociological Review* 58: 819-836.

Morrison, K. 1995. *Marx, Durkheim, Weber: Formations of Modern Social Thought.* London: Sage Publications.

Piliavin, J.A. and H.W. Charng. 1990. "Altruism—A Review of Recent Theory and Research." *Annual Review of Sociology* 16: 27-65.

Simon, H.A. 1955. "A Behavioral Model of Rational Choice." *Quarterly Journal of Economics* 63: 129-139.

Smith, A. 1759 (1982). *The Theory of Moral Sentiments.* Indianapolis: Liberty Classics.

Smith, A. 1776 (1981). *An Inquiry into the Nature and Causes of the Wealth of Nations,* 2 Vols. Indianapolis: Liberty Classics.

Taylor, M. 1987. *The Possibility of Cooperation.* Cambridge: Cambridge University Press.

THE PRODUCTION OF
TRUST IN ONLINE MARKETS

Peter Kollock

ABSTRACT

This paper addresses the question of how groups manage the risks of trade when they do not have access to external enforcement mechanisms. It examines the emergence of endogenous solutions to the problems of risky trade in informal markets. The focus is particularly on informal online markets, that is, person-to-person markets on the Internet that offer no guarantees, warranties, or other third-party enforcement mechanisms. Online markets represent an extraordinary opportunity to study the dynamics of trust and exchange in what seems at first to be a very unpromising environment. Participants in these markets have created an elegant and efficacious set of solutions for managing risk. This paper first discusses general approaches to managing risk in online markets and then examines two classes of systems for using reputations as a risk management tool. It then details the attempts to institutionalize reputation systems by online auction houses. Finally, it concludes with discussions of the prerequisites for an online reputation system and design issues for such systems.

Advances in Group Processes, Volume 16, pages 99-123.
ISBN: 0-7623-0452-9

An economic transaction is a solved political problem. Economics has gained the title of queen of the social sciences by choosing solved political problems as its domain.

—Abba Lerner (1972)

INTRODUCTION

At the heart of any unsecured transaction is a social dilemma. By *social dilemma*, I mean a situation in which behavior that is rational for the individual leads to an irrational collective outcome.[1] In the case of bilateral exchange, the temptation exists to receive a good or service without reciprocation, but if both parties hold back on their side of the exchange, the trade is never consummated and both are worse off. Thus, an unsecured bilateral exchange typically has the structure of a Prisoner's Dilemma.

The temptation to defect in the exchange has led to a wide range of formal and informal mechanisms for managing this risk. The simple act of meeting face to face for the transaction helps reduce the likelihood that one party will end up empty handed. Separating the two sides of the transaction by time or space (such as by purchasing something through the mail or on credit) introduces greater risks. The party who moves second must be considered trustworthy or have some other form of guarantee. The formal infrastructure that exists to manage these risks is vast and includes such elements as credit card companies, credit rating services, public accounting firms, and—if the exchange goes bad—such service as collection agencies or the court system.

Such third-party enforcement mechanisms are inevitably imperfect and impose their own set of costs. Pointing to them as an explanation for how the risks of trade are overcome also begs the question of emergence. When and how are groups able to manage the risks of trade when they do not have access to external enforcement mechanisms? It is the emergence of endogenous solutions to the problems of risky trade that this paper explores; it investigates informal markets that are still very much in the process of solving the political problems of exchange. Although mindful of the distinctions that have been made among markets, hierarchies, and networks, in this paper the term *market* is used, in a very broad sense, to refer to any exchange setting with multiple buyers and sellers, regardless of whether it approximates a formal market.

Online Markets

To study endogenous solutions to the problem of risky trade, the ideal research site would be a collection of large, informal markets in which one was able to observe thousands of transactions, record participants' reactions, and track the development of risk management strategies. Remarkably, such research sites exist in the informal markets that have emerged on the Internet. These markets are striking in terms of their size and the value of goods exchanged.

One set of informal online markets is the collection of Usenet newsgroups in which individuals buy and sell everything from computer equipment to bootleg music tapes. In each newsgroup, participants simply list an item for sale along with a description. Potential buyers then contact the seller via e-mail if they are interested. These markets are very loosely structured. Nevertheless, a detailed Frequently Asked Questions (FAQ) file has been produced. It has gathered the accumulated wisdom of participants concerning such matters as the best way to structure an advertisement or complete the transaction (King 1996). This is also a very large market—it was estimated in 1996 (King 1996) that more than 300,000 individuals from around the world participated in the Usenet *forsale* newsgroups, and the number of participants has grown very significantly since then.

The emergence of the World Wide Web has also made it possible to easily establish informal marketplaces for different goods. In particular, a thriving set of barter markets exist that focus on collectible items, such as game cards. Again, these sites attract a large and global audience.

More structured online auction houses have also emerged. In these, individuals can post items that are then bid on by other market participants. The largest of these auction sites boasts a market with more than two million participants. In terms of gross revenues, the most successful auction houses are starting to rival some financial exchanges.

In fact, it is useful to contrast these informal online markets to financial exchanges, which are the most formalized marketplaces that exist. As Jaycobs (1998) describes it, a financial exchange provides four key services: matching, liquidity, information, and clearing. The financial exchange promotes matching by offering a centralized location where buyers and sellers can meet. The presence of market makers at the exchange mean that buyers and sellers do not need to coordinate when they will arrive at the market; the market makers are there to take the other side of the transaction to assure a liquid market. The financial exchange also serves as a place to aggregate, store, and distribute information, which contributes to its function as a price discovery mechanism. Finally, financial exchanges provide a clearing service to guarantee the transactions and eliminate counterparty risk.

The economies of communication and coordination that exist in online interaction (Kollock 1999a) mean that even informal online markets can excel at the matching and information functions. However, evidence has not yet been seen of market makers in these settings, although there are clearly opportunities for speculation within a market and arbitrage across markets, especially in the more structured sites such as the auction houses. The most important difference between these online markets and formal exchanges is the absence of a formal clearing mechanism or other third-party enforcement mechanism. This distinction is the defining characteristic of an *informal* market.

Risk and Reputation

Although the monetary value of trades in these online markets is small compared to transactions at a financial exchange (at least for now), the risks are still very significant for the individuals involved in the trades.[2] First, there is the fact that one is dealing with a party who may be identified only by an e-mail address and who in all likelihood lives far away, perhaps even in a different country. This is a Prisoner's Dilemma transaction that requires a great amount of trust, given that it may not be possible to track down or even identify the other party and that the two sides of the transaction are likely to be separated in both time and distance. And indeed, there is no shortage of trades that go bad. The National Consumers League[3] has gathered information on Internet fraud since February 1996. It found that online auctions were the third most common source of complaints in 1997 and the number one source in 1998. There are also some infamous examples of large-scale fraud within these informal markets. For example, in 1994, someone with the username "T. Le" posted several ads on one of the Usenet *forsale* newsgroups offering to sell a variety of computer components (Barrett 1996). The postings contained a great deal of information and offered the goods at attractive prices. Approximately 50 interested buyers sent this person money in response to the ads. In returned they received empty boxes, and the person in question disappeared with more than $13,000.

Yet despite such incidents and the absence of formal enforcement schemes, both observation of these markets and reports from the participants indicate that only a small fraction of traders default on their transactions. This is remarkable given the inherent risks in online trades and invites an investigation into these risky exchanges. These markets are, in other words, huge naturally occurring pools of prisoner's dilemma situations. This paper's goal is to explore how cooperation is created and maintained in such a seemingly unpromising setting. In particular, it focuses on the use of reputation reporting systems to encourage trustworthiness in transactions.

The study of reputation as a risk-management technique is directly relevant to both theoretical work on cooperation and trust and the practical issues of designing and running online markets. A *reputation*, as defined by Wilson (1985, pp. 27-28), is a "characteristic or attribute ascribed to one person...by another (e.g., '*A* has a reputation for courtesy'). Operationally, this is usually represented as a prediction about likely future behavior (e.g., '*A* is likely to be courteous'). It is, however, primarily an empirical statement (e.g., '*A* has been observed in the past to be courteous'). Its predictive power depends on the supposition that past behavior is indicative of future behavior."

Having interacted with someone before is, of course, a key source of information and a powerful determinant of that person's reputation. But relying only on direct personal experience is both inefficient and perilous: inefficient, because any one individual will be limited in the number of exchange partners she or he has, and perilous, because one will discover untrustworthy partners only through hard experience. Great gains are possible if information about past interactions is shared and aggregated within a group. This sharing of past interactions can take many forms, including informal gossip networks, institutionalized review systems, and even specialists whose sole job is to consume and evaluate a good or service (e.g., a restaurant critic). Theoretical work (e.g., Raub and Weesie 1990), has demonstrated the beneficial effects of shared reputations, and there is even some experimental work (Rapoport, Diekmann, and Franzen 1995) that demonstrates greater levels of cooperation when reputations are shared.

It is important to note that reputations serve as both a source of information and as a potential source of sanctions (Yamagishi and Yamagishi 1994). For the person deciding whether to enter into a transaction, the partner's reputation is a source of information that can reduce uncertainty and guide the decision of whether to trust the partner. Because of this same dynamic, the existence of shared reputations serves as an incentive for the partner to be trustworthy because of the damaging effects of acquiring a bad reputation. However, the threatened or actual sanction of acquiring a bad reputation will only be effective to the extent that accurate information is collected and disseminated among likely exchange partners. If people do not talk among themselves, if the information exchanged is inaccurate, or if a person can hide his or her identity, then reputation systems will not be an effective means of managing risk.

These concerns highlight the importance of informal online markets as a research site. On the one hand, there are new challenges to managing risk because of the ease of changing identities in online environments. On the other hand, the economies of online interaction mean that the costs of collecting and distributing information can be extremely low, making possible reputation and evaluation systems that could otherwise not be supported (cf. Avery, Resnick, and Zeckhauser forthcoming; Friedman and Resnick 1998).

The following discussion examines general approaches to managing risk in online markets and then studies two classes of systems for using reputations as a risk-management tool. These sections focus on the Usenet markets and Web barter sites. The paper then details the attempts to institutionalize reputation systems by online auction houses and closes with a discussion of the prerequisites for an online reputation system and design issues for such systems. It is important to stress that this is an investigation of a rapidly changing phenomena. Although the general issues and principles discussed will remain relevant, the details about specific markets are inevitably out of date. Web addresses are provided below for the markets under investigation, so that readers can examine the sites as they currently exist.

MANAGING RISK

The numerous hazards faced by individuals in these markets have encouraged participants to sometimes seek out third-party services in an attempt to manage these risks. Although third-party services are an interesting part of online markets, these services do not guard against all risks, impose costs of their own, and are, in fact, usually not used in online trades. Nevertheless, it is useful to briefly survey these risk-management methods before turning to endogenous solutions to the problem of risky trade.

Third-Party Services

Suggestions for the use of third-party services for online transactions have been compiled in a number of documents (e.g., King 1996, Barrett 1996). The first issue is that parties wish to guard against goods or funds that never arrive. At times individuals may also attempt to claim that goods or funds never arrived when in fact they did, as a way of backing out of their part of the exchange. Thus, it is recommended that individuals use certified mail with a return receipt or an express mail service that provides proof of delivery. The fact that a check has been received is small comfort if the check later bounces. The alternative here is to ask the buyer to send funds in the form of a money order. Interestingly, the buyer may resist doing so to preserve the option of stopping payment on the check if the goods are judged inadequate.[4]

There is also the problem that each party would prefer not to be the first to send their half of the exchange, and thereby unilaterally expose themselves to risk. Ideally, the goods and funds would be exchanged simultaneously by a neutral party. This can be accomplished through a COD (collect on delivery) service. However, there are limitations here as well. One cannot open the package to inspect the goods prior to payment, which means there is the threat that the seller has simply sent a "box of rocks." On the seller's side, there is the risk that the buyer will refuse delivery and the fact that the COD service can sometimes take a substantial length of time before delivering the funds. In addition, COD is not available in some countries, and many online markets are global markets.

These limitations and the fact that participants are increasingly dealing in high value items has encouraged the emergence of escrow services that specialize in online markets. Typically, the buyer transfers funds to the escrow service. Once the funds have cleared, the service instructs the seller to ship the goods. The buyer than has some period of time to inspect the goods and approve payment to the seller. These services charge anywhere from 2 to 15 percent of the purchase price.

While escrow services eliminate many of the risks associated with these transactions, they are used only a very small percentage of the time. These services are relatively new, and the significant fees they charge may only make sense for high-value items. Further, there are large markets in which escrow services are not an option. For example, there is a very healthy trade in bootleg audio tapes. The ambiguous legal status of these tapes precludes the use of these services. There are also many markets in which goods are exchanged for goods in barter transactions. The value of these goods may be considerable, but participants are reluctant to spend money on escrow fees, and there is the issue of how escrow agencies would set fees on a noncash transaction or administer the transfer of goods.

The fact remains that the vast majority of online transactions in these markets do not involve escrow services. Thus, the issue is to investigate the manner by which participants have endogenously managed the risks of trade.

Identity and Accountability

A collection of advice and trading tips has been assembled in a variety of documents created by experienced online traders (Kuhn 1997; Mak 1997; Barrett 1996; King 1996). A number of observers have ruefully noted that if a deal seems too good to be true, it probably is being offered as bait in hopes of taking advantage of the other party. Nevertheless, the working assumption is that most individuals can be trusted given reasonable precautions. Miscommunication and misunderstanding, however, often create difficulties among otherwise reputable parties. Hence, several observers stress the importance of frequent communication via e-mail between the buyer and seller to thoroughly describe the items, the shipping and payment terms, when funds have cleared, when a shipment has been sent, when it has arrived, and so on. Another piece of advice given in several markets is that one should start with a small trade when dealing with an unknown participant, and scale up the value of the trades if the initial exchanges go well.[5]

Most of the advice that is given centers on the issues of identifiability and accountability. Participants have a deep understanding of a lesson that is at the heart of work on social dilemmas: cooperation is much less likely when dealing with an anonymous actor. Hence, a variety of trading tips are offered that are directed toward evaluating someone's physical and electronic identity.

As a matter of course, one is advised to ask for a person's full name, address, and phone number, and not to trade with anyone who withholds this information. Along these lines, it is very common to see cautions against sending goods to someone using a post office box. These cautions either recommend that one should never trade in such circumstances or that one should insist on receiving payment before shipping the goods. Several observers recommend calling the other party, both to confirm the phone number and perhaps to also get a better sense of the person with whom one might be trading. A related suggestion is to call back at some random time to guard against the possibility that the person originally gave the number of a public phone and simply waited for one's return call. Finally, some individuals have attempted to eliminate certain risks by only trading with those in the same geographic area. There are, for example, Usenet newsgroups that are specific to certain cities (e.g., *dc.forsale*) as well as Websites that target particular areas (e.g., CityAuction). In such cases, buyer and seller can meet in person to carry out the trade. While this certainly reduces the risks of the transaction, it also imposes costs (at least in terms of the time and effort needed to get together) and eliminates some of the most powerful advantages of online markets, which include access to a vast variety of goods and a global market of potential trading partners.

Participants are, of course, also very concerned about one's online identity. If the interactions have taken place via a Usenet newsgroup or a Website, one is cautioned to always test the other person's e-mail address to ensure it is a valid address and that the potential trading partner responds. It is widely understood that there are reputable as well as questionable neighborhoods online, as indicated by domain names and e-mail addresses. An offer to sell something from a trader with the address kollock@ucla.edu signals something very different than the same offer from pete@crunchy.net. A known university (ucla.edu), company (wsj.com), or government domain (jpl.nasa.gov) implies not just a certain respectability, but also a greater probability that one would be able to track down and hold a person accountable in the case of fraud.[6]

There is also broad suspicion, or at least caution, of individuals using America Online e-mail addresses. The reason is not so much a general prejudice against users of America Online (although this exists) as it is an understanding that identity is not fixed in this system. When a person signs up for an AOL e-mail account, he or she establishes a parent account that cannot be changed and is tied to the user's personal information and credit card number. However, every user is also given a number of secondary accounts. The idea is that an entire family can operate through one account, with the parent account having certain controls over the secondary accounts. The problem is that the user name, and therefore the e-mail address, of any of these secondary accounts can be changed at will and without cost. This makes it very easy to manufacture an e-mail address that can be tossed aside after taking advantage of someone. While one can contact AOL in an attempt to hold the person accountable, this may not be worth the trouble except for high-value items, and the common belief is that one is likely to get a very slow response or even no response from AOL.[7]

An even more difficult situation has been created by the emergence of free e-mail services, which give anyone a free e-mail address on demand (such sites support themselves through advertising revenue). Given that there is no financial relationship between free e-mail services and their users, there is even less hope of actually tracking a person down or holding that person accountable. This is such a serious issue that some observers recommend using extreme care whenever dealing with a party using a free e-mail service. One person reports that 80% of the bad traders at his site used these free e-mail services (Mak 1997). Some market participants have also collected the names of these services so that one can look out for their domain names in e-mail addresses.[8]

The advice discussed above is directed toward managing risks before the execution of the trade. If the trade occurs and something goes wrong, there are also a variety of suggestions that are offered. Given the everyday challenges of one's work and personal schedule, the first piece of advice some people give is to show a little patience and not expect the goods or funds to arrive immediately. Increasingly frequent e-mail and phone queries are recommended as time goes on. If the contact information for one's trading partner was never gathered or is fraudulent, a number of observers recommend trying to track down the phone number and address of the person using a variety of search services available on the Internet.[9] If it is clear the other party does not intend to uphold his or her side of the exchange, one still has the options of posting a report of the fraudulent behavior to other members of the market (discussed below) or pursuing legal action by making a claim of mail fraud to postal authorities or bringing the person to small claims court. However, such legal responses seem to be very rare.

NEGATIVE REPUTATION SYSTEMS

There is little satisfaction in suffering silently. Having experienced a bad trade, the common reaction is to complain publicly, perhaps in the hope that it might motivate one's trading partner to make restitution or at least to warn others to watch out for this person in future trades. In our "offline" world, we might complain to our friends or business colleagues, or to an agency such as the Better Business Bureau in the case of a commercial enterprise. But on the Internet, we can complain to the world, and at almost no cost.

The Internet has radically reduced the costs of distributing information to a global audience. Thus, it is not surprising that individuals take advantage of these extraordinarily low distribution costs to air their grievances.[10] One possibility is to simply set up a Web page with a report of the fraudulent trade. In one case, the author came across a Website in which the person had uploaded scanned images of bad checks, complete with the accused person's name, address, phone number, and e-mail address. However, such untargeted and unorganized displays are likely to be of limited value—one has to seek out this site, which contains the experiences of only a single trader.

In the case of some Usenet trading newsgroups, the common response after a bad trade is to post a report of the trade to the group itself and ask what experience others have had with the questionable trader. This has the advantage that traders in this market all have a chance to view the complaints.[11] An interesting case study in this regard is the newsgroup *alt.music.bootlegs*. This group is devoted to trading bootleg audiotapes and videotapes. Drawing from the group's Frequently Asked Questions file (Kuhn 1997), *bootlegs* are defined as "recordings that have not been released by an artist's main record label. They could be live recordings, studio outtakes, rehearsals, or just jams." The focus of the group is on the trading of tapes for tapes, although sales also occur. Members of the group make a strong distinction between bootlegging and *pirating*, which is "making copies of legitimate releases and selling them as if they were legitimate" (Kuhn 1997). This is a key point for members, who maintain that trading bootleg tapes for personal use is either legal (as it certainly is in the case of groups that permit personal taping of shows—most famously, The Grateful Dead) or at least does no harm. Indeed, attempts to buy or trade pirated tapes are usually met with strong disapproval and flaming within the newsgroup.

Nevertheless, the ambiguous legality of bootleg tapes forecloses the use of an escrow service, and using a COD service does not address the main concern of participants in this market, which is the quality of the tape. Thus, the group must rely on its own devices to manage the risks of trading.

Quality is such a serious issue because of the great variance in skill and equipment among those who tape at live concerts. There is also the question of a tape's *generation* (e.g., a tape of a tape of the original recording is a second-generation tape), given that the quality of even an excellent recording deteriorates significantly with each generation. Thus, the participants face a lemons market (Akerlof 1970) in which goods are purchased before one can definitively ascertain their quality.

One response has been to gather together the accumulated knowledge of the group in a very detailed Frequently Asked Questions file (Kuhn 1997). This document goes on for more than 60 pages, providing extremely detailed specifications about how to tape or what tapes to use, how to prepare the tapes for shipping, and so on. There are even shared grading systems to rate the quality of tapes. In its detail, the document rivals the contract and delivery specifications of commercial commodities.

As helpful as this information is, it certainly does not eliminate bad trades, whether the issue is tapes or funds that never arrived, or receiving a tape of poorer quality than was advertised. One is encouraged to first try to work things out with the other trader, but if such efforts are unsuccessful, it is customary to post a complaint to the newsgroup. This has the advantage of making the report public to participants of the market and is the beginnings of a *negative reputation system*: a public system that distributes information on untrustworthy traders.

However, simply posting reports to the newsgroup has a number of shortcomings. If one is not constantly checking in with the newsgroup, it is possible to miss someone's report on a trade gone bad. Because Usenet posting are automatically deleted after a period of time, the information can be lost even to someone who tries to go over all the messages posted since one's last visit. It is also an inconvenient system in that the information is not aggregated.

Thus, it is not surprising that early in the group's history there emerged efforts to create lists of suspect traders, known as *blacklists*. These list were either posted periodically to the group or posted on a Web page. Blacklists create a kind of durable gossip that can be used as a reference by all group members in managing their risks in trading.[12] While some lists simply noted the names of bad traders, others provided richer information, including the name and e-mail address of both the accused and accuser, as well as an explanation of what went wrong with the trade. And the extremely low information-distribution costs meant that the lists could be made available to an unlimited number of individuals.

Almost immediately, however, participants realized there were problems with negative reputation systems such as blacklists. Both participants in these markets (e.g., Kuhn 1997) and scholars (e.g., Miller and Drexler 1988) have noted the same weaknesses. First, there is the risk that one can be wrongly accused. Most commonly, a person is added to a blacklist solely on the weight of a single person's report, without any further fact finding. In terms of signal detection models, the criterion threshold has been set in this case to err on the side of false alarms: avoiding trades with anyone for whom there is even the hint of untrustworthiness. Given the hazards of the transaction, it is perhaps understandable that any report of untrustworthiness should be enough to stain one's reputation. But the serious danger here is that as a result of a misunderstanding, circumstances beyond an individual's control, or the deliberate desire to damage someone's name, a person will be falsely accused and suffer the consequences. As a result, some blacklists allow the accused to offer a response or even to be removed from the list if the accused reaches a satisfactory resolution with the accuser (the accuser then contacts the manager of the list to say the trade has been settled). Such procedures still leave blacklists open to mistakes and manipulation.

A second weakness in negative reputation systems exists that condemns such systems to failure in most online environments. Blacklists are ineffective to the extent that it is easy for an individual to assume a new identity and so cast off the negative reputation. While this is difficult in the physical world (though not impossible, as witness relocation programs demonstrate), changing identities online is trivially easy, especially given the rise of free e-mail services. Thus, it is probably the case that pure negative reputations systems are doomed to failure in current online environments.[13]

POSITIVE REPUTATION SYSTEMS

An alternative way to structure a reputation system is to base it on positive references. A positive reputation system attends to the other tail in the distribution of trustworthiness. Rather than marking and avoiding untrustworthy traders, the point is to mark and seek out those market participants who have a history of successful trades. This can take the form of individual traders appending a list of positive references (with e-mail addresses) to their post or aggregated lists of good traders with references.

The requirements of a positive reputation system are less onerous than a negative system. The key requisite condition is that one cannot easily claim the identity of another (known as *spoofing* in many online groups), so that one cannot improperly damage or free-ride on that person's reputation. Changing identities serves no purpose if an individual has a positive reputation because that individual cannot carry his or her reputation capital to the new identity. It would still be possible for an untrustworthy trader to continually change identities as a way of at least having a neutral reputation, but if others will only trade with those who have established successful track records or impose additional conditions on those who have no track record (see below), this will not be a successful strategy.

An interesting case study in the use of positive reputation systems can be found in the Web-based trading posts that have been established for game cards. The greatest amount of trading seems to revolve around the game *Magic*, which is a sophisticated strategy card game that inspires a near-obsessive devotion in many of its players. Drawing from a large population of cards, a player assembles a deck of cards that is used in a contest against another player's deck. The skill comes in picking a general strategy among the many that are available, as well as in the tactical decision of how to assemble the deck. The game is constructed such that no one strategy is likely to dominate play; each approach has its strengths and limitations and is particularly useful against certain other families of strategies and particularly vulnerable against others. In addition, the manufacturer of the game periodically releases new cards to keep the game fresh. Given that one purchases a pack of cards without knowing the contents of the pack, assembling a particular deck can be an expensive proposition and can result in many unwanted cards.

For all these reasons, a huge secondary market quickly emerged in which players traded (or sold) cards to each other. For many individuals, trading *Magic* cards is a serious activity that has become more important than the original game. The is no shortage of strategic challenges in trading the cards, and there is the possibility of taking on speculative positions as the value of certain cards ebb and flow. There are even individuals involved in this secondary market for whom selling cards is a significant or primary source of income. A valuable card can command hundreds of dollars, and there is a global market of players.

The sites focused on for this study are concerned with the barter exchange of cards for cards. Hence COD services are irrelevant. Escrow services are also not useful because it is a barter exchange. Thus, the participants in this market must develop their own mechanisms to manage risky exchange. These risks are quite serious. While the dollar value of many transactions may not be that great, the subjective value of the cards to the players is very substantial. Occasionally, large-scale frauds are also committed.

An elegant procedure has been developed based on acquiring positive references from previous trading partners (e.g., Burrows 1997; Mak 1997). The norm is that the person with the fewer references sends his or her cards first. Once the cards are received and inspected, the trader with the greater number of references then sends his or her cards to complete the trade. Traders with approximately equal number of references are expected to "simul-send," that is, send their cards to each other at the same time. Note that this structure means that a neutral reputation (no references) puts one at a disadvantage and so provides a disincentive for switching identities.

Another implication of this structure is that a new entrant in the market will have to send her or his goods first until a reputation is established. Because the newcomer bears a disproportionate amount of the risk in these trades, it is suggested that one begin by proposing trades with those who have established long lists of references as a way of mitigating one's own risk. Further, every attempt should be made to be sure the person with whom one is trading is happy with the terms and execution of the trade so that one might ask to use the person as a reference. As one participant puts it, "Net refs are like golden eggs and should be earned by fairly trading with everyone you trade. Nurture them. Cultivate each trade as though all your future trades depended on each one. They do! They are you[r] ticket to not having always to ship first" (Burrows 1997).

Merely seeing a list of references is not enough. Cases are recounted of traders who simply copied someone else's references in hopes of masquerading as a reputable trader. For this reason, participants are cautioned to always check at least a subset of the references to make sure the e-mail address is valid and that the reference has in fact traded successfully with the person in question. References are discounted or rejected if they are from individuals with e-mail addresses from the same domain as the trader in question. The reason is that it is assumed the references may just be alternate accounts the trader has set up to inflate his or her reputation. References using e-mail address from AOL or one of the free e-mail serves are particularly suspect, for reasons that were discussed above.

It is understood that such efforts can decrease the risks of trade, but not eliminate them. A particularly disturbing strategy for fraud that has been seen in a number of online markets is the person who works hard at establishing a trustworthy reputation and then sets up a whole series of significant trades and defaults on all them, disappearing into a new identity after the fact.[14]

Aggregated lists of trustworthy traders have also been established. Sometimes anyone with positive references are listed, with the names of the references following their name. On other lists, a criterion must be met, such as a minimum of 20 references, all from different domains than one's own and all subject to verification before inclusion on the list (Burrows 1997).

INSTITUTIONALIZED GOSSIP:
ONLINE AUCTION HOUSES

Many of these reputation-based methods of risk management are now being institutionalized by for-profit companies that have set up online auction houses. While some online auctions sell off new merchandise from manufactures, this study focuses on person-to-person auction sites in which individuals are trading with other individuals. These person-to-person auction companies are still informal markets in the sense that there is no formal clearing mechanism, and the companies do not guarantee the terms of the trade.[15]

In exchange for a commission on the sale, and sometimes a listing fee, anyone with Internet access can post an item for auction at these sites. The posting can include an elaborate description and pictures, and interested parties can place bids for the item. Almost any object imaginable has been offered for auction, although illegal goods are banned and adult material is sometimes restricted or banned as well.

The best-designed auction sites address a number of limitations that exist in the Usenet *forsale* newsgroups. In the Usenet groups, it can take time for listings to propagate to all the servers, traders have little control about when a post to a Usenet group will disappear, it can be difficult to estimate the market value of an item, and there is no structured, institutionalize system for collecting and distributing information about participants' reputations. Instead, the better online auction markets offer sites in which:

- Listings appear immediately after they've been posted.
- The seller has direct control over how long the offer is available by specifying the length of an auction in days.
- Buyers get immediate feedback about the current best offer for an item and know exactly when the auction for that item will end.
- Buyers and sellers can get a good sense of fair market value by reviewing the history of auctions for similar items.
- Buyers and sellers are both subject to peer review.[16]

As of autumn 1998, there are thousands of auction sites on the web, and some of these sites are huge and are growing exponentially. Thus, this paper focuses on those person-to-person auction sites that are the largest or have been highly rated for their design and offerings (Hughes 1997).

eBay Auctions

Currently the largest, and one of the oldest (launched September 1995), person-to-person auction houses is eBay.[17] Statistics from autumn 1998 show it has approximately 1 million items for sale on any given day, more than 1.2 million registered users, and had more than 195 million dollars in gross merchandise sales for the third quarter of 1998. Since its inception, more than 30 million auctions have been completed at the site, and eBay boasts a sell-through rate of approximately 60 percent (e.g., the percentage of offered items that result in a sale). It has grown at the rate of 20 percent to 30 percent per month and has been profitable since its inception. The site receives more than 20 million hits per day, and more time is spent at this site by Internet users than at any other commerce site. In fact, only Yahoo! and AOL rank above eBay among all web sites in terms of time spent at the site.[18]

Remarkably, eBay offers no warranties or guarantees for any of the goods that are auctioned off. Buyers and sellers assume all risks for the transaction, with eBay serving as a listing agency. It would seem to be a market ripe with the possibility of large-scale fraud and deceit. Yet, the default rate for trades conducted through eBay is remarkably small. Both eBay and the participants in its market credit an institutionalized reputation system at the site—known as the Feedback Forum—for the very high rate of successful trades.

After every seller's or bidder's name is a number in parenthesis. In the case of a seller, the information is displayed as follows:

Seller   name@company.com (265) ★

           (view seller's feedback) (view seller's other auctions) (ask seller a question)

The number is a summary measure of a person's reputation in the eBay market. Registered users are allowed to post positive, negative, and neutral comments about users with whom they have traded. Each positive comment is given a score of +1; each negative comment is given a score of –1; neutral comments do not affect one's score in either direction. Thus a score of 10 might mean 10 positive comments, or 110 positive comments, 100 negative comments, and any number of neutral comments. At certain levels, market participants are also awarded a color star that marks the number of net positive comments they have received (e.g., a rating of 10-99 receives a yellow star, a rating of 100-499 receives a turquoise star, a rating of 500-999 receives a purple star, a rating of 1,000-9,000 receives a red star, and a shooting star is reserved for those with a rating of 10,000 or higher). An interesting enforcement mechanism is that eBay users with a net negative score of –4 or lower are automatically barred from trading by the software system.

One is able to contact the person via e-mail by clicking on the name; clicking on the number following someone's name leads to their full feedback profile. There one finds the full list of comments, with e-mail links and ratings numbers for every evaluator as well (thus, one can explore the reputation of the evaluators just as one can the evaluated). A typical positive comment might be "Well packaged, fast delivery. Highly recommended. A+." There is also a summary table at the head of the comments (e.g., see Table 1).

Although a user may rate someone an indefinite number of times, he or she can affect that person's rating by at most one point. This restriction prevents both attempts to completely undermine someone's reputation as well as attempts to inflate someone's rating (e.g., a circle of friends pushing each other's ratings up in a never ending spiral).[19] The summary table also notes if some of the comments came from users who are no longer registered participants of the market. Comments from someone who is no longer registered are automatically converted to a neutral rating.

Summary of Most Recent Comments			
Overall profile makeup	Past 7 days	Past month	Past 6 mo.
300 positives. 283 are from unique users and count toward the final feedback rating.	Positive 40	143	300
4 neutrals. 1 are from users no longer registered.	Neutral 0	1	4
1 negatives. 1 are from unique users and count toward the final feedback rating	Negative 0	0	1
	Total 40	144	305

A high feedback rating is an extremely valuable asset. Many participants report that they are more willing to trade, or even that they will only trade, with someone with a high rating. In that sense, some traders create a brand identity that increases their volume of sales or even the price at which they are able to sell items. On a rotating basis, eBay has even featured some of its most highly rated traders on its opening Web page. Such public displays of highly rated traders are likely to be a powerful motivator, both in terms of the status of being marked as a top trader and because it is likely to send more bidders to one's auctions. One auction house, Auction Universe,[20] even maintains a constantly updated list of its top 50 traders based on reputation rating. For all these reasons, users in these auction markets often stress the importance of always adding a positive comment to someone's feedback profile when a trade goes well.

Even a few negative ratings can seriously damage a reputation, and so frequent traders are very careful about nurturing their rating by providing swift execution of honest trades. The potential damage of a negative comment is a subject of great concern among frequent participants. Both eBay and informal Websites that have been set up by users caution that one should post a negative comment only after extensive efforts at trying to resolve the difficulty directly with the other party. The fact that any one user can only affect someone's rating by one point serves as a limit to the amount of damage one can do. Nevertheless, it is inevitable that negative rating are posted (sometimes hastily) that the counterparty regards as illegitimate.

Interestingly, eBay has a policy that once a comment is posted, neither eBay nor any user can delete that comment. One can post a rebuttal to a comment to give the other side of the story,[21] but it is not possible to retract a comment if both parties have reached an understanding later in time. It is also impossible to selectively edit or censor comments. One can choose to make one's entire feedback profile private, but this is a huge disadvantage in a market that relies on these reputations.

Other Online Auction Sites

While eBay is by far the largest person-to-person auction market at this time, it is useful to compare other prominent auction sites to see how their systems are differently structured. Risk management at each of the auctions houses discussed below is also centered around a reputation system.

One such auction site is Haggle Online.[22] Unlike eBay, this auction system disaggregates the single ratings number into two totals: one for positive comments and one for negative comments. In the case of a seller, the following information is displayed:

> **Seller e-mail address:** name@company.com
> **Haggle Online User since:** 1-Jan-1998 14:00 PST
> **Number of listings:** 23 (click for open listings)
> **+ Positive/– Negative comments:** +266/–2

Splitting the positive and negative comments eliminates some of the ambiguity that occurs in eBay's one-number rating. The length of time one has been a participant in this market is also noted. Haggle Online does not display the number of neutral comments in the summary ratings, though of course this could be done very simply.

In fact, another auction site—CityAuction[23]—display totals for positive, neutral, and negative comments after a users name, preceded by the total number of trades in which the user has been involved:

> Seller: name@company.com (365: 265+ / 4 / 2-)
> (view **feedback** on seller) (view seller's **other auctions**) (**contact** seller)

Listing the total number of trades is useful as a comparison to total number of comments to get a sense of what proportion of trades have been rated. Also, having information about *both* length of time in the market and number of trades could be helpful in evaluating the experience of a trader and determining the rate at which the trader participates in auctions.

A different system of arriving at a summary measure of reputation was used by Onsale Exchange. Onsale is a new merchandise auction house that attempted to open up a separate section—known as Onsale Exchange—for person-to-person auctions.[24] In this system, rather than being given a binary choice between coding one's feedback comments as positive or negative (or perhaps neutral), participants were asked to rate their satisfaction with the trade on a scale of 0 to 5. What appeared after the trader's name was his or her average rating, displayed in stars. Thus, in the case of a seller, the format was as follows:

JK of Los Angeles, CA, USA About the Seller Current rating: ★★★★

Giving users something other than a dichotomous choice in categorizing their comments promises a more fine-grained rating system, although the fact that there are only five discrete summary ratings displayed (one cannot display a rating of, e.g., 4.32 stars) means that a lot of information is lost.

Just as in eBay, clicking on the summary rating at each of these auction sites takes one to the actual list of comments. Here again a variety of different formats can be seen. For Haggle Online, the name and e-mail address for each evaluator is include, but not the evaluator's rating. Nor is a summary table of comments for recent time periods given, as is the case on eBay. However, Haggle Online does provide a link for each comment that references the transaction in question, which means one can recover the value of the good, how active the bidding was, and so on.[25] Haggle Online also provides a very different way of processing comments. When a participant submits a comment about a trader, the comment is first sent to that trader, who has the option of publishing the comment or censoring it. If the comment is censored, this is noted on the trader's list of comments. It is also possible for a comment to be retracted by the person who originally made it if, for example, an initially troublesome trade was eventually settled to the satisfaction of both parties. When a comment is retracted, the text disappears, but the fact that a comment has been retracted is explicitly noted on the trader's feedback page.

This different format has a number of implications. Unlike eBay, on Haggle Online it is possible to exercise a "line-item veto," in which only certain comments are censored. It is also possible to repair (at least in part) a negative comment if the evaluator later agrees to retract the comment. That fact that such actions are noted on the trader's feedback page mean that a history of troublesome trades cannot be completely hidden, even if they are not reflected in the summary rating numbers.

The options for handling comments on CityAuction are very similar to eBay. Individuals can respond to the comments evaluators have made or block all their comments from being seen, but currently one cannot selectively censor or retract comments. On Onsale Exchange, such options were not possible, and the site had the curious policy of only listing the most recent comments about an individual. The attempt may have been to avoid information overload or save on storage space, but the absence of a complete feedback history for a trader means a great deal of important information is lost. This is especially true given that the summary reputation measure is an average, and so one has no information about the total number of 5-star, 4-star, and so on comments or the total number of trades in which the person had been involved.

The Impact of Reputation

The efficacy of these reputation systems to manage the risks of unsecured trades seems to be impressive. Two years into its history (summer 1997), eBay released a report stating that of the 2 million auctions that occurred from May through August 1997, only 27 were considered to involve possible criminal fraud (these cases were referred to the U.S. Postal Authority for prosecution as mail fraud). The report by eBay also stated that more than 99.99 percent of auctions attracting bids were successfully complete (reported in Hughes 1997; see Chervitz 1998 for the same low levels of fraud as reported by eBay's CEO in an October 1998 paper).. An online publication (Hughes 1997) that reported on Internet auction sites also stated that its own research found that negative comments on trades were quite rare, accounting for fewer than one percent of feedback on eBay. Once a trader has established a positive reputation there is a very great incentive to maintain and improve on one's rating, and traders with negative reputations are selected out by at least two mechanisms: other market participants will be reluctant to trade with them, and at a certain point (a net negative rating of –4), the software prohibits further trading. Participants in these reputation-based auction markets also claim that the vast majority of trades are successful despite the inherent risk.[26]

Conceptually, reputations should be expected to affect not just rates of cooperation, but also the price of goods in these markets. If these reputation systems do in fact provide useful information and an incentive to behave in a trustworthy manner, buyers should be willing to pay more for a good if it comes from a highly rated seller, at least when the transaction involves significant risk. Preliminary evidence from a quantitative study of reputations on eBay suggests this is in fact the case (Kollock 1999b). At least for some high-value goods, the seller's reputation had a positive and statistically significant effect on the price buyers paid for identical goods of equivalent quality. This effect of reputation seems to diminish or disappear for low value goods.[27]

DISCUSSION

In what seems at first to be a very unpromising environment, participants in informal online markets have created an elegant and efficacious set of solutions for managing risk. Some of these markets have also been elaborated in impressive ways by the participants. Users of eBay have created their own independent Websites in which advice, strategy, and answers to frequently asked questions are collected. Some experienced eBay traders have even set themselves up as for-fee consultants, offering new users advice on how to set up an auction to attract attention. But perhaps more noteworthy are the number of experienced traders who offer free help and advice to others on a continuing basis. While there are undoubtedly some individuals who visit eBay only once or sporadically to buy particular objects, there are also core groups of traders in each category area (e.g., trading cards, coins, antiques, Beanie Babies, etc.) who are there continually and come to know each other. EBay has encourage the formation of these communities of traders by providing message boards so that users can interact with each other. Both casual interaction and serious discussions occur here, covering such issues as spotting counterfeit goods or warnings about rogue traders. Some traders have even created "neighborhood" watch groups that oversee particular categories of auctions for violations of trading rules or suspicious activity. To further encouraging a sense of identity and commitment, eBay has recently begun offering its registered users free personal Web pages, on which traders can post information about themselves and their auctions. The sense of fellowship felt in some of these trading communities is striking. There are even cases of traders contributing goods or money to another participant who could not otherwise afford a particular object. At least for the core users, this is not a market of atomized price-takers.

Requisite Features

As impressive as these risk-management techniques seem to be, it is important to ask what the prerequisites are for an online reputation system. This speaks to the question of how generalizable these solutions are to other settings.

A number of elements must be in place for an online reputation system to work effectively and provide an incentive for trustworthiness in trading. First, the costs for submitting and distributing ratings must be very low. This is, of course, one of the great advantages of online trading—distributions costs can approach zero, and the system software can also be used as an automatic monitoring agent, prohibiting, for example, individuals with low ratings from trading.

Second, to be effective, there must be many alternative trading partners. It is the fact that one can easily go to another trader with a better reputation that serves as a powerful motivator to create and maintain a positive reputation. If a single trader or cartel has near monopoly control over particular desired goods, one may have to trade despite a questionable reputation.

Third, the costs involved in impersonating another trader must be very great to prevent a trader from damaging or free-riding on another trader's reputation.

Finally, the reputation server itself must be trustworthy. Whether an individual or a company is collecting and distributing reputation ratings, they lose their value if it is believed there is negligence or deceit on the part of the owner of the system or if it is believed that the software does not work properly.

Further Studies and Design Issues

The success of these markets reinforces the importance of some recent trends in theoretical and experimental work on social dilemmas. Early work used models in which actors could neither leave the interaction nor choose their partners. More recently, researchers investigating the dynamics of cooperation have relaxed these constraints, examining settings in which actors have the option of choosing new exchange partners (e.g., Hayashi 1993, Yamagishi et al. 1994) or even choosing the game structure (i.e., the value of how much is at risk; Kakiuchi and Yam-agishi 1997). Such options are clearly important to the working of these markets, in which participants can decide with whom to trade or the level of risk they want to assume. The intriguing success of these markets invites controlled experimental studies that tease out the structural features that encourage cooperation.

In addition, as well-structured as some of these reputation systems are, they by no means exhaust the possibilities. Both in terms of designing better systems for actual use and to study these systems rigorously, it is important to lay out the elements of a distributed reputation system and ask about the different ways in which it might be constructed. Below some of the key design issues and some different possible formats are outlined.

Evaluators

The first issue that needs to be addressed is, who is permitted to post an evaluation? "Anyone," is one possible answer. Somewhat more restrictive would be to let only registered participants in a market submit comments about a trader. Some of the auction houses examined further restrict the ability to comment on a transaction to only those who have actually placed a bid.[28] It would be possible to be even more restrictive and only allow those who have completed a trade with someone to comment on that person's trustworthiness. However, there are times when it seems natural to allow at least other bidders to offer feedback even if they have not consummated a trade—for example, to protest a seller ending an auction earlier than scheduled without offering a valid excuse. Other sorts of restrictions might be added: eBay allows an individual to affect another's reputation rating by at most one point, and the rating of comments from a person who is no longer registered are automatically converted to neutral. CityAuction requires a three-day wait after the close of an auction before submitting comments. Presumably, City Auction hopes to diminish the number of comments that might be written in haste and allow the parties a reasonable amount of time to complete the details of the transaction.

Evaluations

A very important issue is how the evaluations themselves should be structured. To date, the common format is to allow a free-form comment that is categorized as positive, negative, or perhaps neutral. Other possibilities include allowing ratings on a continuous scale or perhaps using a structured set of survey questions as a substitute or addition to free-form comments. Given that many of the comments have started to follow a common pattern (e.g., commenting on the quality of goods, how well the goods were packed for mailing, how quickly the other trader answered questions and passed on information, and a grade such as "A+"), it would be reasonably easy to create a set of questionnaire items that the evaluator could fill out. Collecting comments in this way would also permit other sorts of data analyses and ratings, such as separate ratings for quality of packaging or speed of service.

History of Evaluations

The aggregated collection of comments for a trader might simply be put together as one long list. But even in this simple case there are a number of design questions. Should every comment be displayed or only the most recent comments (as was the case for Onsale Exchange)? What information for evaluators should be displayed? Haggle Online, for example, provides the e-mail address for all evaluators, as well as a link to the transaction that is being commented on, while eBay lists each evaluator's reputation rating. Listing the evaluator's rating can be an important way of deciding how much weight to place on a comment, and recipients of negative comments sometimes point out the evaluator's low rating, as a way of discounting the feedback. Some auction houses also try to digest the list of comments to make it easier to evaluate. For example, eBay provides a table showing the breakdown of positive, negative, and neutral comments for the past seven days, past month, and past six months. Tables and other ways of distilling the history of evaluations are likely to become more important over time, as the list of comments for active traders extends into the thousands.

Summary Measures

Each of the auction houses examined also recognized the importance of providing some sort of short, summary measures that could be appended to a person's name. Possibilities here include totals for positive and negative comments, net positive comments (positive—negative), an average evaluation score (as in Onsale Exchange's five-star system), total number of trades, and starting date as a participant in the market. Other criteria and other measures of central tendency could also be explored—for example, might it be useful to report median scores as well as the mean or to weight the rating one receives by the value of the good traded? And apart from the issue of what summary measures should be appended to a trader's name, there is the question of when this information should be displayed: When one is a seller? A buyer? An evaluator? At all times? Finally, highlighting traders with exceptionally impressive reputations is likely to have powerful effects. Auction Universe, as an example, provided a constantly updated list of the 50 traders with the highest ratings.

Modifying Evaluations

Another design issue is the extent to which posted evaluations can be censored, retracted, or commented on. The strictest policy, such as the one eBay follows, is to not allow individuals to censor specific comments or evaluators to retract comments—the only option is to post a reply to a comment. Haggle online, as a contrast, permits both censoring individual comments and the retraction of comments, although in both cases these actions are noted in the trader's permanent history. Another option would be to allow censoring or retracting comments without the "residue" of a note indicating the action.

Evaluating the relative strengths of different designs suggests a whole set of experimental studies. In general, online markets represent an extraordinary opportunity to study the dynamics of exchange and cooperation. In-depth field studies, quantitative analyses of market data, and experimental studies of the efficacy of different reputation systems should all be pursued.

ACKNOWLEDGMENTS

I wish to thank Jason Fisher and John Malonson for their help in this project. I also thank the editors for their comments on an earlier draft.

NOTES

1. For reviews of the research literature on social dilemmas, see Kollock (1998), Messick and Brewer (1983), and Dawes (1980).

2. Even in the case of small-scale exchanges, the value of the trade is almost always greater than what is at risk to subjects in experimental studies of exchange and social dilemmas.

3. http://www.fraud.org/

4. Paying by credit card can also eliminate a number of risks, but one must be an authorized merchant to receive credit card payments, which is rarely the case in these person-to-person transactions.

5. This strategy of beginning with a low-risk exchange and then moving to greater levels of interdependence (i.e., the possibility of both greater profits and greater losses) has only recently begun to be studied in the experimental social dilemma literature (Kakiuchi and Yamagishi 1997).

6. It should be noted, however, that it has become increasingly easy and inexpensive for individuals to register their own .com domain names and thus signal these same qualities, even though *President@first_trust.com* may be only the creative construction of a young student. In contrast, domain names ending in .edu and .gov cannot be easily obtained.

7. The many free disks that AOL has distributed offering free accounts for a period of time has also exacerbated these problems.

8. While avoiding individuals who use free e-mail accounts may be good advice, it may also eliminate an increasingly large number of potential trading partners as free e-mail services become more popular and more respectable.

9. It is the sign of the youth of some of the traders that one of the pieces of advice offered if a trade has gone bad is attempting to contact the trader's parents.

10. Hence the joke that alludes to the tag line from the movie *Aliens*: "In cyberspace, everyone can hear you scream."

11. However, there is a norm against posting such reports in some newsgroups, or at least posting them in a separate, related newsgroup devoted to the discussion of such issues (King 1996). The concern is to make as small a demand on the bandwidth of the network as possible (because of the structure of the Usenet, which is replicated and distributed across many computer servers), but this also

means that valuable trading information may not be seen by the participants. Moving to Web-based trading sites in which all the information is stored on a single server allieviates many of these bandwidth concerns.

12.   Of course, as a public good it also requires that someone is willing to take on the job of creating and maintaining the list.

13.   See the discussion on pseudonym commitments by Friedman and Resnick (1998), as a way of liomiting identity exchanges.

14.   The strategy of building up a reputation to be in a position to defraud others is one that the author has also seen in his experimental studies (Kollock 1994).

15.   Typically at sites selling new mechandise (e.g., Onsale: http://www.onsale.com/), payment is made via credit card, and the new goods come with warranties. These features eliminate many of the risks of a transaction and so make these markets less relevant as a site to study endogenous solutions to the problem of risky trade.

16.   http://www.haggle.com/about.html

17.   http://www.ebay.com

18.   Despite its success, eBay was relatively unknown by the general public until its initial public offering in September 1998.

19.   Note, however, that there is still the danger of using multiple free e-mail accounts to achieve these ends.

20.   http://www.auctionuniverse.com

21.   EBay has announced it will change its Feedback Forum to also allow the evaluator to post a follow-up comment to clarify the original evaluation.

22.   http://www.haggle.com

23.   http://www.cityauction.com/

24.   Originally at http://www.onsale.com/exchange.html, Onsale subsequently closed down its person-to-person auction site, transferring the open auctions to the newly formed Yahoo Auction site (http://auctions.yahoo.com/), with which it had entered into a partnership.

25.   EBay plans to add this feature to its Feedback Forum.

26.   As suggestive as this evidence is, it is, of course, no substitute for controlled studies of reputation and risk.

27.   Again, it is important to stress that these are preliminary findings.

28.   Sometimes this restriction exists only as a norm; other times, it is programmed into the software.

REFERENCES

Akerlof, G.A. 1970. "The Market for 'Lemons': Quality Uncertainty and the Market Mechanism." *Quarterly Journal of Economics* 84: 488-500.

Avery, C., P. Resnick, and R. Zeckhauser. Forthcoming. "The Market for Evaluations." *American Economic Review.*

Barrett, D.J. 1996. "Buying and Selling on the Net." Pp. 83-98 in *Bandits on the Information Superhighway.* Cambridge, MA: O'Reilly & Associates.

Burrows, D. 1997. *Dave's Magic Trading Post.* Website: http://www.cobweb.net/~quail/magic.htm

Chervitz, D. 1998. "IPO First Words." CBS MarketWatch (October 26). Website: http://cbs.marketwatch.com.

Dawes, R. 1980. "Social Dilemmas." *Annual Review of Psychology* 31: 169-193.

Friedman, E., and P. Resnick. 1998. "The Social Cost of Cheap Pseudonyms: Fostering Cooperation on the Internet." Proceedings of the 1998 Telecommunications Policy Research Conference, Washington, DC.

Hayashi, N. 1993. "From Tit-For-Tat to Out-For-Tat: The Dilemma of The Prisoner's Network." *Sociological Theory and Methods* 8, 1(13): 19-32. (Japanese)

Hughes, G.P. 1997. *Auction Land Online Report.* Website: http://www.neomax.com/ (now defunct).

Jaycobs, R. 1998. "The Internet: The Ultimate Solution?" *Futures Industry* 8(4): 11-13.

Kakiuchi, R., and T. Yamagishi. 1997. "The Dilemma of Trust." Seventh International Conference on Social Dilemmas. Cairns, Australia

King, D. 1996. *The Usenet Marketplace FAQ.* Website: http://www.fmn.net/FAQ/index.html

Kollock, P. 1994. "The Emergence of Exchange Structures: An Experimental Study of Uncertainty, Commitment, and Trust." *American Journal of Sociology* 100(2): 313-345.

Kollock, P. 1998. "Social Dilemmas: The Anatomy of Cooperation." *Annual Review of Sociology* 24: 183-214.

Kollock, P. 1999a. "The Economies of Online Cooperation: Gifts and Public Goods in Cyberspace." In *Communities in Cyberspace,* edited by M. Smith and P. Kollock. London: Routledge.

Kollock, P. 1999b. "The Value of Reputation." Working paper, UCLA.

Kuhn, J. 1997. *Official Frequently Asked Questions for alt.music.bootlegs.* FTP: ftp://ftp.visi.com/users/astanley/ambfaq.txt

Lerner, A. 1972. "The Economics and Politics of Consumer Sovereignty." *American Economic Review* 62(2): 258-266.

Mak, I. 1997. *Beyond Dominia.* Website: http://www.bdominia.com/

Messick, D.M., and M.B. Brewer. 1983. "Solving Social Dilemmas." Pp. 11-44 in *Review of Personality and Social Psychology,* Vol. 4, edited by L. Wheeler and P. Shaver. Beverly Hills, CA: Sage.

Miller, M.S., and K.E. Drexler. 1988. "Markets and Computation: Agorics Open Systems" In *The Ecology of Computation,* edited by B. Huberman. Elsevier Science Publishers/North-Holland.

Rapoport, A., A. Diekmann, and A. Franzen. 1995. "Experiments with Social Traps IV: Reputations Effects in the Evolution of Cooperation." *Rationality and Society* 7(4): 431-441.

Raub, W., and J. Weesie. 1990. "Reputation and Efficiency in Social Interactions: An Example of Network Effects." *American Journal of Sociology* 96(3): 626-654.

Wilson, R. 1985. "Reputations in Games and Markets." Pp. 27-62 in *Game-Theoretic Models of Bargaining,* edited by A. Roth. Cambridge: Cambridge University Press.

Yamagishi, T., N. Hayashi, and N. Jin. 1994. "Prisoner's Dilemma Networks: Selection Strategy Versus Action Strategy." Pp. 233-250 in *Social Dilemmas and Cooperation,* edited by U. Schulz, W. Albers, and U. Mueller. New York: Springer-Verlag

Yamagishi, T., and M. Yamagishi. 1994. "Trust and Commitment in the United States and Japan." *Motivation and Emotion* 18(2): 129-166.

PART OF LIFE'S RICH TAPESTRY
STEREOTYPING AND THE POLITICS
OF INTERGROUP RELATIONS

Penelope J. Oakes, Katherine J. Reynolds,
S. Alexander Haslam, and John C. Turner

ABSTRACT

This chapter presents the case for considering social stereotyping as, first and foremost, an intergroup phenomenon. Employing the social cognitive analysis offered by self-categorization theory (Turner 1985), it is argued that accounts of the cognitive processes involved in stereotyping must be developed within a metatheoretical context that explicitly recognizes the importance and distinctiveness of intergroup relations. Following a brief discussion of the nature of the categorization process, the chapter reviews some of our recent research, which attempts to demonstrate (1) that stereotyping distinctively characterizes intergroup as compared to interpersonal contexts, and (2) that the process is a context-sensitive means of both reflecting and shaping intergroup relations. More specifically, we review work on the conditions of stereotype use, perceived group homogeneity, stereotype change, and the influence of power in stereotyping. It is concluded that stereotyping is simply impression formation in

Advances in Group Processes, Volume 16, pages 125-160.
Copyright © 1999 by JAI Press Inc.
All rights of reproduction in any form reserved.
ISBN: 0-7623-0452-9

intergroup contexts. The social-psychological and political implications of our argument are discussed.

This chapter argues that social stereotyping should be understood, first and foremost, as an intergroup phenomenon—an expression of intergroup relations. Although this perspective has always been represented in the range of social-psychological answers to questions about stereotyping, the recent dominance of social cognition has produced analyses in which the realities of intergroup conflict, cooperation, and coexistence play virtually no part. We think that it is time to reemphasize the essential, indeed inalienable, connection between intergroup relations and social stereotyping.

Some of the earliest social-psychological investigations of stereotyping stand as evidence that the process is intimately connected with and responsive to current intergroup dynamics (e.g., Buchanan 1951; Meenes 1943; Seago 1947; Sinha and Upadhyaya 1960; Vinacke 1956). Perhaps most importantly, Sherif's classic field studies of intergroup conflict and cooperation demonstrated that stereotypes are products of intergroup relations, an outcome rather than the initial determinant of the quality of intergroup interaction. In his 1967 overview of the field studies and their implications for the social psychology of intergroup relations, Sherif comments:

> [Stereotypes] are not self-generated psychologically. They are generated in the course of interchanges between people who have formed a sense of identity, as they pursue their goals in a world peopled by others who also have their own aspirations and make their own moves to attain them (Sherif 1967, p. 3).

For Sherif, stereotypes are part of the social-psychological currency in a context defined by differentiating affiliations and conflicts of interest. They emerge within goal-oriented intergroup "interchanges" and perhaps serve important functions for group members as they pursue their identity-related goals.

The development of the field of social cognition brought with it a subtly altered approach to stereotyping in which intergroup dynamics became relatively unimportant. Stereotyping came to be defined as "a category-based cognitive response to another person" (Fiske 1993, p. 623), provoked primarily by internal cognitive demands for economical processing (e.g., Macrae, Milne, and Bodenhausen 1994; see Spears and Haslam 1997; cf. Sherif's comment above). The emphasis was on category use and its psychological determinants, with no necessary reference to group affiliations or contexts.

Sherif's intergroup perspective was, however, carried forward within the stereotyping literature, most explicitly in the work of Tajfel (e.g., 1981). He suggested that our understanding of social stereotypes should follow an "analytical sequence" (p. 163), which began with group processes, group contexts, the group functions of stereotypes, and then considered individual (including cognitive) functions and processes as explicitly defined and constrained by group-level considerations. In other words, and just as Sherif had argued, the realities of group life come first, stereotypes follow. Tajfel concluded that, rather than being part of a "static, stable consensus" underlying observed conflicts and coalitions, stereotypes should be seen as "shifting perspectives closely related to the individuals' evaluation of the equally shifting social situations which are perceived *in terms of the relations between the groups involved*" (Tajfel 1981, p. 166, emphasis in original).

Developing Tajfel's analysis, self-categorization theory (SCT) treats stereotypes as "group products, determined by intergroup relationships" (Oakes, Haslam, and Turner 1994, p. 114). Explicitly countering social cognition's portrayal of stereotyping as an unfortunate but cognitively unavoidable *distortion* of person perception, SCT considers stereotyping as simply impression formation in intergroup contexts, contexts in which individuals' shared and differentiating social group memberships, rather than their individual differences, are salient (Oakes et al. 1994; Oakes and Turner 1990; Oakes, Turner, and Haslam, 1991; Turner et al. 1994). As such, stereotyping is seen as appropriate, psychologically valid, accuracy oriented in just the same way as individuated impression formation is appropriate and accuracy oriented in interpersonal contexts (Oakes and Reynolds 1997). Importantly, the context-dependence of the stereotyping process is emphasized. With Tajfel, the "static, stable consensus" is rejected in favor of an appreciation of stereotypes as shifting, dynamic aspects of the judgment processes through which individuals make sense of and pursue their goals within intergroup contexts (Haslam et al. 1996; Haslam et al. 1992; Oakes, Haslam and Reynolds, 1999; see also Ellemers and van Knippenberg 1997; Hopkins, Regan, and Abell 1997; Reicher, Hopkins, and Condor 1997; Verkuyten 1997; Yzerbyt, Rocher, and Schadron 1997).

This chapter provides an opportunity to draw together various strands of our argument that stereotyping does not represent oversimplified distortion made necessary by processing limitations, but is the rich, complex, and dynamic expression of intergroup relationships. Grounded in self-categorization theory, our analysis is social-cognitive, in that it specifies the cognitive processes, operating in interaction with features of the social context, which we believe underpin stereotyping. Importantly though, the *starting point* of our analysis is recognition of the ubiquity and power of *group* processes in social life. This has led us to a distinctive understanding of the social-cognitive 'mechanics' of the stereotyping process, and we shall begin with a brief discussion of the way in which the categorization process is understood in SCT. We shall then elaborate our intergroup analysis of stereotyping by reviewing work which attempts to demonstrate (a) that stereotyping distinctively characterizes inter*group* as compared to interpersonal contexts, and (b) that the process is a context-sensitive means of both reflecting and shaping intergroup relations.

CATEGORIZATION

Why do we perceive people as members of social categories? For intergroup theorists such as Sherif, Asch, and Tajfel, this question does not really arise—obviously we perceive people as members of social categories because, and to the extent that, social contexts are defined in terms of those categories (e.g., Tajfel 1978). Groups exist, people identify with them. Veridical social perception and appropriate, effective social action require that we perceive this.

Social cognition, on the other hand, emerges at least implicitly from a metatheoretical perspective that denies the psychological (if not social) significance of these social categorical divisions (see Asch 1952; Fiske and Leyens 1997; Haslam et al. 1996; Stroebe and Insko 1989; Turner and Oakes 1986, 1997). Tajfel described the metatheoretical individualism that he felt characterized many analyses of group phenomena as a tendency to treat social reality as if it were made up of "freely-floating individual particles," without regard for "the cognitive and socially-shared *organization* of the system within which the particles float" (Tajfel 1979, pp. 187-188). As Fiske and Leyens put it,

> Social cognition research adopts a nonconflictual view of society from the perspective of the individual. That is, it ignores group conflicts and group membership and concentrates on the essentially asocietal individual…[who] has no reason to believe that anyone worth considering differs from himself in important ways. The ideal society to which this individual belongs is composed only of individuals like him, and it is bad taste to encapsulate people in specific groups because supposedly everyone is essentially the same if one looks hard enough (1997, p. 96).

To explain why we do, frequently and habitually, have the "bad taste" to impose ingroup-outgroup categorizations on this individualized social context, social cognition cites the limited capacity of the human information processing system—"for reasons of cognitive economy, we categorize others as members of particular groups" (Fiske and Neuberg 1990, p. 14); "we categorize people into groups as a means of reducing the amount of information we must contend with" (Hamilton and Trolier 1986, p. 128).

The idea that categorization and stereotyping *simplify* perception has been a continuous theme since the earliest statements by Lippmann (1922), Allport (1954), and Tajfel (1969). With the rise of the "cognitive miser" (Taylor 1981) metatheory within social cognition, it became a social-psychological truism that categorization operates in the interests of information reduction (though this was not the case in cognitive psychology, e.g., see Medin 1988). With it came the argument that we stereotype *because*, and to the extent that, we have to economize cognitively. The end result is an unfortunate but unavoidable distortion of social perception in which the complexity, richness and *accuracy* of individuated impression formation is sacrificed for a less accurate but more efficient alternative—stereotyping (e.g., see Brewer 1988; Fiske and Neuberg 1990; Pendry and Macrae 1994). The social group, and intergroup relations, have become redundant in the explanation of stereotyping, for which an almost entirely intra-psychic rationale is proposed. Thus, recent research has attempted to show that it is under conditions where our cognitive capacity is otherwise engaged that we are most likely to stereotype (e.g., Bodenhausen 1990; Bodenhausen and Wyer 1985; Gilbert and Hixon 1991; Macrae, Hewstone, and Griffiths 1993; Stangor and Duan 1991), and the effects of other factors such as mood (e.g., Bodenhausen 1993), interdependence (e.g., Neuberg and Fiske 1987) and power (Fiske 1993) on stereotyping have been explained through their alleged impact on processing capacity (see below). The contextual relevance or specific quality of relations between the *groups* to which the assessed stereotypes apply are not considered in these studies (cf. Nolan et al., in press; Spears and Haslam 1997; Reynolds and Oakes, in press (a)).

How can we reconcile these two views? Can we understand stereotyping in a way that emphasis both the intergroup context and the obviously relevant and powerful cognitive process of categorization? Self-categorization theory (SCT) has attempted to do this by reconceptualizing the nature and functions of categorization within an explicitly intergroup approach to stereotyping. We have discussed these issues at length elsewhere (e.g., Haslam et al. 1996; Oakes 1996; Oakes et al. 1994; Oakes and Reynolds 1997; Turner et al. 1994) and for present purposes the argument can be summarized in terms of four important points:

1.   SCT views *all* person perception as the outcome of a process of categorization. It is not that stereotyping involves categorization whereas individuated perception does not. The latter view necessitates the introduction of special conditions (such as limited capacity) to explain why we sometimes categorize and at other times do not. It also implies that there is a form of person perception that may be more "direct," less affected by cognitive mediation than stereotyping, and therefore more accurate, preferred. In SCT, the difference between stereotypical and individuated perception is simply the level of abstraction—intergroup or interpersonal—at which categorization is operating. Intergroup categorizations define similarities within and differences between collectivities of people (women and men, Australians and Americans, tennis players and cricketers, etc.), whereas interpersonal categorizations involve differentiation within group categories which define individual uniqueness (Pat Rafter, Pete Sampras, Steffi Graf, etc.). The same content, and to some extent the same labels can apply at both levels; the crucial difference is the level of abstraction or inclusiveness at which similarity and difference are defined.

2.   When will categorization be intergroup (and impression formation stereotypical), when interpersonal (and impression formation individuated)? SCT does not view the categorization process as a matching of isolated inputs with cognitive structures, as suggested in current views which conceptualize it as a form of schema activation (e.g., Fiske and Taylor 1991). Rather, categorization is seen as

inherently *comparative*, driven by patterns of perceived similarity and difference across the stimulus context as a whole. It involves judgments of *relative* similarity and difference, operating to maximize perceived similarity within and difference between categorizations at varying levels of abstraction. This idea is formalized in the concept of metacontrast, and the principles of comparative and normative fit as the determinants (in interaction with perceiver readiness) of category salience (e.g. see Oakes, 1987; Turner, 1985).

Briefly, SCT argues that the formation and salience of categories is in part a function of the *metacontrast* between interclass and intraclass differences. That is, with respect to a frame of reference comprised of salient stimuli, any given collection of stimuli will be perceived as a categorical entity to the extent that their difference from each other is seen to be less than the difference between them and all other stimuli. So, for example, an apple and a pear are more likely to be categorized as sharing a common categorical identity (as fruit) when they are on a shopping list that also includes meat. Similarly, Pat Rafter and Pete Sampras are more likely to see themselves as sharing identity as tennis players in a context that includes cricketers rather than tennis players alone, but as differentiated by their nationalities where Australian and American tennis players comprise the context. Metacontrast (comparative fit) combines with the principle of normative fit (the content aspect of the match between category specifications and the instances being represented) and the variable of perceiver readiness to define the context specific salience of social categories (Oakes 1987; cf. Bruner 1957). In summary, to categorize a group of people as Australians rather than Americans, they must not only appear to differ (in attitudes, actions, etc.) from Americans more than from each other (comparative fit), but must also be perceived to do so in the right direction on specific content dimensions of comparison (Australians should, for example, support Pat Rafter rather than Pete Sampras at the U.S. Open). Under these conditions impression formation will involve stereotyping. Where individuals differ within more than between groups categorization will be interpersonal and impression formation individuated.

3. It follows that categorization is understood to be entirely context-specific, dependent as it is upon perceived contrasts amongst current stimuli (e.g., see Turner et al. 1994, p. 456). Categories are not thought of as relatively stable cognitive structures, preformed and ready to be activated by the presence of "consistent" cues. They emerge within contexts, in interaction with perceivers' generalized "background theories" (Medin, Goldstone, and Gentner 1993) in such a way that the perceiver is able to make sense of currently relevant patterns of thought and action.

4. The crucial implication of the fit hypothesis outlined in (2) above is that categorization into groups, and social stereotyping, occur in distinctively *inter-group* contexts, contexts in which shared and differentiating category memberships, rather than individual differences, are salient (see Oakes 1987; Oakes et al. 1991; van Knippenberg, van Twuyver, and Pepels 1994). Further, the crucial

implication of the context dependence of categorization outlined in (3) above is that the parameters and content of social stereotypes are specific to the intergroup context in which they emerge, and to the values, goals and aspirations of group members within those context (cf. Sherif 1967, p. 3, quoted above).

In summary, SCT argues that it is the active interpretation of social reality—a reality that includes *group* loyalties, goals, and patterns of action—that drives social categorization. We would argue that this emphasis on context cannot be viewed as an optional add-on for intrapsychic, capacity-based approaches to categorization. It is fundamental to the nature and purposes of the process, such that we cannot separate analysis of the "cognitive functions" of stereotyping from that of the intergroup reality in which they operate (Tajfel 1981).

We now turn to brief overviews of some recent empirical work in which we have attempted to demonstrate the critical determining role of intergroup contexts in the general incidence and specific quality of social stereotyping.

USING STEREOTYPES: INFORMATION PROCESSING CAPACITY OR INTERGROUP CONTEXT?

Following the arguments outlined above, one of our most important empirical projects in recent years has been to test our assumption that stereotyping occurs in distinctively intergroup contexts and that it is the meaningful interpretation of such contexts, rather than capacity limitations, that underlies stereotypical perception. We have approached this issue in several ways (e.g., Nolan et al. in press; Oakes et al. 1991; Spears and Haslam 1997), but for present purposes we shall address the argument, as presented in Fiske and Neuberg's (1990) continuum model, that stereotyping is more likely when perceivers do not invest sufficient attention in the impression formation process. We shall outline a study in which this prediction was juxtaposed with the competing prediction from SCT that the crucial determinant of stereotyping is a salient intergroup (rather than interpersonal) context (see Reynolds and Oakes, in press (a)).

The continuum model is the most comprehensive account of the impression formation process, including stereotyping, within the social cognition literature. Briefly, Fiske and Neuberg (1990; see also Fiske, Lin, and Neuberg, in press) distinguish between individuated impressions formed through piecemeal integration of attributes and stereotyping based on categorization, placing these at opposite ends of an impression formation continuum. Movement along the continuum, that is, between fully individuated and fully stereotypical impressions, is dependent upon attention; the more attention the perceiver is able or prepared to invest in the impression formation process the more they will actually analyze current attribute information rather than rely on predigested category-based information, increasing the likelihood of individuation over stereotyping. Conversely, lack of attentional investment increases reliance on categorization and produces stereotyping.

One factor thought to increase attentional investment in impression formation, and therefore reduce the likelihood of stereotyping, is interdependence (e.g., Erber and Fiske 1984; Neuberg and Fiske 1987; Ruscher and Fiske 1990). Neuberg and Fiske (1987) suggest that interdependence (i.e., outcome dependency) between individuals "increases perceivers' attention to attribute information with the goal of increasing accuracy" (p. 440). They suggest that perceivers are particularly concerned about forming accurate impressions of others on whom their outcomes depend because they need to be able to predict and perhaps control their behavior. To this end, they avoid categorization and invest attentional capacity in the task of discovering the other's "true attributes." Both positive and negative interdependence, that is, both cooperative and competitive relationships with a target, are expected to have this individuating effect, because both should instigate accuracy-oriented attention to individual attributes.

In this analysis then, the significance of interdependence is cognitive—it is relevant to (the reduction of) stereotyping because of its hypothesized effects on attention. In other contexts, however, social psychologists have emphasized the social, functional, and interactional significance of interdependence, and from this perspective it has been seen as a potentially critical factor in the transformation of interpersonal into intergroup contexts (e.g., Sherif 1967; Turner 1981; cf. Bourhis, Turner, and Gagnon 1997; Turner and Bourhis 1996). For example, we have known for a long time that inter*group* negative interdependence (i.e., intergroup competition) tends to produce highly stereotypical rather than individuated impressions of opponents (e.g., Sherif 1967). This apparent inconsistency with predictions from the continuum model has been confronted by Ruscher and colleagues (1991), who attempt to accommodate the differential effects of intergroup and interpersonal competition on the impression formation process within the categorization-as-simplification approach.

Ruscher and colleagues initially predicted that, irrespective of contextual factors, interdependent individuals should allocate attention to impression formation and individuate. In their first experiment, however, they found that interpersonal competitors tended to individuate their opponents to a greater degree than did intergroup competitors. Their interpretation of this was that, "individuation of opponents during intergroup encounters is hampered because perceivers use their attentional resources to individuate teammates" (p. 601). A second study tested this interpretation, predicting that individuating processes (indicated by attention to and dispositional inferences about stereotype-inconsistent attributes and more variability in impressions formed) would be used more in forming impressions of teammates than opponents.

This prediction was confirmed—analysis of the number of seconds subjects spent considering information about teammates and opponents revealed that indeed more attention was paid to stereotype-inconsistent (i.e., individuating) than consistent information about teammates. However, it also revealed that more attention was paid to stereotype-consistent than inconsistent information about opponents, and overall there was no difference in the amount of attention paid to teammates and opponents. In other words, there was evidence suggesting relatively individuated impressions of teammates and relatively stereotypical impressions of opponents, but this could not be attributed to the hypothesized enhanced attention to teammates. A similar pattern of findings had been reported by Ruscher and Fiske in 1990. Ruscher and colleagues interpret their findings thus:

> Situational constraints (created by being in an experiment or otherwise) may require some attention to attribute information....given one has to attend to something beyond the category, but also given a lack of major motivation to be accurate, a perceiver may simply focus on category-consistent attributes to reconfirm the category....intergroup competitors were unwilling to expend the major effort to incorporate inconsistent information into their impressions of opponents. However, they complied with the experimenter's requirement to form impressions of their opponents by simply reconfirming their expectancies...through increased attention to expectancy-consistent information (1991, p. 603).

But why is attention to consistent information simply compliance with experimenter demands, whereas attention to inconsistent information represents effort towards accuracy? Both types of information were presented as descriptive of the targets by the experimenter. Also, there is actually no evidence at all that individuation required a "major effort" relative to stereotyping—the apparently individuated impressions of teammates and apparently stereotypical impressions of opponents required, by the evidence of Ruscher and colleagues' reading time measures, exactly the same amount of attention.

Alternatively, we could offer a self-categorization interpretation of Ruscher and colleagues' findings, one that takes into account the *real, qualitative difference* between impression formation in interpersonal and intergroup contexts. We would argue that judgments of teammates represented interpersonal differentiations within an ingroup, and therefore focused on characteristics that could differentiate between group members—inconsistent information—and were relatively variable. On the other hand, judgments of opponents were made on an ingroup-outgroup basis, and focused on characteristics that differentiated between the ingroup and the outgroup—consistent, stereotypical attributes—and were less variable.

We have explored the validity of this reinterpretation in a recent series of experiments which have juxtaposed continuum model (CM) and SCT predictions (Reynolds 1996; Reynolds and Oakes, in press (a)). The aim of the first experiment was to test whether individuation and stereotyping would vary with the interpersonal versus intergroup nature of the comparative context (SCT) or with variations in attention to target information (CM). As in previous research, interdependence was used to manipulate attentional resources. Comparative context was also manipulated such that judgments of a target person were made in either an interpersonal or an intergroup context. In interpersonal conditions the participant and the target were members of the same group whereas they were members of different groups in intergroup conditions (see Ruscher et al. 1991). SCT predicts a main effect for comparative context (more stereotyping in intergroup contexts) and the CM predicts a main effect for interdependence (more stereotyping with no interdependence).

Experimental participants were told that the study concerned the effect of competition on problem solving. A pretest had ostensibly identified them as either logical or lateral problem solvers, and in the main study they were told they would complete a further set of problem-solving tasks but this time in the presence of another person—their opponent (the target person)—and that a prize of $20 was available.

At this point the comparative context variable was manipulated. Following SCT, the aim in the interpersonal condition was to create a purely ingroup context within which interpersonal differentiation would be most salient (see the definition of metacontrast above). In this condition there was no explicit contrasting outgroup; participants were told that everyone in the session had a lateral problem-solving style and no reference was made to logical problem solving. In contrast, participants in the intergroup conditions were led to believe that some of those present were lateral and others logical problem solvers.

Participants were then handed a booklet that included information about their opponent. As noted above, in interpersonal conditions participants were told that all those in the session, including themselves and their opponent, had a lateral problem-solving style. In intergroup contexts participants were led to believe that they were logical problem solvers but their opponent was lateral. In this way the identity of the target (opponent) was held constant while group membership was shared in interpersonal conditions, differentiating in intergroup conditions. Manipulation checks revealed that participants were equally accepting of their designated problem solving style, regardless of whether it was lateral or logical.

Competitive interdependence was manipulated using the technique adopted by Ruscher and Fiske (1990; Ruscher et al. 1991). In the interdependent conditions, participants were told that their score would be compared with their opponent's and that the person with the highest score would be entered into a draw for the $20 prize. In contrast, noninterdependent participants were told that all scores would be collated and that those scoring above the 50th percentile would be entered into the draw for the prize. Manipulation checks confirmed that participants in interdependent conditions felt that they were significantly more outcome dependent on their opponent than did those in noninterdependent conditions.

In addition to participants being given information about their own and their opponent's problem-solving style, they were also given six statements that described their opponent. These had supposedly been generated from pretest items completed by all participants. In fact, a constant set of two statements consistent with a pretested stereotype of lateral problem solvers, two stereotype-inconsistent and two neutral statements were presented. For example, a stereotype-consistent statement was "be open to novel solutions" and a stereotype-inconsistent statement was "use ordered thinking." Participants were asked to read through the information provided about their opponent and then answer a few questions before moving on to the competition. Once these questions were completed, the session was terminated and participants were debriefed about the aims of the experiment.

One of the novel features of this study was that the main dependent variable was an impression content measure. In previous research investigating the impact of motivational factors, the main dependent variable has been the time participants spend looking at information about the target—more specifically, gaze duration (e.g., Erber and Fiske 1984; Ruscher and Fiske 1990; Ruscher et al. 1991). It has been assumed that longer gaze durations for stereotype-inconsistent information correspond to more individuated impressions, but actual variations in impression content have received little attention. In contrast, we were interested in exploring the outcome of the impression formation process, and to this end included a checklist assessment of impressions formed. Participants were asked to read through a list of 15 words, underline those that were typical of their opponent, and then select the 5 most typical words from those underlined. The main measure is the relative frequency with which stereotype-consistent compared to stereotype-inconsistent information was selected in each condition.

Consistent with SCT predictions, participants' impressions were significantly more stereotypic in the intergroup conditions compared to the interpersonal conditions. There were no significant effects for interdependence. Our interpretation of these findings is that the tendency to individuate or stereotype varied with the salient level of abstraction—interpersonal versus intergroup. Level of abstraction was, however, confounded with whether the target was an ingroup or outgroup member in this experiment. This issue was addressed in a second study (see Reynolds and Oakes in press (b)) which added a condition in which participants formed impressions of an ingroup member in an intergroup context, and in which attention was manipulated through a direct instruction to form accurate impressions in half the conditions (high attention; Neuberg and Fiske 1987). Overall, results were consistent with SCT predictions: there was a clear relationship between impressions and salient comparative context (more stereotyping of both ingroup and outgroup members in intergroup contexts), but not between impressions and exhortations to accuracy.

In summary, both the findings reported by Ruscher and colleagues (1991) and those from our own recent studies confirm our earlier arguments and evidence (e.g., Oakes 1987; Oakes et al. 1991) that the crucial determinant of stereotyping is a salient intergroup context. It appears that, as Sherif (1967, p. 3) argued, stereotyping is not "self-generated psychologically" through internal factors, such as depleted cognitive capacity or insufficient attention. Rather, stereotyping happens when intergroup relations happen. It is simply impression formation in intergroup contexts.

STEREOTYPICAL HOMOGENEITY: COGNITIVE STRUCTURE OR INTERGROUP CONTEXT?

We have also applied our emphasis on the critical role of the salience of intergroup relations in stereotyping to analysis of perceived group homogeneity. The homogenizing effects of the categorization process have been noted and investigated since the earliest days of stereotyping research. We know that categorization produces an accentuation of similarity within categories (and difference between them), but does it do this evenhandedly? Both anecdote and evidence suggest that outgroups are rather more vulnerable to homogenization than ingroups. As Gordon Allport put it:

> We [Americans] know...that not all Americans are dollar-worshipers, breezy or vulgar. Nor are they all friendly and hospitable. On the other hand, Europeans, who know us less well, often view us as one big monolithic unit having all these qualities" (1954, p. 172).

This 'outgroup homogeneity effect' has been repeatedly demonstrated in more recent social cognitive research. For example, Park and Rothbart (1982) asked male and female participants to estimate the proportions of males and females who would endorse each of 54 attitudinal and behavioral items which varied in their relevance to sex stereotypes. As predicted, opposite-sex estimates were more sex-stereotypical than same-sex estimates. For example, men's estimates of the proportion of women endorsing stereotypic items was higher than women's estimates of the same proportion.

The implication is that we stereotype outgroups to a greater extent than ingroups, and the social cognitive explanation of this pattern has focused, again, on internal psychological factors—in this instance, on potential differences in the way in which information about outgroups and ingroups is represented in memory (for a review, see Haslam et al. 1996). Essentially, it is argued that ingroups are represented by more complex, differentiated cognitive structures than outgroups, at least partly because we are thought to be more familiar with ingroups than outgroups (e.g., see Linville, Salovey, and Fischer 1986; Park, Judd, and Ryan 1991)

This emphasis on fairly stable aspects of category structure can be contrasted with the entirely context-dependent acts of categorization posited by SCT. According to our analysis, salient intergroup contexts should produce homogeneity—as a prime indicator of group rather than individual level impression formation—in perceptions of both ingroup and outgroup, whereas interindividual variability should be emphasized where interpersonal categorizations are salient.

How can the apparently ubiquitous asymmetry in perceived ingroup and outgroup homogeneity be understood from this perspective?

In fact, and following directly on from our analysis of the role of comparative fit in social category salience, it can be shown that the operation of meta-contrast may be one very important determinant of outgroup homogeneity effects (see Haslam and Oakes 1995; Haslam et al. 1995, 1996; Oakes et al. 1994, Chapter 7). If, as SCT predicts, personal categories become salient in the context of intra-group comparison and social categories become salient in the context of inter-group comparison, then ingroup members should tend to be individuated more than outgroup members when judgment of those ingroup members is made in the absence of a salient intergroup division.

To clarify this point by means of an example, we can imagine three scenarios in which some men are asked to make judgments of (1) some women, (2) each other, or (3) each other in comparison to women. If we assume that scenarios 1 and 3 are both intergroup by virtue of the fact that they involve comparisons between ingroup and outgroup categories (the former implicit the latter explicit), then SCT predicts that the social categorical properties of the judged group would be more salient in these scenarios than in the intragroup scenario (2). Accordingly, when the male ingroup is judged alone (scenario 2) it should be seen as less homogeneous than the female outgroup (scenario 1). Other things being equal though, there should be no such asymmetry in perceived homogeneity when the ingroup is judged in comparison to the outgroup (scenario 3).

It turns out that the first two of these scenarios are common in investigations of group homogeneity where subjects typically make ratings *either* just of the outgroup *or* just of the ingroup (e.g., Linville 1982; Linville and Jones 1980; Linville, Fischer, and Salovey 1989; Park and Rothbart 1982; Quattrone and Jones 1980; Wilder 1984). It follows from the above analysis that when the subjects in these studies made judgments of outgroups they should have tended to make implicit *inter*group comparisons between that group and their own ingroup that led to the salience of social categories *within* which similarities were accentuated (as per scenario 1). Conversely, when subjects judged ingroups in the absence of a salient outgroup, they should have been more likely to make *intra*-ingroup comparisons leading to the salience of personal categories *between* which differences were accentuated (as per scenario 2).

In an attempt to provide a direct test of this analysis, we conducted two studies (Haslam et al. 1995) in which subjects in one set of conditions judged both an ingroup *and* an outgroup (both judgments thus being made in an explicitly inter-group context), while subjects in other conditions followed the common proce-dure of judging *either* an ingroup or an outgroup. Our general hypothesis was that group homogeneity judgments would vary with the categorization process, as determined by comparative context, rather than with ingroup-outgroup status. More specifically, it was predicted that on stereotypic dimensions the ingroup and outgroup would be perceived as equally homogeneous in the two-group comparative context (where both groups were salient for subjects). On the other hand, an outgroup homogeneity effect was expected where groups were judged alone, as this would represent an intergroup context for the outgroup judgment, but an intragroup context for the ingroup judgment.

In the first experiment participants initially used a checklist to assign traits either to an ingroup (Australians) or an outgroup (Americans). As previous research led us to expect, participants stereotyped their ingroup more positively than the outgroup. Australians were typically described as sportsmanlike, pleasure loving, and happy-go-lucky, while Americans were generally described as extremely nationalistic, materialistic, and ostentatious. Having assigned traits in this manner, participants then either estimated the percentage of people in the stereotyped group alone who had the assigned traits or estimated the percentage of people both in this group and in the other comparison group who had the traits (i.e., in these two-group conditions participants estimated the percentage of Americans and Australians to whom the traits selected to describe Americans applied, or the percentage of Australians and Americans to whom the traits selected to describe Australians applied). As predicted, when one of the two groups was judged alone, an outgroup homogeneity effect emerged: stereotypic traits were seen to apply to more Americans (75%) than Australians (57%). However, when both groups were judged at the same time, this effect was eliminated: the traits selected to describe Australians were seen to apply to 74 percent of Australians and the traits assigned to Americans were seen to apply to 74 percent of Americans.

In addition to the explicit manipulation of comparative context, one very important procedural difference between our studies and those demonstrating outgroup homogeneity is that our participants *chose for themselves* the dimensions on which ingroup and outgroup were judged. In our experiment, then, we can be sure not only that particular traits were stereotypical of the groups involved, but also that they were explicitly recognized as such by the participants. In other words, the *normative fit* of stereotypic traits was high for both ingroup and outgroup. This meant, among other things, that there was a relationship between the *favorableness* of traits and their ingroup/outgroup stereotypicality. As noted above, traits selected for ingroup judgments were more favorable than those seen as applicable to the outgroup. Again, this is a departure from normal research practice in this area. For example in the experiment reported by Judd, Ryan, and Park (1989), each group was represented by one positive and one negative trait and one positive and one negative attitude statement, so that the favorableness of the dimensions used did not differ systematically between groups.

This procedure might appear to add symmetry and control to an experimental design, but it may also introduce *asymmetry* and systematic bias into the judgmental process because ingroup social categories are made differentially *unsalient* (leading to perceived ingroup heterogeneity) by asking subjects to define the ingroup in negative terms. Although experimental participants may be quite willing to see both positive and negative characteristics as applicable to the outgroup, they may be much more reluctant to see relatively negative characteristics as generally (i.e., homogeneously) applicable to the ingroup. Overall, this would contribute to an outgroup homogeneity effect. There was some evidence consistent with this argument in our first study, and a second experiment (Haslam et al. 1995, Experiment 2) was conducted in order both to replicate the effect for comparative context obtained in the first study, and to examine this motivational account of the link between perceived variability and trait favorableness more rigorously.

The design of the study was very similar to the initial experiment, although the favorableness of traits included in the checklist was introduced as an additional factor. That is, participants characterized Australians or Americans in either a single-group or a two-group context but did so with respect to a checklist that included either only positive traits, only negative traits, or both positive and negative traits. Predictions for the comparative context effect were the same as those for the first experiment, and two related effects were expected to arise from participants' reluctance to apply negative traits to the ingroup, as discussed above. First, it was predicted that the ingroup would be represented as more homogeneous when the checklist included all positive rather than all negative traits. Second, we expected the outgroup to be represented as more homogeneous than the ingroup when the checklist included only negative traits.

All these predictions were supported. A significant interaction between stereotyped group and comparative context on the stereotypical ratings replicated the effect found in the first experiment; there was outgroup homogeneity when Americans and Australians were judged alone, but no difference in perceived homogeneity in the context of explicit intergroup comparison. Other interaction effects also provided support for both predictions relating to trait favorableness. The ingroup was seen as more homogeneous when it had to be described using all positive rather than all negative traits, and the outgroup was seen as more homogeneous than the ingroup when only negative traits could be assigned.

In summary, stereotypical homogenization appears to define perceptions of both outgroups and ingroups in salient intergroup contexts—again, we would suggest that it is an aspect of normal impression formation under conditions where people are being defined as group members rather than unique, differentiated individuals. Our work in this area has also demonstrated the motivational aspects of homogeneity judgments. They are definitional statements about the nature of human groups and on some occasions, therefore, statements about the self as a group member. The variable processes of self-definition—as individual or group member, positive or negative—seem to be crucial inputs to homogeneity judgments, and those judgments themselves look more like motivated communications about relations as currently defined than the preset output of a more or less differentiated internal structure.

STEREOTYPE CHANGE:
INFORMATION OR MEANING?

Our argument thus far has been that stereotyping reflects context-specific intergroup comparison. In recent work, we have applied this argument to the issue of stereotype change. Given the common association between stereotyped beliefs and prejudiced, discriminatory intergroup attitudes, the question of change has always been at the forefront of research in the area. From the earliest investigations of the contact hypothesis to the most recent analyses of relevant cognitive processes, the assumption has been that stereotype content misrepresents groups, and that we need to find ways in which to replace that distorted content with less damaging information.

At the same time, stereotypical beliefs have been widely portrayed as rigid, unresponsive to reality, and generally resistant to change. This was the view long before the cognitive analysis was developed (e.g., Fishman 1956; Lippmann 1922) and perhaps contributed to the construal of stereotypes as cognitive structures with built-in processing defenses against disconfirmation. Importantly, the view of stereotypes as relatively stable cognitive entities has meant that attempts at stereotype change have usually taken the form of assaults on the content of the relevant cognitive structures. In his excellent recent overview of stereotype change research, Miles Hewstone comments that a "focus on *information processing* is the hallmark of cognitive analyses of intergroup relations" (1996, p. 338; emphasis added), and one manifestation of this focus is an approach to stereotype change that emphasizes *the processing of disconfirming information*, the management of data inconsistent with cognitively represented stereotypical expectations (Hewstone, 1989, 1994). Thus, researchers present perceivers with *information* (content) that allegedly applies to a member of a given category, and then examine the receptiveness of that category to that (allegedly) relevant content. This section reviews some of Hewstone and colleagues' recent investigations of stereotype change. We suggest that, rather than indicating a revision of cognitive structures in response to "information," the stereotype variation reported in these studies might reflect the fact that stereotyping functions as a context-specific construal of an intergroup relationship. Some of our own relevant research is also outlined.

Hewstone and colleagues have reported a program of research testing the "prototype subtyping" model (1996, p. 340) of the processing and effects of stereotype disconfirming information. The model develops Rothbart and John's (1985) prototype analysis of categorization, in which they argue that it is goodness of fit to a category prototype, "the degree to which the individual's attributes match those of the category" (1985, p. 90), that determines categorization (cf. the fit hypothesis in SCT; see above). By definition, an exemplar carrying category disconfirming information is not highly prototypical, may not be securely categorized as a member of the category it disconfirms, and may not, therefore, have any impact on the representation of that category. Building on these ideas, and on the work of Weber and Crocker (1983), Hewstone and his colleagues argue that stereotypes are "hierarchical structures" (1996, p. 339) that can respond to disconfirming information by becoming more internally differentiated. Specifically, subtypes develop within the higher level category (e.g., Black lawyers; aggressive women) such that disconfirming information is assimilated without revision of the overall stereotype (of lawyers as white; of women as gentle).

In Hewstone's studies a constant amount of stereotype disconfirming information is presented to participants in varying patterns (e.g., Hewstone, Hopkins, and Routh 1992; Johnston and Hewstone 1992; for a review, see Hewstone 1994). For example, in the first study reported by Johnston and Hewstone (1992), participants (psychology students) were presented with both confirming and disconfirming information about members of an outgroup, physics students. The patterning of the information across outgroup members was varied, such that disconfirmation was either *concentrated* in two out of the eight members presented or *dispersed* across six members (there was also an intermediate condition in which disconfirmation was dispersed across four members). The confirming information described physics students as interested in new technology and hard working, whereas the disconfirming information referred to their fashion consciousness and involvement in student politics. Johnston and Hewstone predicted more stereotype change under dispersed than concentrated conditions because disconfirming stimulus group members were more prototypical when disconfirming information was dispersed. They were, therefore, more likely to be categorized as "physics students," and to import their disconfirming attributes into that category. This prediction was confirmed, and the authors conclude that dispersal of disconfirming information enhances stereotype change *because* dispersed disconfirmers are more prototypical, and they are more prototypical *because* "prototypicality...is determined by the amounts of confirming and disconfirming information used to describe a member" (Hewstone 1994, p. 81).

These findings are clearly consistent with the notion of subtyping as a cognitive response to category disconfirmation. In line with the prevailing view of categories and stereotypes as cognitive structures, Hewstone interprets both observed change and observed stability as reflections of the state of the relevant structure—the overall category has assimilated some new information (change), or (more often) a subtype has been constructed to accommodate the new information, perhaps with the deliberate intent of preserving the established meaning and value connotations of the overall category (stability; see Hewstone 1996 p. 340; Yzerbyt, Rocher, and Coull 1997). Hewstone comments that, because subtyping is such an ever-ready response to stereotype disconfirmation, the model is "more a model of non-change...than change" (1994, p. 73), and he feels that his studies add up to "depressing support for the view that the persistence of stereotypes is cognitively overdetermined" (1994, p. 101).

Self-categorization theory suggests a different view of this research, a view that has led us to question both the extent to which stereotypes really are "persistent," and the extent to which the persistence we do observe can be considered "*cognitively* overdetermined.*" As we have outlined above, SCT rejects the idea of categories as preformed, waiting-to-be-activated cognitive structures in favor of an emphasis on the categorization *process* as a context-dependent, variable means of representing current stimulus relationships. In turn, we have outlined an alternative to the attribute-matching approach to the categorization process. Rather than being a matter of referring the attributes of each stimulus to a cognitive representation, and membership decisions following from calculation of the "hits" and "misses" by confirming and disconfirming attributes respectively, we argue that categorization involves interpreting, with reference to background theories and expectations, the *pattern of similarities and differences between stimuli across the context as a whole*. This process is specified in the fit hypothesis discussed above.

The cognitive subtyping account of stereotype change in the disconfirming information paradigm rests heavily on an attribute matching view of categorization. It argues that change is mediated by the relative typicality of the disconfirmers under dispersed and concentrated conditions, and that relative typicality depends on "the degree to which the individual's attributes match those of the category" (Rothbart and John 1985, p. 90). Given that we have presented an alternative to this view of categorization, what does our analysis imply for the process of stereotype change? We shall discuss implications both for the specific interpretation of results in the disconfirming information paradigm and for the general issue of stereotype stability and change.

Thus far this chapter argues that a salient intergroup context provides the essential condition for stereotyping. SCT also hypothesizes that the specific nature of that intergroup context importantly defines the content and parameters of emergent stereotypes (e.g., Haslam et al. 1992). As part of this analysis, SCT defines category prototypicality in a way which goes beyond the attribute-matching approach. We assume that *the nature of relevant comparison outgroups* plays a major role in defining both prototypicality and category meaning more generally.

To elaborate this point, let us return to the first study reported by Johnston and Hewstone (1992), outlined above, in which psychology students read both confirming (interested in new technology, hard working) and disconfirming (fashion conscious, involved in student politics) information about physics students, presented under concentrated or dispersed conditions. As predicted, Johnston and Hewstone found more stereotype change under dispersed than concentrated conditions and attributed this finding to the comparatively strong prototypicality of dispersed disconfirmers, commenting that "prototypicality...is determined by the amounts of confirming and disconfirming information used to describe a member" (Hewstone 1994, p. 81). Interestingly, though, a close reading of Johnston and Hewstone's article reveals that their procedure involved presentation of the physics student stimulus group in *explicit comparison* with drama students. In effect, then, a specific *inter*group context was defined in the study, the categorization in action was *physics students as compared to drama students*. A sartorially challenged, apolitical, hardworking technologist clearly did represent the prototypical physics student in the context of this contrast between physics and drama, but what if computer science or engineering majors rather than drama students had been introduced into the comparative context? According to SCT, this should affect the definition, including the prototype, of the "physics student" category, perhaps even to the extent of physics students being defined as *comparatively* politically aware and well dressed. In other words, it might be misleading to think of "fashion conscious" as a piece of "information" with a constant (disconfirming) relationship to the category "physics student." Rather, the *meaning* of the attribute, the meaning of the category, and the relationship between them, may have been implicitly but crucially specific to the intergroup context made salient in the study. This may, in turn, have contributed to the relative impact of dispersed versus concentrated disconfirmation on subjects' reported stereotypes. Perhaps there are comparative contexts in which Johnston and Hewstone's well-dressed concentrated disconfirmers would actually gain in perceived typicality over the hardworking dispersed disconfirmers, and the usual dispersed/concentrated effect might be reversed under these conditions.

We have tested this possibility in a program of studies in which manipulations of the comparative context are introduced into the dispersed/concentrated disconfirmation paradigm (Oakes and Dempster 1996; Oakes, Haslam, and Reynolds 1999). In the first of these, the target group was students attending the Australian Catholic University (ACU), a former teacher-training institution with a local campus. These catholic students were generally perceived by our participants (students at the Australian National University; ANU) as conservative, conventional, and tradition loving. The manipulation of comparative context involved either presenting the ACU group alone (*restricted* context), or leading participants to believe that they would also be reading about members of the Call to Australia (Fred Nile) Party (*extended* context). The Call to Australia Party (CTA) is a right-wing religious group led by the Reverend Fred Nile. It is extremely conservative and campaigns vigorously on moral issues, declaiming what it sees as the evils of homosexuality, abortion, and prostitution. In its campaign material for the 1996 Australian Federal Election, CTA described itself as "pro-God," "profamily" and "promoral," and its slogan was "For God and the Family." Thus, the salient comparative dimension within the experimental context was *conservatism*, with the three groups involved in the study—the ANU student participants, the ACU stimulus group, and the CTA comparison group—varying along this dimension such that the ANU participants were toward the nonconservative extreme, the CTA highly conservative, and the ACU group in between.

Table 1. Percentage of Subjects Assigning Listed
Traits to Students of the Australian Catholic University[*]

Frame	Control		Information Dispersed		Concentrated	
Restricted	Religious	62	Religious	37	Religious	62
	Conservative	56	Multifaceted	37	Conservative	56
	Conventional	56	Intelligent	37	Conventional	50
	Tradition-loving	50	Conservative	37	Loyal to family	44
	Loyal to family	37	Conventional	37	Traditional-loving	37
	Neat	37	Courteous	31	Honest	37
	Quiet	31	Honest	31	Courteous	31
	Honest	25	Tradition-loving	31	Intelligent	31
	Straightforward	19	Loyal to family	25	Neat	31
	Practical	19	Neat	10	Multifaceted	25
	Multifaceted	19				
	Methodical	19				
	Courteous	19				
Extended	Conservative	50	Conservative	50	Religious	37
	Honest	50	Conventional	37	Multifaceted	37
	Loyal to family	50	Multifaceted	37	Conservative	37
	Religious	44	Religious	31	Intelligent	37
	Tradition-loving	37	Tradition-loving	31	Loyal to family	37
	Conventional	37	Neat	31	Progressive	37
	Courteous	37	Intelligent	31	Conventional	31
	Straightforward	31	Honest	31	Honest	31
	Progressive	25	Courteous	25	Practical	25
	Practical	25	Loyal to family	25	Courteous	25
	Intelligent	25	Rebellious	25	Complex	19
	Neat	19	Straightforward	19	Straightforward	19
			Irreligious	19		
			Complex	19		

Note: [*]Table only includes traits assigned by 19 percent of subjects in a particular condition

Participants read about six students attending the Australian Catholic University, each of whom was described in terms of six attributes. Stereotype disconfirming attributes, which portrayed them as progressive, frivolous, and rebellious, were either concentrated in the descriptions of three group members or dispersed across all six. Control participants did not receive any information and simply described the stimulus group under either restricted or extended comparison conditions.

Following the metacontrast principle outlined above, and in particular the relevant work by Haslam and colleagues (Haslam and Turner 1992, 1995), we expected that the introduction of the extremely conservative CTA group into the comparative context would affect the overall comparative relations between the groups. Specifically, the relative positions of the ingroup (ANU) and the catholic students should be affected such that under restricted conditions the catholic students would be contrasted from the ANU and seen as highly conservative, but in

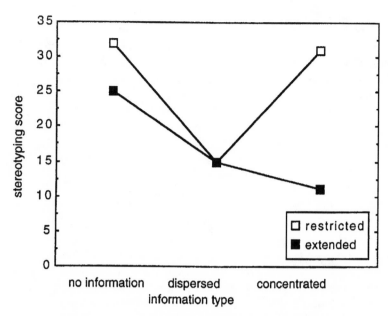

Figure 1. Relative Stereotypicality of Checklist Traits Selected as "Most Typical of ACU Students"

the extended context they would be contrasted from the CTA (and assimilated to the ANU) and seen as significantly less conservative. As part of this process of context-specific category definition, the *prototype* of catholic students should shift away from the conservative extreme under extended conditions, creating the possibility that the less conservative *concentrated* disconfirmers could have more impact on judgments of the category as a whole than the relatively conservative dispersed disconfirmers under these conditions. In short, we predicted a reversal of the usual dispersed/concentrated effect under extended comparison conditions.

Experimental participants read the descriptions of the six Catholic students, with extended participants expecting subsequent presentation of CTA members. All participants completed a series of dependent measures, with those in the control condition completing only those items which referred to ACU students in general rather than the stimulus group itself. Stereotyping of the ACU group was assessed in two ways—participants selected the five traits they felt were "most descriptive" of a typical student at the ACU from a checklist and rated ACU students in general on a series of bipolar trait scales including both stereotype consistent and inconsistent items.

The checklist trait selections are presented in Table 1. Qualitative consideration of these frequencies provides some initial support for our prediction. Within the restricted range conditions, dispersed disconfirmation clearly had more impact on stereotype content, relative to restricted/control, than did concentrated disconfirmation (e.g., see frequencies for religious, conservative, conventional). In contrast, the extension of the frame of reference to include Call to Australia greatly reduced the impact of dispersed disconfirmation, whereas there is evidence of significant change in the extended/concentrated condition (see again, religious, conservative, conventional). To quantify the stereotypicality of checklist responses we carried out a log linear analysis on the frequency with which the four most stereotypically consistent and four most inconsistent traits (as identified in pretesting) were selected as descriptive of a typical ACU student. For each condition we calculated a relative stereotyping score by subtracting the inconsistent frequency from the consistent frequency, and the resulting pattern is presented in Figure 1. As predicted, we observed the usual impact of dispersed but not concentrated disconfirming information under restricted comparison conditions. However, the extension of the comparative context in itself produced the expected shift away from conservatism (see results under control conditions) and consequent impact of the concentrated disconfirmers in the extended context. Planned comparisons indicated that, under restricted conditions dispersed but not concentrated disconfirmation produced a significant shift from the stereotype expressed by control subjects. For extended context participants, the control-concentrated comparison was significant, but not the control-dispersed comparison. A very similar pattern of findings emerged from analysis of the rating scales.

Briefly, a second study in this program involved a very similar design, but varied the stimulus and comparison groups. This time, participants (students) were presented with short written extracts allegedly taken from interviews in which volunteer bushfire fighters outlined their reasons for going to fight devastating bushfires in and around Sydney in January 1994. Participants expected to read about either the group of firefighters alone or the firefighters followed by a group of World Vision volunteers. The relevant comparative dimension was selflessness, with the student participants towards the selfish pole, World Vision volunteers defining the selfless extreme, and bushfire fighters in between. Stereotype confirming information described the firefighters as brave, dedicated, selfless, helpful, while the inconsistent information (which was either concentrated in three of the six firefighters presented, or dispersed across all six) portrayed them as apathetic, irresponsible, and selfish. As in the first study, we expected the introduction of the extremely selfless World Vision group to shift the definition of the firefighter category, and the prototypical firefighter, towards apathy and selfishness, relative to the restricted condition. This, in turn, was expected to enhance the influence of the relatively selfish concentrated disconfirmers under extended conditions, while the usual effectiveness of dispersed disconfirmation was expected in restricted conditions. These predictions were confirmed on both checklist and stereotypic trait rating assessments of participants' stereotypes of "bushfire fighters in general."

It appears, then, that dispersed disconfirmers do not have any privileged status in the stereotype change process. Hewstone's conclusion that it is "the amounts of confirming and disconfirming information used to describe a member" (1994, p. 81) that defines their effectiveness as change agents clearly does not give us a full picture of the relevant factors in stereotype variation of the kind observed in both his studies and our own. In our experiments, the combination of an extended comparative context and the presentation of some extremely "disconfirming" group members produced as much stereotype change as did the presentation of only slightly "disconfirming" group members in the restricted context. Relative "amounts of confirming and disconfirming information" characterizing given group members could not account for emergent stereotypes in isolation from the context in which that information was given meaning.

The information processing approach to categorization tends to assume that attributes are rather concrete, absolute aspects of stimulus reality, that they are also represented in categories, and that categorization is a matter of the relevant stimulus attributes triggering the relevant cognitive category. One example is the role of consistent and inconsistent attributes in Fiske and Neuberg's (1990) continuum model. The attribute-category relationship is fixed and predictable in this view, producing the straightforward definition of some attributes as confirming" (consistent) for a given category, and others as "disconfirming" (inconsistent). Our findings suggest, however, that *the comparative context can alter the category-attribute relationship*, that the categories were not defined in the same way across context conditions, even in the absence of any new or "disconfirming" information (see results for control subjects in Figure 1; see also Haslam et al. 1992). This suggests to us that the idea of "confirming" and "disconfirming" attributes as definable in any abstract, acontextual manner may need to be reconsidered (Reynolds 1996). Was "progressive," for example, disconfirming or confirming for the Catholic student category in our first study? Apparently, it could be either depending on context (see Table 1). It was selected as one of five traits "most descriptive" of ACU students by 25 percent of subjects in the extended-control condition and by 37 percent in the extended-concentrated condition, but by no subjects at all in the restricted context conditions. We would argue that stereotype definition is always *relative*, always an expression of a context-specific intergroup relationship, and therefore that there is no fixed relationship between certain categories and certain attributes.

Of course, any argument for this degree of context dependence immediately confronts the manifest stability of many stereotypes—as we noted above, rigidity and insensitivity to context have long been considered defining features of social stereotypes. Although evidence contradicting this view has been available since the earliest days of stereotyping research (see Oakes et al. 1994, Chapter 2), it is nonetheless obvious that relative stability characterizes many stereotypes. But stability is not evidence against context-depen-

Table 2.   Data from Control Studies of Introductory
Psychology Students' Australian Self-Stereotypes (1992–1997)

Year (N)	Study	Favourableness (−5 to +5)	Uniformity (U: max = 2.5)	Consensus (P_a)	Content[*]	%
1992 (16)	Homog. (Exp1) *BJSP* (1995)	1.94	7.00	.21	Happy-go-lucky Straightforward Sportsmanlike Reserved Talkative	56 50 44 31 31
1994 (20)	Influence and consensus *BJSP* (1996)	2.00	7.25	.21	Happy-go-lucky Sportsmanlike Pleasure-loving Straightforward Talkative	50 50 45 35 31
1995 (20)	Consensual-ization (Exp1) *EJSP* (UR)	1.70	8.00	.21	Sportsmanlike Happy-go-lucky Straightforward	65 35 35
1996 (46)	Consensual-ization (Exp3) *EJSP* (UR)	2.01	8.28	.20	Sportsmanlike Straightforward Pleasure-loving	54 43 39
1997 (20)	Control	1.20	9.00	.15	Happy-go-lucky Pleasure-loving Straightfoward	40 40 40

Note: [*]Table only contains traits assigned by more than 30 percent of subjects

dence. Indeed, we see the intergroup approach to stereotyping that we have
been forwarding in this chapter as offering a rather more plausible and parsi-
monious account of stereotype stability than arguments about cognitively
determined "resistance" to "information." Stable contexts, in particular stable intergroup realities and stable explanatory theories about what those realities mean, produce stable emergent categories and stereotypes. It is when the
material conditions and/or the social interpretation of intergroup relations
change that stereotypes change.

We have recently found evidence of this process occurring in our studies of perceived group homogeneity, discussed above. In the course of that research program, we have assessed Australian students' national self-stereotypes under
single-group conditions (i.e., without explicit manipulation of the comparative
context) on five occasions across a time period of six years (see Haslam et al. in
press). As can be seen from Table 2, the stereotypes elicited in four different studies between 1992 and 1996 were remarkably stable in terms of their favorableness, uniformity, consensuality, and substantive content. There is every reason to
believe that aspects of group life related to national identity were also relatively

stable for this population over this time (cf. Meenes 1943; Seago 1947; Sinha and Upadhyaya 1960).

In the 1997 data, however, there is a clearly discernable shift in all aspects of the stereotype. In terms of substantive content, the usually strongly endorsed "sportsmanlike" (which refers in part to a belief in an egalitarian, sporting sense of fair mindedness and all playing by the same rules) has disappeared, and there are significant changes in favorableness (the stereotype is less favorable), uniformity (the stereotype is more complex) and consensuality (there is less agreement between subjects)—these students' national self-stereotype has become more negative, and there is more disagreement, more uncertainty, about what it means to be Australian.

To explore these findings further, we presented the data (in graphical form) relating to favorableness and consensus to a group of the students who had taken part in some of our stereotyping research in 1997 and asked them to "list any and all factors that you feel may be responsible for the less positive and less consensual view of Australians that emerged this year." Many of the students' responses made reference to events following the Australian Federal Election of March 1996, in which the party of government changed for the first time in 13 years (from Labor to Liberal, i.e., "conservative"), and several explicitly racist candidates, including Pauline Hanson, an Independent from Queensland, were elected to the federal parliament. This change of political direction provoked unprecedented questioning of Australians' capacity for tolerance and acceptance of diversity—salient and valued aspects of the national self-image. Subsequent events relating, in particular, to Aboriginal Australians (e.g., conflict between Aboriginals and farmers over land rights; debate over compensation for the forced adoption of Aboriginal children) together with expressions of concern from some overseas leaders about increasingly overt racism in Australia, contributed to a sense of deteriorating intergroup relations both within the country and between Australia and its international neighbors. Approximately 60 percent of our participants' responses alluded to these factors as responsible for the observed impact on the favorableness and consensuality of the national self-stereotype (52 percent mentioned Hanson explicitly). The following statements are typical:

> The fact that John Howard is Prime Minister and Pauline Hanson is a member of One Nation Party states that there isn't much to be proud of about our country. We are seen as racist and a joke. A lot of us see ourselves (the country) this way as well. How can we have a positive outlook of [sic] Australia with people like this ruling us?

> People are not as 'proud' of being Australian due to Pauline Hanson and Howard government's portrayal overseas as Australians being backward economically, environmentally, socially (racist and human rights).

Australian society has undoubtedly become more divided, and it seems that this has changed the way in which some citizens are able to define (to stereotype) themselves as "Australian." Importantly, this is happening despite consistent official political messages ("information") to the contrary—the Government's rhetoric is of national unity (the Liberals' election slogan was "For all of us"), and Hanson's party is called "One Nation." But it appears that this does not count as "information" with any validity for the student population taking part in our studies. The reduced favorableness and consensuality of their national self-stereotypes can be seen as an attempt to communicate their rejection of this rhetoric, to comment on the political and social realities of national life as they experience them, and as those whose opinions they respect interpret and evaluate them (see Haslam 1997; Haslam et al. 1998). And, of course, we would expect the very same national political shifts to have quite different effects on national self-stereotyping for those who identify with the government agenda and the monocultural vision of Hanson and her followers.

Intergroup images play a crucial role in almost all aspects of social and political life, and there are frequently very good reasons for trying to change some of them. Just as Sherif argued 30 years ago, our point in this section has been to emphasize that "attitudes towards other groups and images of them are *products* of particular relationships between groups, *not their original cause*" (Sherif 1967, p. 25, emphasis added; see also Rothbart 1981, p. 177). Much stereotype change research seems to be motivated by the belief that changing the way groups stereotype each other will change the way they relate to each other. We suspect that the reverse process is far more prevalent and powerful, and that it is changing intergroup realities, and the available ideological interpretations of those realities, that effects changes in the process of social stereotyping.

STEREOTYPING AND POWER: INFORMATION PROCESSING OR POLITICS?

Thus far, we have argued that stereotyping is simply impression formation in intergroup contexts, contexts in which the parameters of identity are defined by intergroup differentiation and intragroup assimilation, rather than interindividual differentiation. We have portrayed stereotypes as emergent, context-specific images, serving to represent salient aspects of the intergroup relationship as currently defined. We have not, however, dealt with the issue of power. Modern societies, probably without exception, comprise groups in relations of unequal control over resources and outcomes. How do such asymmetries in power relations between groups influence stereotyping? Is it possible that the view of the stereotyping process we have outlined thus far applies only to the powerful, who are able to dictate identity boundaries and meanings, whereas the powerless are victims of a process they cannot control? This is, in fact, the argument developed in two recent analyses of the relationship between power and stereotyping.

Fiske (1993) and Jost and Banaji (1994) discuss the impact of power on the stereotyping process. Although emerging from different perspectives, both articles argue that stereotyping is an instrument wielded primarily by the powerful in a way which furthers their interests to the detriment of the powerless. Fiske's argument develops straightforwardly from the interdependence-attention relationship outlined in the continuum model, discussed above. In hierarchical situations of differential power, of one-way dependence rather than mutual interdependence, Fiske argues that attention tends to be directed *up* the hierarchy. Because of their dependence on the powerful, the powerless need to predict and understand them, so they pay attention and do not stereotype. The powerful, on the other hand, are too busy, too unconcerned with accuracy, and possibly too dominance-oriented to invest any attention in their appraisals of the powerless. They tend, therefore, to form highly stereotypical impressions of those over whom they can exert power (Depret and Fiske 1996; Fiske, Morling, and Stevens 1996). Because, in Fiske's view, being stereotyped "limits [people's] freedom and constrains their outcomes, even their lives" (1993, p. 621), this asymmetrical use of the stereotyping process contributes to social domination and exploitation as much as it emerges from it.

Taking a more explicitly intergroup perspective on stereotyping, Jost and Banaji (1994) present a wide-ranging analysis of the role of stereotypes in system justification, "the psychological process by which existing social arrangements are preserved in spite of the obvious psychological and material harm they entail for disadvantaged individuals and groups" (p. 10). Clearly, and in contrast to the functional consequences of the self- and group-justification processes also discussed in their article, system justification is not an adaptive or particularly rational perspective for powerless groups to adopt. They do it, Jost and Banaji suggest, because of the ideological domination exerted by powerful groups. Those with power can control ideas, beliefs, stereotypes in the same way as they control other social and material resources, and can thereby instill a "false consciousness" in the powerless such that they become complicit in their own disadvantage. Specifically, disadvantaged groups are induced to "ascribe to themselves and others traits which are consonant with their social position...rather than question the order or legitimacy of the system which produced such an arrangement" (1994, p. 11).

In both of these accounts, stereotyping emerges as a fairly unambiguously negative force within social relations characterized by power differentials—it contributes to control, constraint, distortion, domination, and false consciousness. In contrast, the intergroup perspective we have elaborated in this chapter implies a more unstable, context-specific, and potentially symmetrical involvement of stereotyping in power-related interactions. Elsewhere, we have suggested that stereotypes can function as "instruments of social conflict" (Haslam et al. 1996, p. 218; see also Oakes et al. 1994, Chapter 8; Oakes and Reynolds 1997) owned, controlled, and used by all parties in conflict, the powerful and the powerless. This approach views stereotyping as impression formation *motivated* by the politics of group goals and values. It is one of the principal mechanisms through which those goals and values are expressed and acted upon by group members under appropriate circumstances:

> We see the cognitive processes implicated in [stereotyping] not as constricting social perception, but as appropriately *facilitating collective action*. Viewed in this light, [stereotyping] itself is not an obstacle to valid perception, but a necessary feature of defining oneself and others that allows people to express and apprehend different social perspectives and different political and ideological motivations associated with them...representations of groups in stereotypic terms are part of the political process through which different groups assert and communicate their competing world views (Haslam et al. 1996, pp. 217-218; emphasis added),

Thus, while group definition in terms of traits "consonant with...social position" (Jost and Banaji 1994; see above) will occur under some intergroup conditions, under other circumstances groups may act to challenge that social position and, in so doing, generate stereotype content which defines and justifies the challenge, and facilitates collective action (Reicher et al. 1997). In other words, our intergroup analysis of the stereotyping process suggests that it can work for social change and resistance to domination just as much as it can contribute to the maintenance of such domination. This is because it represents, at all times, a dynamic expression of context-specific group identities and the current goals and values of group members—if those goals and values include a challenge to the status quo, this will be reflected in the stereotyping process.

Social identity theory (Tajfel and Turner 1979) argues that *collective* challenge to low status and powerlessness is likely to occur where group boundaries are perceived to be impermeable and the status hierarchy is seen as illegitimate and/or unstable. In contrast, permeable boundaries encourage attempts at individual mobility up the status hierarchy and a decreased emphasis on group membership (e.g., see Ellemers 1993; Tajfel 1978; Wright, Taylor, and Moghaddam 1990). Extending this analysis to social stereotyping, our most recent series of experiments has investigated the stereotyping processes engaged in by less powerful, disadvantaged group members under conditions where they responded to their disadvantage with either acceptance, attempts at individual mobility, or collective protest (Oakes et al., under review).

To create these conditions, we adapted the procedure used in a highly imaginative study of responses to disadvantage by Wright, Taylor, and Moghaddam (1990). Participants in two studies were assigned to a low status group (a group of "unsophisticated" decision makers) and given an opportunity to rise into a higher status ("sophisticated") group on the basis of performance on a decision making task. High status group members were required to be creative, rigorous, complex, analytical, and conscientious, so performance was allegedly assessed on these dimensions. All participants failed to gain promotion to the high status group, ostensibly because of either inadequate performance (open condition) or because, despite having performed at the required level, the high status group had rejected their attempt at upward mobility. Under quota conditions, participants were told that only 10 percent of those achieving required scores were to be admitted to the high status group, whereas under closed conditions no-one was to be admitted. Thus, the intergroup boundary varied in permeability, from completely open, through a "tokenist" permeability (see Wright et al. 1990), to completely closed.

Major dependent variables were participants' choice of response to their rejection by the high status group—acceptance, individual mobility, or collective action—and the stereotypical images they formed of both the high status outgroup and their low status ingroup. In both experiments, participants in the open and quota conditions tended to opt for acceptance of disadvantage and reported fairly consensual stereotypes in terms of traits "consonant with...social position": the high status group was described as analytical, rigorous, straightforward, and also rule-bound, while the ingroup was practical, conscientious, creative, and straightforward. Under closed conditions, however, there was significantly more support for collective protest, and participants' stereotype of the high status group reflected this challenge, becoming far more negative. In addition to analytical and rule bound, sophisticated group members were now described as cold, hostile, and mean, while the ingroup was conscientious, friendly, open, and pleasant. As we had predicted, conditions which increased the likelihood of collective action against disadvantage also affected stereotyping—an outgroup to be challenged was defined in a way which justified this challenge, which expressed group members' rejection of current status relations between the groups. We are currently conducting and planning further studies designed to explore the way in which asymmetries of power affect the stereotyping process (e.g., Reynolds et al. 1998).

In contrast, then, to the perspectives outlined above, we do not see stereotyping as a weapon largely owned and wielded by the powerful, nor do we see it as an overwhelmingly negative force in power-based intergroup relations. Although there clearly are conditions under which consensually accepted group images work in the interests of the powerful, to the disadvantage of the powerless, we would argue that resistance to oppression also and crucially involves acts of stereotyping, that crafting stereotypes of both ingroup and outgroup which define resistance as possible is perhaps the critical first step towards social change (see Sherif 1967, chap. 1). This was certainly a process recognized by African American activist Malcolm X who tried, in many of his writings and speeches, to manipulate the stereotypes held by African Americans, both of themselves and of whites, so that the intergroup relationship was defined as amenable to challenge and to change (e.g., see Perry 1989).

CONCLUSION

This chapter has presented evidence from four areas of our recent research program. We have demonstrated that stereotyping follows variation in the salient comparative context (intergroup or interpersonal) rather than variation in level of attentional investment; that stereotypical homogenization characterises descriptions of both ingroups and outgroups in contexts in which intergroup relations are salient; that the content of stereotypes changes markedly with the intergroup context in which they are expressed; and that stereotype content varies with the specific quality of intergroup relations as affected by factors such as differential power and the permeability of intergroup boundaries.

In our view, the overall message of these findings is that stereotyping is simply the form person perception takes in intergroup contexts, contexts where individuals think, act, and feel in terms of group identities rather than individual personalities. The word 'simply' appears in that sentence to signal the idea that this process does not involve distortion, bias, or error to a greater extent than any other form of person perception. We do not wish to suggest, however, that stereotyping is in any sense 'simple,' or 'simplifying.' Quite the reverse. It reflects the full richness, complexity, and dynamic character of the intergroup relationships which provoke it. It is, as our title comments, part of life's rich tapestry—as long as there are social groups, with differences of opinion and interest, disparate aims, goals, values, priorities, there will be stereotypes to, as Sherif put it (1967, p. 3), "codify" our relevant actions and attitudes.

Social psychology has a long tradition of denigrating stereotypes as impoverished distortions of the "true" complexity of human individuality. Our argument here has been for a rehabilitation of stereotypes as expressions of the true complexity of intergroup relations—conflict, contempt, disagreement, and denigration included, for it is these manifestations of the process which seem to drive our theories. In a sense, stereotyping has become a scapegoat for some aspects of social and political reality that we perhaps prefer not to confront (see Mackie 1973; Oakes and Reynolds 1997). Groups engaged in struggle do vilify each other (e.g., Bar-Tal 1988, 1990) and do develop sometimes strikingly divergent understandings of the issues at hand (Reicher 1996). Social psychologists have consistently accounted for this by diagnosing psychological problems—dysfunctions of the personality, shortcomings of cognition. However, these "special pleadings" become redundant when one accepts intergroup relations as a real, powerful and distinctive aspect of social life, and stereotyping as a rational consequence. In Sherif's words:

> Images of other groupings...are invariably formulated from the point of view of the in-group's interests and goals, as parties to the intergroup relationship...the images are appropriate to *their* position vis a vis the others, or the position they desire to achieve. From the point of view of the people possessing the image, it is rational and logical, given the premise that the others

must stand in a certain relationship to them, if they themselves are to attain cherished goals (Sherif 1967, p. 27, emphasis in original).

We need to revitalize this view of stereotyping as a rational expression of inter-group relations, while also recognizing that intergroup relations are at the core of political life, often premised upon disagreement about fundamental values, rights and wrongs. As a consequence, stereotypes can become vehicles for the expression of values we find objectionable. For example, Bar-Tal (1988) found that many Israeli Jews see Palestinians as primitive criminal murderers, while Palestinians characterised Jews as Nazi imperialist oppressors. We may well feel moved to challenge one or both of those stereotypes, but in doing so we should nonetheless acknowledge that they both arise from the same rational processes underlying our own value-based judgments of them. They express positions in an intergroup relationship, as do our own views. This is not a defense of social or political relativism; rather we wish to emphasise the inherent, inescapable *relativity* of human perception, a relativity which other social-psychological processes can work to correct, but which cannot be defused by calling it error," "bias" and so forth (see Oakes et al. 1994, chap. 8; Oakes and Reynolds 1997).

Our argument here has more than academic significance. Explanatory recourse to personality dysfunction and cognitive deficit have tended to retard our discipline's ability to make effective contributions to problems of racism, discrimination, bigotry in general (see also Hopkins, Reicher, and Levine 1997; Reicher 1986). In characterizing stereotyping as a psychological mistake we underestimate its power (for both bad and good), and our attempts to redress injustice attack the wrong target—we try to correct the psychological mistake with "information" (e.g., Donovan and Leivers 1993) and "facts" (ATSIC 1998), often without regard for the real political and social differences in perspective which drive intergroup images and give them their power. Our work in areas such as stereotyping may have far greater and more constructive (Hopkins et al. 1997; Leach 1998) social impact if we begin by taking seriously group-based relativities of perspective, and the power of group processes to influence individuals' interpretations of social reality.

REFERENCES

Allport, G.W. 1954. *The Nature of Prejudice*. Cambridge, MA: Addison-Wesley.

Asch, S.E. 1952. *Social Psychology*. Englewood Cliffs, NJ: Prentice Hall.

ATSIC. 1998. *As a Matter of Fact: Answering the Myths and Misconceptions about Indigenous Australians*. Aboriginal and Torres Strait Islander Commission, Canberra, Australia.

Bar-Tal, D. 1988. "Delegitimizing Relations Between Israeli Jews and Palestinians: A Social Psychological Analysis. Pp. 217-248 in *Arab-Jewish relations in Israel*, edited by J. Hoffman. Bristol, IN: Wyndham Hall.

Bar-Tal, D. 1990. *Group Beliefs*. New York: Springer-Verlag.

Bodenhausen, G.V. 1990. "Stereotypes as Judgmental Heuristics: Evidence of Circadian Variations in Discrimination." *Psychological Science* 1: 319-322.

Bodenhausen, G.V. 1993. "Emotions, Arousal, and Stereotypic Judgments: A Heuristic Model of Affect and Stereotyping." Pp. 13-27 in *Affect, Cognition and Stereotyping: Interactive Processes in Group Perception*, edited by D.M. Mackie and D.L. Hamilton. San Diego: Academic Press.

Bodenhausen, G.V., and R.S. Wyer. 1985. "Effects of Stereotypes on Decision Making and Information-Processing Strategies." *Journal of Personality and Social Psychology* 48: 267-282.

Bourhis, R.Y., J.C. Turner, and A. Gagnon. 1997. "Interdependence, Social Identity and Discrimination." In *The Social Psychology of Stereotyping and Group Life*, edited by R. Spears, P. Oakes, N. Ellemers, and S.A. Haslam. Oxford: Blackwell.

Brewer, M.B. 1988. "A Dual Process Model of Impression Formation." Pp. 1-36 in *Advances in Social Cognition*, Vol. 1, edited by T.K. Srull and R.S. Wyer. Hillsdale, NJ: Lawrence Erlbaum.

Bruner, J.S. 1957. "On Perceptual Readiness." *Psychological Review* 64: 123-152.

Buchanan, W. 1951. "Stereotypes and Tensions as Revealed by the UNESCO International Poll." *International Social Science Bulletin* 3: 515-528.

Donovan, R.J., and S. Leivers. 1993. "Using Paid Advertising to Modify Racial Stereotype Beliefs." *Public Opinion Quarterly* 57: 205-218.

Ellemers, N. 1993. "The Influence of Socio-Structural Variables on Identity Enhancement Strategies." *European Review of Social Psychology* 4: 27-57.

Ellemers, N., and A. van Knippenberg. 1997. "Stereotyping in Social Context." In *The Social Psychology of Stereotyping and Group Life*, edited by R. Spears, P. Oakes, N. Ellemers, and S.A. Haslam. Oxford: Blackwell.

Erber, R., and S.T. Fiske. 1984. "Outcome Dependency and Attention to Inconsistent Information." *Journal of Personality and Social Psychology* 47: 709-726.

Fishman, J.A. 1956. "An Examination of the Process and Function of Social Stereotyping." *Journal of Social Psychology* 43: 27-64.

Fiske, S.T. 1993. "Controlling Other People: The Impact of Power on Stereotyping." *American Psychologist* 48: 621-628.

Fiske, S.T., and E. Depret. 1996. "Control, Interdependence and Power: Understanding Social Cognition in Its Social Context." Pp. 31-61 in *European Review of Social Psychology*, Vol. 7, edited by W. Stroebe and M. Hewstone. Chichester, England: Wiley.

Fiske, S.T., and J.P. Leyens. 1997. "Let Social Psychology Be Faddish or, at Least Heterogeneous. In *The Message of Social Psychology*, edited by C. McGarty and S.A. Haslam. Oxford: Blackwell.

Fiske, S.T., and S.L. Neuberg. 1990. "A Continuum of Impression Formation, from Category-Based to Individuating Processes: Influences of Information and Motivation on Attention and Interpretation." Pp. 1-73 in *Advances in Experimental Social Psychology*, Vol. 23, edited by M.P. Zanna. New York: Random House.

Fiske, S.T., and S.E. Taylor. 1991. *Social Cognition*. New York: McGraw-Hill.

Fiske, S.T., M. Lin, and S.L. Neuberg. In Press. "The Continuum Model: Ten Years Later." In *Dual Process Theories in Social Psychology*, edited by S. Chaiken and Y. Trope. New York: Guilford.

Fiske, S.T., B.A. Morling, and L.E. Stevens. 1996. "Controlling Self and Others: A Theory of Anxiety, Mental Control, and Social Control. *Personality and Social Psychology Bulletin* 22: 115-123.

Gilbert, D.T., and J.G. Hixon. 1991. "The Trouble of Thinking: Activation and Application of Stereotypic Beliefs. *Journal of Personality and Social Psychology* 60: 509-517.

Hamilton, D.L., and T.K. Trolier. 1986. "Stereotypes and Stereotyping: An Overview of the Cognitive Approach." Pp. 127-163 in *Prejudice, Discrimination, and Racism*, edited by J.F. Dovidio and S.L. Gaertner. New York and Orlando, FL: Academic Press.

Haslam, S.A. 1997. "Stereotyping and Social Influence: Foundations of Stereotype Consensus." In *The Social Psychology of Stereotyping and Group Life*, edited by R. Spears, P. Oakes, N. Ellemers, and S.A. Haslam. Oxford: Blackwell.

Haslam, S.A., and P.J. Oakes. 1995. "How Context-Independent Is the Outgroup Homogeneity Effect? A Response to Bartsch and Judd." *European Journal of Social Psychology* 25: 469-475.

Haslam, S.A., and J.C. Turner. 1992. "Context-Dependent Variation in Social Stereotyping. 2: The Relationship Between Frame of Reference, Self-Categorization and Accentuation." *European Journal of Social Psychology* 22: 251-278.

Haslam, S.A., and J.C. Turner. 1995. "Context-Dependent Variation in Social Stereotyping. 3: Extremism as a Self-Categorical Basis for Polarized Judgement." *European Journal of Social Psychology* 25: 341-371.

Haslam, S.A., P.J. Oakes, J.C. Turner, and C. McGarty. 1995. "Social Categorization and Group Homogeneity: Changes in the Perceived Applicability of Stereotype Content as a Function of Comparative Context and Trait Favourableness." *British Journal of Social Psychology* 34: 139-160.

Haslam, S.A., P.J. Oakes, J.C. Turner, and C. McGarty, C. 1996. "Social Identity, Self-Categorization, and the Perceived Homogeneity of Ingroups and Outgroups: The Interaction Between Social Motivation and Cognition. In *Handbook of Motivation and Cognition*, Vol. 3, edited by R.M. Sorrentino and E.T. Higgins.. New York: Guilford.

Haslam, S.A., J.C. Turner, P.J. Oakes, C.A. McGarty, and B.K. Hayes. 1992. "Context-Dependent Variation in Social Stereotyping. 1: The Effects of Intergroup Relations as Mediated by Social Change and Frame of Reference." *European Journal of Social Psychology*, 22: 3-20.

Haslam, S.A., J.C. Turner, P.J. Oakes, C. McGarty, and K.J. Reynolds. 1998. "The Group as a Basis for Emergent Stereotype Consensus. Pp. 203-239 in *European Review of Social Psychology*, Vol. 8, edited by W. Stroebe and M. Hewstone. Chichester, England: Wiley.

Haslam, S.A., P.J. Oakes, K.J. Reynolds, and J. Mein. In Press. "Rhetorical Unity and Social Division: A Longitudinal Study of Change in Australian Self-Stereotypes." *Asian Journal of Social Psychology*.

Hewstone, M. 1989. Changing stereotypes with disconfirming information. Pp. 207-223 in *Stereotyping and Prejudice*, edited by D. Bar-Tal, C.G. Graumann, A.W. Kruglanski, and W. Stroebe. New York: Springer-Verlag.

Hewstone, M. 1994. "Revision and Change of Stereotypic Beliefs: In Search of the Elusive Subtyping Model." Pp. 69-109 in *European Review of Social Psychology*, Vol. 5, edited by W. Stroebe and M. Hewstone. Chichester, England: Wiley.

Hewstone, M. 1996. "Contact and Categorization: Social Psychological Interventions to Change Intergroup Relations." Pp. 323-368 in *Foundations of Stereotypes and Stereotyping*, edited by C.N. Macrae, C. Stangor, and M. Hewstone. New York: Guilford.

Hewstone, M., N. Hopkins, and D.A. Routh. 1992. "Cognitive Models of Stereotype Change. 1: Generalization and Subtyping in Young People's Views of the Police." *European Journal of Social Psychology* 22: 219-234,

Hopkins, N., M. Regan, and J. Abell. 1997. "On the Context Dependence of National Stereotypes: Some Scottish Data." *British Journal of Social Psychology* 36: 553-563.

Hopkins, N., S. Reicher, and M. Levine. 1997. "On the Parallels Between Social Cognition and the 'New Racism'." *British Journal of Social Psychology* 36: 305-329.

Johnston, L., and M. Hewstone. 1992. "Cognitive Models of Stereotype Change. 3: Subtyping and the Perceived Typicality of Disconfirming Group Members." *Journal of Experimental Social Psychology* 28: 360-386.

Jost, J.T., and M.R. Banaji. 1994. "The Role of Stereotyping in System-Justification and the Production of False-Consciousness." *British Journal of Social Psychology* 33: 1-27.

Judd, C.M., C.S. Ryan, and B. Park. 1989. "Accuracy in the Judgement of In-Group and Out-Group Variability." *Journal of Personality and Social Psychology* 61: 366-379.

Leach, C.W. 1998. "Comments on Hopkins, Reicher and Levine." *British Journal of Social Psychology* 37: 255-258.

Linville, P.W. 1982. "The Complexity-Extremity Effect and Age-Based Stereotyping." *Journal of Personality and Social Psychology* 42: 193-211.

Linville, P.W., and E.E. Jones. 1980. "Polarized Appraisals of Outgroup Members." *Journal of Personality and Social Psychology* 38: 689-703.

Linville, P.W., G.W. Fischer, and P. Salovey. 1989. "Perceived Distributions of the Characteristics of In-Group Members: Empirical Evidence and a Computer Simulation." *Journal of Personality and Social Psychology* 57: 165-188.

Linville, P.W., P. Salovey, and G.W. Fischer. 1986. "Stereotyping and Perceived Distributions of Social Characteristics: An Application to Ingroup-Outgroup Perception." Pp. 165-208 in *Prejudice, Discrimination and Racism*, edited by J.F. Dovidio and S.L. Gaertner. New York and Orlando, FL: Academic Press.

Lippman, W. 1922. *Public Opinion*. New York: Harcourt Brace.

Mackie, M. 1973. "Arriving at 'Truth' by Definition: The Case of Stereotype Inaccuracy." *Social Problems* 20: 431-447.

Macrae, C.N., M. Hewstone, and R.J. Griffiths. 1993. "Processing Load and Memory for Stereotype-Based Information." *European Journal of Social Psychology* 23: 77-87.

Macrae, C.N., A.B. Milne, and G.V. Bodenhausen. 1994. "Stereotypes as Energy-Saving Devices: A Peek Inside the Cognitive Toolbox." *Journal of Personality and Social Psychology* 66: 37-47.

Meenes, M. 1943. "A Comparison of Racial Stereotypes of 1935 and 1942." *Journal of Social Psychology* 17: 327-336.

Medin, D.L. 1988. "Social Categorization: Structures, Processes and Purposes. Pp. 119-126 in *Advances in Social Cognition*, Vol.1, edited by T.K. Srull and R.S. Wyer. Hilldale, NJ: Lawrence Erlbaum.

Medin, D.L., R.L. Goldstone,. and D. Gentner. 1993. "Respects for Similarity." *Psychological Review* 100: 254-78.

Neuberg, S.L., and S.T. Fiske. 1987. "Motivational Influences on Impression Formation: Outcome Dependency, Accuracy-Driven Attention, and Individuating Processes." *Journal of Personality and Social Psychology* 53: 431-44.

Nolan, M.A., S.A. Haslam, R. Spears, and P.J. Oakes. In Press. "An Examination of Resource-Based and Fit-Based Theories of Stereotyping under Cognitive Load and Fit." *European Journal of Social Psychology*.

Oakes, P.J. 1987. "The Salience of Social Categories." In *Rediscovering the Social Group: A Self-Categorization Theory*, edited by J.C. Turner et al. Oxford/New York: Basil Blackwell.

Oakes, P.J. 1996. "The Categorization Process: Cognition and the Group in the Social Psychology of Stereotyping." In *Social Groups and Identity: Developing the legacy of Henri Tajfel*, edited by P. Robinson. Oxford: Butterworth Heineman.

Oakes, P.J., and A.A. Dempster. 1996. *Views of the Categorization Process, with an Example from Stereotype Change*. Paper presented at the Annual Meeting of the Society of Australasian Social Psychologists, Canberra, 2-5 May.

Oakes, P.J., and K.J. Reynolds. 1997. "Asking the Accuracy Question: Is Measurement the Answer?" In *The Social Psychology of Stereotyping and Group Life*, edited by R. Spears, P. Oakes, N. Ellemers, and S.A. Haslam. Oxford: Blackwell.

Oakes, P.J., and J.C. Turner. 1990. "Is Limited Information Processing Capacity the Cause of Social Stereotyping?" Pp. 111-135 in European Review of Social Psychology,. Vol. 1, edited by W. Stroebe and M. Hewstone. Chichester, England: Wiley.

Oakes, P.J., S.A. Haslam, and J.C. Turner. 1994. *Stereotyping and Social Reality*. Oxford: Blackwell.

Oakes, P.J., J.C. Turner, and S.A. Haslam. 1991. "Perceiving People as Group Members: The Role of Fit in the Salience of Social Categorizations." *British Journal of Social Psychology* 30: 125-144.

Oakes, P.J., S.A. Haslam, and K.J. Reynolds. 1999. "Social Categorization and Social Context: Is Stereotype Change a Matter of Information or of Meaning?" In *Social Identity and Social Cognition*, edited by D. Abrams and M.A. Hogg.. Oxford: Blackwell.

Oakes, P.J., K.J. Reynolds, S.A. Haslam, M. Nolan, and L. Dolnik. Under review. "Responses to Powerlessness: Stereotyping as an Instrument of Social Conflict."

Park, B., and M. Rothbart. 1982. "Perception of Outgroup Homogeneity and Levels of Social Categorization: Memory for the Subordinate Attributes of In-Group and Out-Group Members." *Journal of Personality and Social Psychology* 42: 1051-1068.

Park, B., C.M. Judd, and C.S. Ryan. 1991. "Social Categorization and the Representation of Variability Information." Pp. 211-245 in *European Review of Social Psychology*, Vol. 2, edited by W. Stroebe and M. Hewstone. Chichester, England: Wiley.

Pendry, L.F., and C.N. Macrae. 1994. "Stereotypes and Mental Life: The Case of the Motivated But Thwarted Tactician." *Journal of Experimental Social Psychology* 30: 303-25.

Perry, B. 1989. *Malcolm X: The Last Speeches* New York: Pathfinder.

Quattrone, G.A., and E.E. Jones. 1980. The Perception of Variability within Ingroups and Outgroups: Implications for the Law of Small Numbers." *Journal of Personality and Social Psychology* 38: 141-152.

Reicher, S. 1986. "Contact, Action and Racialization: Some British Evidence." Pp. 152-168 in *Contact and Conflict in Intergroup Encounters*, edited by M. Hewstone and R. Brown. Oxford: Blackwell.

Reicher, S. 1996. "The Battle of Westminster: Developng the Social Identity Model of Crowd Behavior in Order to Deal with the Initiation and Development of Collective Conflict." *European Journal of Social Psychology* 26: 115-134.

Reicher, S., N. Hopkins, and S. Condor. 1997. "Stereotype Construction as a Strategy of Social Influence." Pp. 94-118 in R. Spears, P.J. Oakes, N. Ellemers, and S.A. Haslam (Eds.) *The Social Psychology of Stereotyping and Group Life*. Oxford: Balckwell.

Reynolds, K.J. 1996. *Beyond the Information Given: Capacity, Context and the Categorization Process in Impression Formation*. Unpublished PhD thesis, Australian National University.

Reynolds, K.J., and P.J. Oakes. In press (a). "Understanding Impression Formation: A Self-categorization Theory Perspective." In *Progress in Asian Social Psychology*, Vol. 2, edited by T. Sugiman, J. Lui, M. Karasawa, C. Ward, and U. Kim.

Reynolds, K.J. and Oakes, P.J. In press (b) "Variability in Impression Formation: Investigating the Role of Motivation, Capacity, and the Categorization Process." *Personality and Social Psychology Bulletin.*

Reynolds, K.J., Oakes, P.J., Haslam, S.A., Spears, R. and Wegener, R. 1998. *Does Having Power Always Lead to Stereotyping? Investigating Cognitive Capacity and Group-Based Accounts of the Stereotyping Process*. Paper presented at the 4th Meeting of Australasian Social Psychologists, Christchurch, New Zealand, April 1998.

Rothbart, M. 1981. "Memory Processes and Social Beliefs." Pp. 145-182 in *Cognitive Processes in Stereotyping and Intergroup Behavior*, edited by D.L. Hamilton. Hillsdale, NJ: Lawrence Erlbaum.

Rothbart, M., and O.P. John. 1985. "Social Categorization and Behavioral Episodes: A Cognitive Analysis of the Effects of Intergroup Contact." *Journal of Social Issues* 41: 81-104.

Ruscher, J.B., and S.T. Fiske. 1990. "Interpersonal Competition Can Cause Individuating Processes." *Journal of Personality and Social Psychology* 58: 832-843.

Ruscher, J.B., S.T. Fiske, H. Miki, and S. Van Manen. 1991. "Individuating Processes in Competition: Interpersonal versus Intergroup." *Personality and Social Psychology Bulletin* 17: 595-605.

Seago, D. W.1947. "Stereotypes: Before Pearl Harbor and after." *Journal of Social Psychology* 23: 55-63.

Sherif, M. 1967. *Group Conflict and Co-operation: Their Social Psychology*. London: Routledge and Kegan Paul.

Sinha, A.K.P., and O.P. Upadhyaya. 1960. "Change and Persistence in the Stereotypes of University Students toward Different Ethnic Groups during Sino-Indian Border Dispute." *Journal of Social Psychology* 52: 31-39.

Spears, R., and S.A. Haslam. 1997. "Stereotyping and the Burden of Cognitive Load." Pp. 171-207 in *The Social Psychology of Stereotyping and Group Life*, edited by R. Spears, P. Oakes, N. Ellemers, and S.A. Haslam. Oxford: Blackwell.

Stangor, C., and C. Duan, C. 1991. "Effects of Multiple Task Demands upon Memory for Information about Social Groups." *Journal of Experimental Social Psychology* 27: 357-378.

Stroebe, W., and C.A. Insko. 1989. "Stereotype, Prejudice, and Discrimination: Changing Conceptions in Theory and Research." Pp. 3-34 in *Stereotyping and Prejudice: Changing Conceptions*, edited by D. Bar-Tal, C.F. Graumann, A.W. Kruglanski, and W. Stroebe. New York: Springer-Verlag.

Tajfel, H. 1969. "Cognitive Aspects of Prejudice." *Journal of Social Issues* 25: 79-97.

Tajfel, H., ed. 1978. *Differentiation Between Social Groups: Studies in the Social Psychology of Intergroup Relations*. London: Academic Press.

Tajfel, H. 1979. "Individuals and Groups in Social Psychology." *British Journal of Social and Clinical Psychology* 18: 183-190.

Tajfel, H. 1981. "Social Stereotypes and Social Groups." Pp. 144-167 in *Intergroup Behaviour*, edited by J.C. Turner and H. Giles. Oxford: Blackwell; Chicago: University of Chicago Press.

Tajfel, H., and J.C. Turner. 1979. "An Integrative Theory of Intergroup Conflict." In *The Social Psychology of Intergroup Relations*, edited by W.G. Austin and S. Worschel. Monterey, CA: Brooks/Cole.

Taylor, S.E. 1981. "A Categorization Approach to Stereotyping." Pp. 88-114 in *Cognitive Processes in Stereotyping and Intergroup Behavior*, edited by D.L. Hamilton. Hillsdale, NJ: Lawrence Erlbaum.

Turner, J.C. 1981. "The Experimental Social Psychology of Intergroup Behaviour." In *Intergroup Behaviour*, edited by J.C. Turner and H. Giles. Oxford: Blackwell; Chicago: University of Chicago Press.

Turner, J.C. 1985. "Social Categorization and the Self-Concept: A Social Cognitive Theory of Group Behaviour. In *Advances in Group Processes*, Vol. 2, edited by E.J. Lawler. Greenwich, CT: JAI Press.

Turner, J.C., and R.Y. Bourhis. 1996. "Social Identity, Interdependence and the Social Group: A Reply to Rabbie et al." Pp. 25-63 in *Social Groups and Identities: Developing the Legacy of Henri Tajfel*, edited by P. Robinson. Oxford: Butterworth-Heinemann.

Turner, J.C., and P.J. Oakes. 1986. "The Significance of the Social Identity Concept for Social Psychology with Reference to Individualism, Interactionism and Social Influence." *British Journal of Social Psychology* 25: 237-252.

Turner, J.C., and P.J. Oakes. 1997. "The Socially Structured Mind." In *The Message of Social Psychology*, edited by C. McCarty and S.A. Haslam. Oxford: Blackwell.

Turner, J.C., P.J. Oakes, S.A. Haslam, and C.M. McGarty. 1994. "Self and Collective: Cognition and Social Context." *Personality and Social Psychology Bulletin* 20: 454-463.

Van Knippenberg, A., M. Van Twuyver, and J. Pepels. 1994. "Factors Affecting Social Categorization Processes in Memory." *British Journal of Social Psychology* 33: 419-432.

Verkuyten, M. 1997. "Discourses of Ethnic Minority Identity." *British Journal of Social Psychology* 36: 565-586.

Vinacke, W.E. 1956. "Explorations in the Dynamic Process of Stereotyping." *Journal of Social Psychology* 43: 105-132.

Weber, R., and J. Crocker. 1983. "Cognitive Processes in the Revision of Stereotypic Beliefs." *Journal of Personality and Social Psychology* 45: 961-977.

Wilder, D.A. 1984. "Predictions of Belief Homogeneity and Similarity Following Social Categorization." *British Journal of Social Psychology* 23: 323-333.

Wright, S.C., D.M. Taylor, and F.M. Moghaddam. 1990. "Responding to Membership in a Disadvantaged Group: From Acceptance to Collective Protest." *Journal of Personality and Social Psychology* 58: 994-1003.

Yzerbyt, V.Y., A. Coull, and S.J. Rocher. 1997. "The Cognitive Costs of 'Refencing': The Role of Atypicality Judgments in the Maintenance of Stereotypes." Manuscript under review.

Yzerbyt, V.Y., S. Rocher, and G. Schadron. 1997. "Stereotypes as Explanations: A Subjective Essentialistic View of Group Perception." Pp. 20-50 in *The Social Psychology of Stereotyping and Group Life*, edited by R. Spears, P. Oakes, N. Ellemers, and S.A. Haslam. Oxford: Blackwell.

BOUNDED GENERALIZED RECIPROCITY
INGROUP BOASTING AND INGROUP FAVORITISM

Toshio Yamagishi, Nobuhito Jin, and Toko Kiyonari

ABSTRACT

This chapter discusses theoretical implications of seven experiments conducted in Japan by Jin, Yamagishi, and their colleagues. All of those experiments involved the minimal group paradigm originally developed by Tajfel
and his colleagues in the early 1970s. The major findings from those experiments are: (1) Ingroup favoritism in reward allocation is not a mere reflec-
tion of "ingroup boasting" or the tendency to perceive ingroup members
more positively than outgroup members. (2) Ingroup favoritism in reward
allocation in the minimal group situation requires the expectation that they
would be favorably treated by other members of their own group, but not by
outgroup members. A logical analysis of the minimal group experimental
paradigm revealed the existence of a generalized kind of interdependency.
Based on these findings and the logical analysis, an alternative theory to
explain ingroup favoritism is proposed that emphasizes the role of generalized exchanges which themselves are both the cause and the product of
ingroup favoritism.

Advances in Group Processes, Volume 16, pages 161-197.

INTRODUCTION

The so-called "minimal group" experiments originally conducted by Tajfel and his associates in the early 1970s (Tajfel, Billig, Bundy, and Flament 1971) have been a source of inspiration for the later development of social psychology. The startling finding that people give more favorable treatment to those who share a trivial, *nominal* social category and less favorable treatment to those who do not provided the impetus for Billig and Tajfel (1973) to develop a theory of intergroup behavior called social identity theory. According to this theory, the ingroup-outgroup bias often observed in real as well as laboratory groups—the tendency for people to treat ingroup members more favorably than outgroup members—is a product of universal human motivation for maintaining a positive self-identity. Because one's self-identity partly derives from social identity, identity with the group, or a social category with which one is associated, one is motivated to establish positively valued distinctiveness for such a group or category. From this perspective, participants of the minimal group experiment treat ingroup members more favorably than outgroup members; this makes their group positively distinct.

The success of social identity theory went far beyond the initial impact of the minimal group experiment (MGE) (Tajfel et al. 1971) and encouraged researchers to work on problems related to intergroup relations, producing an impressive array of literature on intergroup relations from the social identity perspective (cf. Messick and Mackie 1989; Hogg and Abrams 1988, for reviews of this literature). More recently, because of the seminal effort by Turner and his associates (Turner et al. 1987) to broaden the scope of social identity theory, social categorization theory, an offspring of social identity theory, has spread out its influence beyond the range of intergroup relations into other areas of social psychology (cf. Brown 1988; Hogg and Abrams 1988; Turner et al. 1987; Hogg 1992).

The success of social identity theory, however, was not achieved without battling criticisms. The theory has been challenged on many grounds. Some of the criticisms have valid points, and empirical evidence has now been accumulated against the theory's basic assumptions. This study delineates logical implications of some of the valid criticisms so far addressed against social identity theory, proposes an alternative explanation of ingroup favoritism observed in the minimal group situation, and finally examines larger theoretical implications of our alternative theory of ingroup favoritism. Although some of the experimental works reported in this article have already been published, most of them were published in Japanese and thus are hard for non-Japanese readers to access. Therefore, this chapter reports those works in a greater more detail than the works published in English.

EXPLAINING INGROUP BIAS: EARLIER FORMULATIONS

Conflicts among various forms of social groups have been a major concern throughout the history of humanity. They are still one of the major concerns of our time. Reflecting on the importance of the problem, social psychologists have traditionally treated it as one of their major research topics. And, ingroup-outgroup bias—the tendency shared by many people to perceive members of the same group as superior and to give more favorable treatments to one's own group members—has been the core of discrimination against outgroup members and has almost always played an important role in the social psychologists' effort to explain intergroup conflict. Social identity theory, advanced by Tajfel and his associates (Billig and Tajfel 1973; Tajfel and Turner 1979; Tajfel 1982), represents a more recent and one of the most successful efforts by social psychologists to explain this phenomenon. The purpose of this paper is to critically examine the theory. Before starting, however, let us briefly summarize the earlier theoretical efforts to explain ingroup-outgroup bias.

Earlier Theories of Ingroup-Outgroup Bias

Perceived Similarities/Differences of Attitudes

One of the early explanations of discriminatory attitudes against outgroup members offered by social psychologists is one based on the perceived similarities and differences of attitudes and beliefs. People tend to like those who share similar attitudes and beliefs and dislike those who have different attitudes and beliefs (Byrne 1969). At the same time, people tend to overestimate similarities when they compare their own attitudes and beliefs to those of members of the same group and underestimate similarities with outgroup members (Rokeach 1960). According to Rokeach, this constitutes a mechanism through which discriminatory attitudes against outgroup members emerge. This account of ingroup-outgroup bias, however, leaves critical questions intact. Why do people perceive similarities with ingroup members and differences with outgroup members, and why do people like others who are similar to themselves? Unless answers to those problems are provided, the account of ingroup bias based on similarities/differences of attitudes is simply a tautological statement. Furthermore, results of the MGE (Billig and Tajfel 1973) show that ingroup-outgroup bias emerges even when people do not perceive similarities in attitudes.

Displaced Aggression

Another early explanation of ingroup-outgroup bias was based on the frustration-aggression hypothesis (Dollard et al. 1939), which regarded unfavorable behavior against outgroup members as displaced aggression. Although some studies show that aggression and/or discrimination against outgroup members (mostly minorities) is more likely to occur among those who are experiencing frustration (e.g., Bettelheim and Janowitz 1949; Wilson, Chun, and Kayatani 1965), the psychodynamic notion of displaced aggression is generally considered to be too general and thus insufficient as an explanation of ingroup-outgroup bias.

Realistic Conflicts

The famous Robber's Cave experiment by Sherif and colleagues (1961) is a classic in inter-group relations literature. In that work, Sherif and his associates proposed the realistic conflict theory of ingroup-outgroup bias. According to their view, negative attitudes toward outgroup members are a result of social conflict between one's own group and the other group over control of resources. Thus, the existence of a shared goal whose attainment requires cooperation of all the people involved, including members of both groups, alleviates the negative attitudes created by social conflict between the two groups. Although no one would dare to deny the relevance of this theory for understanding many of the real world examples of social conflict, social practice of ingroup favoritism and nepotism, as well as discrimination against outgroup members, its power as the general account of ingroup-outgroup bias has been challenged because of increasing evidence generated by the social identity researchers, demonstrating that categorization alone produces ingroup-outgroup bias even when no real conflicts are involved.

Shared Fate

Members of a social group share many elements. The social category that plays the central role in social identity theory is one of those elements that characterize shared group membership. In an effort to identify the particular element that is critical for the emergence of ingroup-outgroup bias, Rabbie and Horwitz (1969) conducted an experiment in which they divided the participants into two groups, Blues and Greens, on an arbitrary basis. In one condition, one of the two groups was randomly selected to receive attractive rewards. In the other, neither of the two groups received rewards. The results showed that ingroup-outgroup bias emerged only in the first condition. That is, subjects gave more favorable evaluation to ingroup members than to outgroup members when, and only when, they were to share the same fate, that is, receiving or not receiving attractive rewards. Based on this finding, Rabbie and Horwitz concluded that sharing a common fate is the cause for the emergence of ingroup-outgroup bias. The shared fate promotes we-*ness* and a common identity among the members of the group. The sense of cohesion and solidarity provides the basis for the higher evaluation of ingroup members. More recently, however, Horwitz and Rabbie (1982) found that ingroup-outgroup bias exists even among the control condition in the aforementioned experiment in which no rewards are provided, when the sample size was increased substantially. Furthermore, results of the MGE mentioned earlier provide evidence that social categories alone are sufficient to produce the ingroup-outgroup bias, implying that shared fate is not the critical factor for the emergence of ingroup-outgroup bias.

Minimal Group Experiments

Tajfel and colleagues (1971) were the first to conduct an MGE. The original purpose was to identify the critical factor responsible for the emergence of ingroup-outgroup bias, a further extension of Rabbie and Horwitz's (1969) experiment. Tajfel and his associates set up the minimal group consisting of people who shared only a social category as a "control condition" in which no social interactions are allowed. Specifically, minimal groups were created in their laboratory by dividing subjects into two groups based on a trivial criterion, such as the tendency to overestimate or underestimate the number of dots displayed on a screen or a preference for Klee's as opposed to Kandinski's paintings. There is absolutely no social interaction or communication in those minimal groups, either within each group or across the two, and thus no reason for ingroup-outgroup bias to emerge according to the explanations for the bias presented above—no similarities, no frustration, no conflict of interests, and no shared fate. They had planned to use this "control condition" to examine what extra factor would produce ingroup-outgroup bias. What they found, instead, was that no extra factor was needed for the emergence of ingroup-outgroup bias. Subjects who were asked to allocate money gave more money to an ingroup member than to an outgroup member despite the fact that the grouping was made on a completely arbitrary basis and absolutely no social interactions existed either within or across groups. That is, the result indicated that mere categorization alone, not matter how trivial the categorization involved, was sufficient for the emergence of ingroup-outgroup bias in reward allocation.

Another impact of this MGE by Tajfel and associates (1971) came from the finding that subjects preferred to maximize the difference in the reward ingroup members and outgroup members received even when it meant a smaller reward to ingroup members. In other words, subjects in their experiments were willing to sacrifice own group member's rewards to gain a *relative* advantage in relation to rewards given to members of the other group. To those subjects, how much ingroup members received was not as important as *how much more* they received in relation to outgroup members. None of the earlier theories mentioned sufficiently explains both of the findings—the findings that mere categorization produces ingroup-outgroup bias and that relative gain is more important than absolute gain. The answer to the theoretical challenge posed by those findings Tajfel and his associate provided is social identity theory.

Social Identity Theory

The social identity theory that Tajfel and his associates (Billig and Tajfel 1973; Tajfel 1982) proposed to explain the ingroup-outgroup bias in the minimal group situation is based on the assumption that people are motivated to give self a positively distinct identity. An implication of this assumption is that people are motivated to maintain a positive social identity—that is, people who derive a part of their self-identity from the group membership are motivated to give the group positive distinctiveness. Given the fact that a group is distinct only with regard to other groups, a desirable social identity is achieved by making (or perceiving) the group with which they are associated favorably different or positively distinct from the other groups. In sum, according to social identity theory,

1. People are motivated to establish positively valued distinctiveness for groups with which they identify from relevant outgroups, and
2. When social identity in terms of some group membership is unsatisfactory, members will attempt to leave that group (psychologically or in reality) to join some more positively distinct group and/or to make their existing group more positively distinct. (Turner et al. 1987, p. 30)

The social identity theory briefly summarized above can successfully explain ingroup favoritism in reward allocation in MGE. Subjects in MGE have a group identity forced upon them. The trivial social category they were assigned by the experimenter is the only salient category for their group identity in the laboratory environment. They are also limited in the value dimension that distinguishes their group from the other group; it consists only of those provided by the experimenter, such as money, points, or evaluation scores. Given those constraints, they try to give positive value to their own group on the only dimension available. Thus, they allocate more money to ingroup members than to outgroup members. Furthermore, because the goal of their behavior is to make their own group positively distinct from the other group, relative difference is more important than the absolute level of reward.[1]

CRITICAL ASSESSMENTS OF SOCIAL IDENTITY THEORY

Considering the impact the original MGE (Tajfel et al. 1971) had, it is natural that it stirred up heated disputes over its interpretations. Most of the disputes have centered on the validity of the social identity theoretic interpretation of the finding.

Critiques of social identity theory have raised concerns on experimental procedures, especially the design features that invite demand characteristics, and proposed alternative interpretations of the finding, such as generic norms and residue of interdependency. We will examine each of the criticisms and how social identity theory defended itself against those criticisms.

Demand Characteristics and Generic Norm of Group Behavior

One possible interpretation of the ingroup favoritism that occurs in an MGE is that subjects are simply doing what they think is expected of them. "What is the point in allocating money between an ingroup member and an outgroup member?" "It is much simpler if the experimenter him/herself allocated the money, and yet, why does the experimenter let me allocate the money?" These would be questions that naturally come to the minds of subjects. It would not be surprising if at least some of the subjects answer that the experimenter is interested in how differentially people treat ingroup and outgroup members—"All right, I will treat ingroup members more favorably since that is what is expected of me." Gerard and Hoyt (1974) and Berkowitz (1994) pointed out the possibility that demand characteristics such as mentioned above can explain ingroup favoritism in MGEs.

This alternative explanation of ingroup favoritism in MGEs is based on the assumption that there is a "generic norm" of group behavior according to which people should give more favorable treatment to ingroup members than to outgroup members. In the absence of such a norm, subjects would not think that practicing ingroup favoritism is what is expected of them. In fact, a "'generic' social norm of ingroup-outgroup behaviour" is what Tajfel and colleagues (1971) originally proposed as an explanation of ingroup favoritism in MGEs.[2] Later, Tajfel and his colleagues discarded the "generic" norm as the explanation of ingroup favoritism in MGEs because they found experimental evidence to be inconsistent with such an explanation. For example, Billig (1973) reports that subjects who are aware of the norm exhibit ingroup favoritism less than those who are not aware of it. Tajfel and Billig (1974) found that subjects who were supposed to rely on the norm more strongly—subjects who faced an unfamiliar situation and feeling anxious—exhibited a lower level of ingroup favoritism than did others. St Claire and Turner (1982) let the subjects estimate how much of ingroup favoritism others would practice and found that subjects exhibited a higher level of ingroup favoritism than the expected level.

Residue of "Real" Interdependence with Utilitarian Implications

Another criticism of the social identity theoretic interpretation of ingroup favoritism in MGEs concerns the "minimal-ness" of the minimal group. Tajfel and his colleagues (1971) created the minimal group through a process of elimination; they eliminated characteristics of "real" groups such as communication, intergroup conflict, utilitarian consequence, and so on, and finally ended up with the skeleton of a group consisting only of categorization. They thus believed that the minimal group is endowed with nothing but categorization. As pointed out by Kerr and Stone (1993), this method of elimination, however, may not provide a guarantee for their claim. The inappropriateness of the method of elimination to guarantee "minimal-ness" can easily be understood when we think of alchemists who concluded, through a process of eliminating "all" other materials, that the minimal condition for burning to occur are combustible and ignition; they just could not think of oxygen as an indispensable element in the minimal burning condition. Similarly, an element that Tajfel and his colleagues failed to conceive of may play the critical role in producing ingroup favoritism in MGEs.

Rabbie, Schot, and Visser (1989), in fact, thought that the minimal group is not as minimal as Tajfel and his colleagues believed. Although interdependence of interest in the sense that one's action affects others' action and, through the altered action of others, indirectly affects one's own interest—mutual behavior control, using Thibaut and Kelley's (1959) terminology—does not exist in the minimal group, subjects' self-interests in an MGE are in fact dependent on other subjects' action. Subjects in an MGE allocate rewards between an ingroup member and an outgroup member. The allocation choice by the subject has no utilitarian consequence to the allocator him/herself as claimed by Tajfel and his colleagues. However, Rabbie and his colleagues claim that Tajfel and his coworkers overlooked the fact that the subject's rewards are determined by other subjects. They allocate money and, at the same time, are allocated money by others. Each subject's pay is dependent upon other subjects' choices. Rabbie et al. (1989) reasoned that this implicit interdependence of interests is the critical factor for the emergence of ingroup favoritism, and they demonstrated the critical role this interdependence of interest plays for the emergence of ingroup favoritism in MGEs by manipulating who allocates money for the subject. In this experiment, subjects whose pay was determined by outgroup members gave more money to outgroup members, while those whose pay was determined by ingroup members gave more to ingroup members. Rabbie and Lodewijkx (1994) concluded that the ingroup favoritism in MGEs is a strategic behavior motivated by utilitarian goals; that is, subjects of an MGE treated ingroup members more favorably than outgroup members because they expected similar favorable treatment from other ingroup members.

While admitting the existence of interdependence of interest in MGE as suggested by Rabbie and his colleagues, we should be aware of the fact that the interdependence takes the form of *mutual fate control* rather than mutual behavior control (Thibaut and Kelley 1959). That is, each member's payoff in an MGE depends on other members' choices, but the payoff is independent of his/her own choice. In this sense, the subject's choice cannot have any utilitarian consequence to the subject him/herself as claimed by Tajfel and his colleagues. And yet, experimental evidence repeatedly shows that the kind of interdependence that takes the form of mutual fate control is critical in the production of ingroup favoritism in MGE (Jin and Yamagishi 1997; Jin, Yamagishi, and Kiyonari 1996; Karp et al. 1993; Ng 1980; Rabbie et al. 1989). The following sections will first provide recent experimental findings showing that mutual fate control is critical in the production of ingroup favoritism in MGEs, and then introduce our account of ingroup favoritism in MGEs. Our account is basically a combination of the two alternative explanations discussed above—(1) a "generic" social norm of group behavior and (2) interdependence in the form of mutual fate control. We will present results from seven experiments we conducted with our colleagues; these experiments clearly demonstrate that ingroup favoritism in MGEs is not a matter of mere categorization.

MINIMAL GROUP IS NOT SO MINIMAL AFTER ALL

Experiment 1: Multilateral Fate Control

The first of the series of experiments Jin, Yamagishi, and their associates conducted in 1991 (Experiment 1), was published in Karp et al. (1993). The goal was to demonstrate that the minimal group created in the laboratory following the procedure proposed by Tajfel and colleagues (1971) is not as minimal as originally considered. They demonstrated this by comparing the original minimal group condition with a *more minimal* condition. In the original minimal group condition, ingroup-outgroup bias in reward allocation emerged as in the original experiment (Tajfel et al. 1971). In the *more minimal* minimal group condition, no ingroup-outgroup bias emerged.

The original minimal group condition used in this experiment was almost a complete replication of the work of Tajfel and his colleagues (1971), except that subjects allocated 500 yen (approximately 5 dollars) between one ingroup member and one outgroup member, instead of using a series of allocation matrices. This change in the procedure was justified because the goal of the experiment was to demonstrate that the ingroup-outgroup bias in reward allocation would disappear once the last remnant of interdependency among group members was removed; it was *not* important to determine whether the bias was the result of maximization of absolute gain or of relative gain. Karp and colleagues (1993) reasoned, following Rabbie and associates (1989), that the original minimal group condition was not as free from interdependence of utilitarian interest as social identity theorists had assumed. Subjects in the original minimal group condition had "multilateral fate control." A subject determines, at least partly, the reward of an ingroup and an outgroup member. At the same time, his/her reward is determined by ingroup and outgroup members. Logically, this should not affect the subject's choice because the choice is completely anonymous. Empirically, however, it did, as is shown below.

Karp et al. (1993) eliminated this "multilateral fate control" aspect in the *more minimal* minimal group condition by setting the amount of money the subject received at a fixed rate. Subjects in their "unilateral" allocation condition (i.e., the more minimal minimal group condition), subjects allocated money (500 yen) between an ingroup member and an outgroup member. However, they were not a target of other subjects' allocation behavior. Instead, they received a predetermined amount (300 yen) directly from the experimenter. The rest of the procedures were identical. Thirty-six students (17 males and 19 females) recruited from an introductory psychology class at a major national university participated in the experiment in six-person groups. The result was clear-cut. Subjects in the original minimal group condition gave significantly more than a half of 500 yen to an ingroup member (an average of 283.44 yen, sd = 53.56) and 216.56 yen to an outgroup member, successfully replicating the ingroup-outgroup bias observed by Tajfel and colleagues (1971). On the other hand, no ingroup-outgroup bias emerged in the "unilateral" allocation condition; subjects in this condition gave an average of 250.07 yen (sd = 20.00) out of the total of 500 yen to an ingroup member and 249.93 yen to an outgroup member. The difference was neither statistically significant nor substantially meaningful.

Those results clearly indicate that the ingroup-outgroup bias in reward allocation requires the "multilateral fate control" in reward allocations. This conclusion is also consistent with the conclusion from the experiment by Rabbie and his coworkers (1989). Rabbie and his associates' reasoning was similar to ours. It is the fact that subjects in MGE are targets of other subjects' allocation decisions that is critical for the emergence of ingroup-outgroup bias in reward allocation. We demonstrated this by eliminating the "multilateral fate control" in the unilateral allocation condition. Rabbie and colleagues (1989) demonstrated this by adding another condition in which subjects were the target of allocation decisions either by ingroup members or by outgroup members. When the subjects were the target of allocations by ingroup members alone, they allocated more money to an ingroup member than to an outgroup member. However, when the subjects were targets of allocations by outgroup members alone, they allocated more money to an outgroup member than to an ingroup member.

Experiment 2: Ingroup Favoritism and Ingroup Boasting

Although the above result of the experiment by Karp and associates (1993) that ingroup-outgroup bias in reward allocation required the "multilateral fate control" seemed clear cut, it is premature to accept this conclusion because an alternative interpretation is possible. According to the alternative interpretation, subjects in the unilateral allocation condition did not share the same social category with the rest of the ingroup members. Following the original MGE procedure, subjects estimated the number of dots projected on a screen several times, and then, were divided into the "overestimators" and the "underestimators." Each subject then allocated 500 yen to one overestimator and one underestimator. To the subject who was classified as an over- or underestimator, the other over- or underestimators were ingroup members and the under- or overestimators were outgroup members. This feature was common both in the multilateral allocation condition (i.e., the original minimal group condition) and the unilateral allocation condition. However, the fact that the subjects made the allocation decision but were not the target of other subjects' allocation decisions might have put them in yet another group, the group of allocators. If allocator/recipient difference was more salient than the over-/underestimator difference, subjects in the unilateral allocation condition were actually allocating 500 yen between two outgroup members or between two recipients (rather than between an overestimator and an underestimator). This, rather than the lack of multilateral fate control, may explain the lack of ingroup-outgroup bias in the unilateral allocation condition.

Jin and colleagues (1996) conducted another experiment (Experiment 2) to eliminate this alternative explanation by demonstrating that "ingroup boasting" (which they called "ingroup evaluation"), but not ingroup favoritism, existed in both multilateral and unilateral allocation conditions. They defined *ingroup favoritism* as allocation of reward of some utilitarian value in favor of ingroup members. Ingroup favoritism of this kind existed both in the original MGE (Tajfel et al. 1971) and in the original minimal group condition of Karp and colleagues' (1993) experiment. In contrast, they defined *ingroup boasting* (or ingroup evaluation) on a purely nonmaterialistic ground, as more favorable evaluation given to ingroup members than to outgroup members. Jin and coworkers (1996) argue that *ingroup boasting* may be produced by simply categorizing people on a trivial criterion, but that multilateral fate control is needed for the emergence of *ingroup favoritism*. Let us review the results of their experiment before further discussing theoretical implications of this statement.

The experiment was almost a complete replication of that of Karp and colleagues (1993). The only difference was that subjects in Jin and colleagues' (1996) experiment evaluated an ingroup member and an outgroup member on a set of semantic differential scales, in addition to the task of allocating 500 yen. The reward allocation aspect of the experiment was identical to that of Karp and coworkers' experiment. Forty-four students (29 males and 15 females) selected from the subject pool of about 1,000 first year students at a major national university participated in the experiment. The result in reward allocation was also almost identical. Subjects in the multilateral allocation condition gave an average of 282.27 yen (sd = 54.42) out of 500 yen to an ingroup member, leaving 217.73 yen to an outgroup member. The difference was significant. In contrast, subjects in the unilateral allocation condition gave an average of 247.77 yen (sd = 58.51) to an ingroup member, leaving 252.23 yen to an outgroup member. The difference was not statistically significant. The critical role of multilateral fate control in the production of ingroup favoritism was again clearly demonstrated.

When it came to ingroup boasting rather than ingroup favoritism, however, the effect of the experimental manipulation disappeared, as predicted. The average semantic differential responses to three evaluative pairs of adjectives, trustworthy-untrustworthy, likable-unlikable, intelligent-unintelligent, on a seven-point scale was used. Subjects gave a more favorable personal evaluation to an ingroup member than to an outgroup member, as indicated by a marginally significant main effect of target membership, $F(1, 42) = 3.66, p < .07$. Neither the main effect of the experimental condition nor the interaction effect was far from the significant level. The result that subjects gave more favorable evaluation to an ingroup member is clearly against the alternative explanation that allocator/recipient difference was more salient than overestimator/underestimator difference, and thus they were allocating money between two outgroup members (i.e., two recipients).

A seeming inconsistency of the above findings from Experiments 1 and 2 and those from Gagnon and Bourhis (1996) should be discussed here. At about the same time that Karp and colleagues (1993) conducted Experiment 1, Gagnon and Bourhis (1996)[3] conducted a similar experiment using almost the same design to test the same hypothesis. They compared two conditions. The first was the original minimal group condition. The second, "autonomous" condition was almost identical to our "unilateral allocation" condition. Subjects in the autonomous condition received five percentage grade points directly from the experimenter, and allocated the same amount of points between one ingroup member and one outgroup member. Subjects in the original minimal group condition allocated the same amount of grade points while understanding that they themselves are a target of other participants' allocation decisions. Their subjects gave more points to an ingroup member than to an outgroup member in both original minimal group condition (which they called the interdependent condition and Karp et al. 1993, called the multilateral fate control condition) and in the "autonomous" or "unilateral allocation" condition. Their conclusion, thus, was diagonally opposite to ours.

This seeming inconsistency between our findings from Experiments 1 and 2 and their findings may be reconciled once the distinction between ingroup boasting and ingroup favoritism is acknowledged. Our subjects allocated real money, 500 yen, and thus the utilitarian consequence of their allocation behavior was transparent. Those who gave more than 250 yen to an ingroup member was practicing ingroup *favoritism*, not simply ingroup boasting. We found that ingroup favoritism to occur only in the multilateral fate control condition (or what they called interdependent condition); no ingroup favoritism at all occurred in the unilateral allocation (or autonomous) condition. On the other hand, ingroup boasting occurred in both conditions. Whether or not our findings and Gagnon and Burhis' (1996) findings are inconsistent depends on how seriously Gagnon and Burhis' subjects perceived utilitarian consequences of their allocation behavior. Five percentage grade points may be important to students, as Gangon and Burhis claim. On the other hand, their data suggest that their subjects did not fully understood the utilitarian consequences of their behavior. They report that subjects in the interdependent condition expected to receive an average of 5.11 points from ingroup members. Because the total number of points to be allocated is five, the majority of their subjects expected to receive from ingroup members more than the total amount available! The fact that the majority of their subjects had unrealistic expectations strongly suggests the possibility that they did not fully understand the nature of their allocation behavior. Given the lack of clear understanding concerning the nature of their allocation behavior, the points their subjects allocated would better be considered to have symbolic rather than utilitarian value. In other words, their subjects showed "ingroup boasting" in both conditions, but not ingroup favoritism.[4]

The evidence from the above two experiments indicates that the psychological processes involved in ingroup favoritism (allocation of resource of utilitarian value) are not the same as those involved in ingroup boasting, and that ingroup favoritism in reward allocation cannot be directly derived from ingroup boasting that seems to be based on mere categorization. Social identity theory may be able to defend itself by saying that it is a theory of ingroup boasting, not of ingroup favoritism. This defense does not devalue the importance of social identity theory as a theory of social perception. However, by using such a line of defense, social identity theory can no longer claim to be the major player in intergroup conflict. The importance of the original MGE was derived from the fact that subjects *acted* in a discriminatory manner against outgroup members despite no logical or historical reasons to do so. What the result of Experiment 2 suggests is that positive feelings derived from membership in a superior group do not necessarily lead to acting in an outright discriminatory manner. For example, feeling superior based on skin color is far different from sending people of the other skin color to a gas chamber. Jin and colleagues (1996) argue that social identity theory placed too much emphasis on the minimalness of MGE and prematurely closed the gap between discriminatory action (i.e., ingroup favoritism in reward allocation of some utilitarian consequences) and self-boasting feelings (i.e., ingroup boasting).

THE ILLUSTION OF CONTROL HYPOTHESIS

The results of Experiments 1 and 2 indicate that multilateral fate control is needed for the emergence of ingroup favoritism in reward allocation, but not of ingroup boasting. If the subject's desire to be associated with a superior social category is not the reason for ingroup favoritism as assumed in social identity theory, what then is the cause? Karp and colleagues (1993) proposed the "illusion of control" hypothesis to answer this question. Briefly, it is a hypothesis that subjects expected that the favor they gave to an ingroup member would somehow be reciprocated. They call this idea the "illusion of control" hypothesis because subjects were hypothesized to expect favors they gave to ingroup members to be reciprocated, while that expectation was not grounded in the true nature of the relationship; because other subjects had no chance to see if the subject gave a favor to an ingroup member, they could not respond to the action of the subject.

The illusion of control hypothesis is similar to the explanation offered by Rabbie and coworkers (1989) and Rabbie and Lodewijkx (1994). They reasoned that subjects who face the minimal group situation favor an ingroup member in exchange for expected return. They tried to justify this explanation by demonstrating that subjects gave more to an outgroup member than to an ingroup member when their own reward depended on outgroup members. The only difference between Rabbie and his associates' "interdependency" hypothesis and Karp and colleagues' "illusion of control" hypothesis is in that the latter emphasizes the "illusory" nature of the interdependency. Using Thibaut and Kelley's (1959) terminology, subjects in MGEs have mutual fate control but not mutual behavior control. Rabbie and his associates call the mutual fate control "interdependency" and do not make the distinction between the two types of control explicit. Karp and his colleagues (1993) call it "multilateral fate control," implying that one can control the reward the target receives but not the behavior of the target (and thus own payoff to be provided by the target).[5] Despite this difference, Karp and his associates and Rabbie and his associates share the same fundamental idea; the idea that ingroup favoritism in reward allocation in the minimal group situation is based on their expectations of their favors to be reciprocated.

Experiment 3: Those Who Have and Those Who Do Not Have the Illusion of Control

Jin and his associates (1996) conducted another experiment (Experiment 3) to demonstrate that only the subjects who harbored the "illusion of control"—the expectation that the favor they gave to an ingroup member would be reciprocated—would practice ingroup favoritism. The experiment, with 39 students selected from a large subject pool at a major national university, was an almost exact replication of the second experiment.[6] The results clearly supported the illusion of control hypothesis. In the analysis, subjects were divided into two groups, those who had the illusion of control and those who did not, according to their responses to a postexperimental questionnaire item, "Did you think that your own group members would allocate you more if you allocated more to a member of your own group?" Eleven subjects responded positively to this question, and they in fact practiced ingroup favoritism, giving an average of 314.55 yen (sd = 49.27) of 500 yen to an ingroup member leaving only 185.45 yen to an outgroup member. The difference was statistically significant. On the other hand, twenty-eight subjects who responded negatively to the above question gave an average of 246.43 yen (sd = 69.29) to an ingroup member and 253.57 yen to an outgroup member. The difference was not statistically significant. Ingroup favoritism in this MGE was produced by a minority (about 30 percent) of the subjects who had an illusory expectation that giving a favor to an ingroup member would invite the favor to be reciprocated by their group members.

Letting the Subjects Wait

After the initial success in demonstrating that ingroup favoritism disappeared once the last remnant of interdependency was eliminated in Karp et al.'s (1993) experiment, the same research team that conducted that experiment under the leadership of Yamagishi started a series of follow-up experiments. The first thing they did was to streamline experimental procedures. In the original experiment (Karp et al. 1993) some subjects arrived far after the appointment time and thus the other subjects had to wait 10 to 20 minutes before the experiment began. By improving telephone conversations for scheduling subjects, we became successful in bringing subjects to the laboratory on time. As the experimenters became accustomed to the procedure, the experiment itself ran faster and more smoothly than in the original experiment. Then, we faced a problem: Ingroup favoritism did not emerge even in the standard minimal group condition. We failed to replicate the effect that we did in the original replication experiment (Karp et al. 1993). The only change we introduced to the standard minimal group condition was the above streamlining of the procedure. We were at a loss at that time and tried every possible alteration to the procedure. We used Klee and Kandinski's paintings instead of the dot estimation task. It did not make any difference. We dressed the experimenter in a white laboratory garment instead of jeans and a T-shirt. It did not make any difference. We replaced young-looking experimenters with older-looking experimenters. It did not make any difference. We compared males and females. There was no difference. We improved readability of the instructions. It did not make any difference. We used the original instructions and protocol instead of the streamlined ones. It did not make any difference. We increased the money to be divided from 500 yen to 1,500 yen. It did not make any difference. The last thing we did in this lengthy series of pretesting was to let subjects wait by introducing a confederate who arrived 10 minutes after the appointment time. It made a difference; we succeeded in replicating ingroup favoritism in the standard minimal group condition. Experiment 2 (Jin et al. 1996) had this feature of a "lazy confederate" incorporated in its design.

The question is why such a "trivial" feature had so great an effect. Our tentative answer was that ingroup favoritism in reward allocation was an *unfair* deed, and subjects had to have an excuse for engaging in such an unfair practice. The unfair nature of ingroup favoritism may have been concealed in the original design by Tajfel and his colleagues (1971) by the use of a series of complicated decision matrices and the game-like feelings those complicated matrices brought with them. The task used in our experiment of letting subjects divide 500 yen made the unfair nature of ingroup favoritism more salient. Subjects in the series of pretesting may have hesitated in engaging in such a grossly unfair practice. But, why did the extra waiting make the subjects suddenly engage in the same unfair practice? The experimental findings of Cook and Yamagishi (1983) and Yamagishi (1986b) provide an answer to this question. They show that subjects allocate more to themselves and less to the partner only when their "locally unfair" reward allocation is at least justified in the "referential comparison." The local comparison is the comparison of input and reward between particular people. For example, it is "locally" unfair if one of two people who have worked together with the same level of effort and productivity gets the lion's share. However, even the underrewarded partner may yet be getting a reward above the ongoing and thus "referentially" fair level. What the results of the above experiments by Yamagishi and Cook indicate is that subjects are not likely to claim more than half of the pooled reward when half of the pooled reward is insufficient to reach the referentially fair level. Suppose, for example, two students worked on the same experimental task for an hour and were given a total of $100 to divide. Compare this with another scenario in which two students worked on the same experimental task for 10 hours and were given a total of $100. Suppose one of them is given some reason to claim more than half; maybe, for example, he/she is more senior or needs money more desperately. He/she would not feel as bad if he/she takes $75, leaving $25 for the partner if it is for only an hour's work, even the partner is getting a far better deal than most students would get for working an hour. On the other hand, he/she would feel more guilty if he/she takes $75 for ten hours' work, leaving the partner only $2.50 per hour, which is less than what ordinary students "referentially" deserve for an hour's work. The partner will be more upset in the latter case than in the former. In the former case, the referential comparison provides at least a partial fairness to the underrewarded subject's pay.

The extra waiting time, we speculated, gave the subjects a referential ground for claiming more than half of 500 yen, or 250 yen. With the extra waiting time and the frustration, it is referentially fair for a member to receive more than 250 yen, although claiming more than half of 500 yen was not locally fair. Experiment 2 (Jin et al. 1996) had this feature of an "irresponsible confederate" built in. Furthermore, the "work load" for the subjects was also increased; subjects performed the "dot estimation" task 50 times instead of 30 in the first experiment (Karp et al. 1993). The increase in the work load and the extra waiting time, we believe, made the subjects feel that they deserved good monetary reward.

The third experiment was conducted, in addition to demonstrate the aforementioned difference between ingroup boasting and ingroup favoritism, to test if the extra work load and the longer waiting time was in fact critical for the emergence of ingroup favoritism in reward allocation. For this purpose, we ran a low work load condition in which subjects performed the dot estimation task 20 times. Furthermore, the "irresponsible confederate" was not used in this added condition. This condition ($n = 17$) was compared with the "mutual fate control" condition in the second experiment, in which subjects performed the dot estimation task 50 times after being forced to wait for an "irresponsible confederate" to arrive. Thus, the "mutual fate control" condition in the second experiment served as the "high workload" condition in the third experiment, and the newly run condition was treated as the "low workload" condition. The "mutual fate control" nature of the task was retained in the low work load condition. It was predicted that the ingroup favoritism in reward allocation would be weaker in the low workload condition than in the high workload condition.[7] The result of the third experiment unambiguously supported the prediction. Subjects in the high work load condition gave an ingroup member an average of 282.27 yen (sd = 54.42), leaving an average of 217.73 yen to an outgroup member. On the other hand, subjects in the low work load condition gave an ingroup member an average of 244.12 yen (sd = 84.56), leaving an average of 255.88 yen to an outgroup member. The difference in results between the high and low workload conditions was statistically significant.

Thus, the three experiments show that categorization alone is sufficient to make subjects give a more positive evaluation to ingroup members than to outgroup members, and yet, it is not sufficient to make them give more money to ingroup members than to outgroup members. We decided to call the former "ingroup boasting" and the latter "ingroup favoritism." The social identity processes may be responsible for the ingroup boasting, and yet, the results of the three experiments consistently indicate that having positive feelings toward ingroup members is not the same as treating ingroup members more favorably. Implicit expectations of reciprocation of the favor given to ingroup members and a minimum level of justification for such an unfair practice are required for ingroup favoritism in reward allocation to occur, at least among the Japanese college students who participated in our experiment in the 1990s. Social identity theory is powerless in explaining ingroup favoritism patterns in those experiments.

Self-Enhancement versus Self-Interest:
Do Subjects in MGEs Maximize the Difference?

The results of the three experiments presented so far strongly point to a new interpretation of ingroup favoritism in MGE. It is a means to enhance self-interest rather than to enhance self-esteem. This alternative interpretation of ingroup favoritism, however, will have to face a challenge from the traditional, self-esteem camp. The challenge is that it is inconsistent with the finding that subjects of MGEs prefer to maximize the difference in rewards received by ingroup and outgroup members, even if that means sacrificing the absolute amount of reward provided to ingroup members (Tajfel et al. 1971). According to Karp and his colleagues' (1993) "illusion of control" interpretation, subjects of MGEs should not sacrifice ingroup member's reward to maximize the difference with the outgroup member's reward.

Validity of the finding (Tajfel et al. 1971) that subjects prefer to maximize difference even when it entails sacrificing ingroup members' rewards, however, has been strongly challenged. For example, Brewer and Silver (1978) pointed out that the matrices Tajfel and his associates (1971) used to measure subjects' preferences for reward allocation failed to purely isolate the preference for maximizing difference. Locksley, Ortiz, and Hepburn (1980) suggested that their matrices were in favor of detecting ingroup favoritism. Bornstein and his colleagues (1993) contended that the matrices used by Tajfel and coworkers unnecessarily restrict subjects' voluntaristic allocation. They also pointed to the possibility that repeated use of numerous matrices led subjects to "balance" their choices across matrices. Furthermore, Bornstein and coworkers (1983) demonstrated that other types of preferences, such as minimizing difference or maximizing one's own, can be obtained in MGEs with the use of a different set of matrices.

In response to these challenges to the validity of the finding indicating the preference for maximizing difference and against the use of a specific set of matrices in particular, Turner (1983a, 1983b) claims that the matrices of Tajfel and his associates are less vulnerable to influences of social desirability and social norms. Thus, they are more sensitive to the individuals' internal motivations and preferences. This is not a place to evaluate the validity of those matrices as a means to measure subjects' preference for maximizing difference between ingroup and outgroup members. What we would like to emphasize here is, first, that the finding that subjects of MGEs prefer to maximize the difference between ingroup members' and outgroup members' rewards even at a cost of rewards to ingroup members is not as strongly established as social identity theorists claim. Second, and more importantly, the maximizing difference motivation, if it exists at all, is a very weak one that is easily overwhelmed by other factors, such as social desirability or social norms. If the motivation is so weak that it can be detected only with a highly sophisticated methodology, it must be of very little use in accounting for real life intergroup conflict.

Experiment 4: Maximization of Difference
When Subjects Know What They Are Doing

With the last point in mind, we conducted the fourth experiment[8] to examine if subjects of MGEs do in fact reveal a preference for maximizing difference in a meaningful way. The question we addressed in the fourth experiment is whether subjects prefer maximizing difference between ingroup members and outgroup members when they are fully aware of the implications of their choice. For this purpose, we fixed the rewards given to an ingroup (or outgroup) member and let the subject decide how much to give to an outgroup (or ingroup) member. Sixty subjects (30 males and 30 females) selected from a large subject pool at a major national university participated. They first went through the standard dot estimation task and then the money allocation task. In one condition (ingroup-fixed condition), the subject was told that the reward an ingroup member received had been determined to be 250 yen and were asked to decide, within the upper limit of 500 yen, how much an outgroup member should receive. The outgroup member was said to receive the amount the subject decided to give. If the subjects were motivated by the maximization of the difference, they should have given less than 250 yen to the outgroup member. Similarly, subjects in the other condition (outgroup-fixed condition) were told that the reward an outgroup member received had been determined to be 250 yen and were asked to decide, again within the upper limit of 500 yen, how much an ingroup member should receive. Either motivation, maximizing difference or maximizing own should lead to reward over 250 yen to an ingroup member. Subjects in both conditions were further told that how much they would receive would be determined by another subject; whether an ingroup member or outgroup member would determine the subject's reward was not specified as in the multilateral fate control condition used in the previous experiments (including Tajfel et al.'s original MGE).

The result was clearly against the maximizing difference prediction. Subjects in the ingroup-fixed condition gave on average 326.93 yen (sd = 143.01) to an outgroup member. The amount was significantly greater than the predetermined amount for the ingroup member (250 yen). Furthermore, only two out of 30 subjects in this condition gave less than 250 yen to an outgroup member. The amount, 320.34 yen (sd = 111.65) that subjects in the outgroup-fixed condition gave to an ingroup member was also significantly greater than 250 yen (the amount the outgroup member received). The amount given to an outgroup member in the ingroup-fixed condition and that given to an ingroup member in the outgroup-fixed condition were not significantly different from each other. The results of this experiment clearly indicate that seeing that making the ingroup positively distinct in relation to the outgroup or maximizing the difference between the two groups was not the major motivational force in the reward allocation when subjects clearly knew what they were doing. People may have the motivation to maximize the difference between ingroup and outgroup members, but that motivation, if it exists at all, has been demonstrated to be much too weak to surface when people are fully aware of the consequences of their choices, although it may surface when the use of a complicated set of allocation matrices prevents subjects from clearly realizing implications of their behavior.

COOPERATION WITH AN INGROUP MEMBER AND AN OUTGROUP MEMBER IN THE PRISONER'S DILEMMA

The results of the four experiments presented above provide the evidence that ingroup favoritism in reward allocation in MGE is a matter of self-interest rather than self-esteem. Subjects in those experiments allocated more money to an ingroup member than to an outgroup member when and only when they expected the favor they gave would invite a reciprocal favor from ingroup members. In this section, we apply the same logic to another phenomenon that has traditionally been explained by social identity theory: cooperation with an ingroup member and an outgroup member in the prisoner's dilemma.

In the prisoner's dilemma, especially in its one-shot version, defection is the dominant choice. That is, in a one-shot prisoner's dilemma, in which there is no shadow of a future (Axelrod 1984), self-interested behavior should result in defection. Thus, cooperation in a one-shot prisoner's dilemma game has traditionally been attributed to nonegoistic motivation, such as altruistic or cooperative motivation (e.g., Kuhlman, Camac, and Cunha 1986; Kuhlman and Marshello 1975; Liebrand 1984; McClintock and Liebrand 1988; Messick and McClintock 1968). One of the factors promoting such nonegoistic motivation and, thus, cooperation in the prisoner's dilemma and the social dilemma (the n-person version of the prisoner's dilemma) is group identity. Given the effect of group identity on reward allocation in the minimal group situation and the social identity explanation of the effect, it is natural to expect a higher level of cooperation in a prisoner's dilemma when it is played between ingroup members than between outgroup members. And, this prediction has been consistently confirmed (Brewer and Kramer 1986; Kollock 1997; Kramer and Brewer 1984; Wit and Wilke 1992). Through a series of three experiments presented below, we challenged the group identity explanation of this phenomenon of higher level of cooperation among ingroup members. As we did in the series of MGEs presented above, we offer an alternative explanation based on expectations of reciprocity.

Experiment 5: The Higher Level of Cooperation with Ingroup Members Disappears When Expectations of the Partner's Cooperation Are Statistically Controlled

The purpose of the fifth experiment[9] was to demonstrate that the effect of group identity on cooperation in the prisoner's dilemma would disappear once expectations of reciprocity are statistically controlled. A total of 88 subjects (42 males and 46 females) selected from a large subject pool at a major national university was assigned to one of the following three conditions: ingroup condition, outgroup condition, and the control condition. Subjects first participated in a "perception" experiment in which they compared the sizes of a white fan displayed on a black background and a black fan displayed on a white background. Subjects were then classified into two groups, the "black fan group," who were supposed to perceive the angle of black fans to be wider than the angle of white fans, and the "white fan group," for whose members the angle of white fans was supposed to be wider. Then, they participated in the "second experiment" that was supposed to be independent of the "perception" experiment.[10] Subjects played a prisoner's dilemma game with one ingroup member, one outgroup member, and one member whose group identity was not known. When the partner was either an ingroup member or an outgroup member, they were told of the group identity of the partner but not of the partner's personal identity. In the prisoner's dilemma game, subjects decided how much of 200 yen (initial endowment) to give to the partner in increments of 10 yen. The contributed money was doubled and given to the partner.

The result of this experiment successfully replicated the previous finding that players of the prisoner's dilemma game cooperated more with an ingroup member than with an outgroup member (Brewer and Kramer 1986; Kollock 1997; Kramer and Brewer 1984; Wit and Wilke 1992). Subjects gave an average of 99.20 yen (sd = 71.55) to an ingroup member and 80.34 yen (sd = 67.44) to an outgroup member. When the group identity of the partner was not known, the amount they gave to the partner was 91.70 yen (sd = 69.73). The effect of the partner's group identity was statistically significant. The question addressed in this experiment was if this effect of the partner's group identity would disappear when subjects' expectations of the partner's willingness to reciprocate was statistically controlled. For this purpose, we used the following item in the postexperimental questionnaire; "Did you think that your partner would give more to you if you gave more to him/her?" The average response to this question, provided on a five-point scale ranging from one (not at all) to five (strongly), was significantly different among the three group identity conditions; the expectations of reciprocity measured with this item was the strongest in the ingroup condition, 3.47 (sd = 1.91), the weakest in the outgroup condition, 2.39 (sd = 1.50), and in-between the two extremes in the control condition, 2.99 (sd = 1.89). Subjects in this experiment felt that giving a favor to the partner would invite a reciprocal favor from the partner more strongly when the partner was an ingroup member than when the partner was an outgroup member. They had an intuitive understanding that favors given to ingroup members would be more likely to be reciprocated than favors given to outgroup members. Finally, and most importantly, the effect of the group identity on the level of cooperation almost completely disappeared when the response to the post-experimental questionnaire item was entered as a covariate, $F(2, 173) = 0.09$, ns.

Experiments 6 and 7:
Does the Partner Know My Membership?

The result of the above experiment is consistent with the explanation that people cooperate more in the prisoner's dilemma when they play it with an ingroup member because they believe that cooperation is more likely to be reciprocated by an ingroup member. However, the result of the above experiment may reflect the subjects' tendency to project own behavior onto others. They cooperate more with ingroup members and then project the higher level of their cooperative behavior onto ingroup members. Similarly, they cooperate less with outgroup members and then project the lower level of their cooperative behavior onto outgroup members. This tendency to project own behavior onto the partner is more pronounced, according to Kelley and Stahelski (1970), among defectors than among cooperators; that is, defectors are likely to regard everyone as defectors. This may reduce the defector's sense of control of the partner's behavior and thus explain the lower level of "illusion of control" in the outgroup condition in the above experiment.

The strong correlation between own behavior and expectations of other participants' behavior in prisoner's dilemma and social dilemma experiments is one of the most well established findings in experimental gaming literature.[11] On the other hand, there is no consensus concerning the cause of this correlation. Some argue that the correlation is caused by the subjects' tendency to cooperate when and only when the partner cooperates as well (i.e., subjects subjectively transform the PD matrix into an Assurance Game matrix; see Kollock 1997; Pruitt and Kimmel 1977; Yamagishi 1986a, 1990, for examples of this argument). Others argue that the correlation is produced by the subjects' tendency to project own behavior onto others (see Dawes 1980, 1989, for examples of this argument). The results of the above experiment, while consistent with our theoretical tenets, are thus not sufficient to critically compare our approach with the group identity approach in the prisoner's dilemma context. We, therefore, conducted the sixth experiment.

Each of the 70 subjects (38 males and 32 females), who were selected from a large subject pool at a major national university, participated in the sixth experiment (Jin and Yamagishi 1997). The group identity was manipulated through a "separate experiment" on "perception" conducted before the prisoner's dilemma experiment. Subjects were classified into two groups supposedly according to their preferences for Klee's versus Kandinski's paintings (cf. Tajfel et al. 1971). They then played the same prisoner's dilemma game five times, once in each of the five within-subject conditions to be explained below. Two of the five experimental conditions were the standard ingroup/outgroup conditions. In the ingroup condition, subjects played the prisoner's dilemma game with a member of their own group; in the outgroup condition, they played the same game with a member of the other group. They were informed of the membership of the partner, but not of the partner's personal identity. The third condition was a control condition in which subjects played the prisoner's dilemma game with a partner whose group identity was not known. These three conditions were basically replications of the fifth experiment and similar other experiments on group identity and cooperation in the prisoner's dilemma. The unique feature of the sixth experiment was the addition of two conditions. In the fourth condition, subjects played a prisoner's dilemma game with an ingroup member, but they were told that the partner (who was an ingroup member) would not know the group identity of the subject. That is, the subject knew that the partner was an ingroup member, but the partner did not know the group identity of the subject. Similarly, subjects in the fifth condition played a prisoner's dilemma game with an outgroup member who did not know the group identity of the subject. Thus, except for the control condition in which subjects did not know the group identity of the partner, group identity of the partner was crossed with the knowledge the partner had about the subject's group identity. Summarizing the five conditions, in the ingroup/mutual knowledge condition both the subject and the partner knew that they were in the same group; in the outgroup/mutual knowledge condition both of them knew that they belonged to different groups; in the control condition neither knew of the other's group identity; in the ingroup/unilateral knowledge condition the subject knew that the partner was a member of the same group and yet the subject was informed that the partner did not know the subject's group identity; and finally in the outgroup/unilateral knowledge condition the subject knew that the partner was an outgroup member and yet was informed that the partner did not know the subject's group identity. In each of the five prisoner's dilemma games, each subject was given 100 yen as an endowment and was asked how much of it to give to the partner (in increment of 10 yen). The amount contributed by the subject was doubled in value and was given to the partner.

Should the knowledge that partner has about the subject's group identity matter? If the elevated level of cooperation with an ingroup member and the depressed level of cooperation with an outgroup member are consequences of sharing the same group identity per se, whether the partner knows of the subject's group identity or not should not affect the subject's behavior (although it should affect the partner's behavior). This is because the subject knows that they both share the same group identity and the fact that they share the same group identity is all that should matter. Thus, from the social identity theoretic perspective, only the main effect of the partner's group identity (ingroup versus outgroup) is predicted; partner's knowledge of the subject's group identity is predicted to have no effect at all. Our prediction based on the notion of expectations of reciprocity from ingroup members is quite contrary to this. From this theoretical point of view, people give favor to ingroup members because they implicitly expect that the favor is more likely to be reciprocated from ingroup members than from outgroup members. What should matter, then, is the expected behavior of the partner; the partner's group identity should not matter unless it affects the expected behavior of the partner. It is clear that group identity (of both the subject and the partner) can have an effect on the partner's behavior only when the partner has information about it; group identity should have no effect when the partner has no information about the subject's group identity. Thus, from our theoretical perspective, an interaction effect between the partner's group identity and the partner's knowledge about it is predicted in such a way that the partner's group identity has an effect on the subject's cooperation level only when the partner knows about the subject's group identity; the partner's group identity is predicted to have no effect when the partner has no knowledge about the subject's group identity. This experimental design thus provides a critical test of the two theoretical perspectives.

The results of the experiment, as shown in Table 1, are consistent with our prediction and inconsistent with the social identity theoretic prediction. According to the social identity theoretic prediction, the partner's group identity should have an effect regardless of the knowledge the partner has about the subject's group identity. In contrast, according to the expectations of reciprocity reasoning, the former

Table 1. Average Yen out of the Endowment of 100 Yen
Subjects Contributed in Jin and Yamagishi's (1997) Experiment

Condition		
Partner's Group Identity	*Partner's Knowledge*	*Average contribution*
Ingroup	Yes	30.69 (sd = 23.02)
Ingroup	No	23.69 (sd = 20.64)
Outgroup	Yes	20.50 (sd = 21.90)
Outgroup	No	19.04 (sd = 18.00)
Control (partner's identity unknown)		20.74 (sd = 20.97)

is predicted to have an effect only when the partner knows of the subject's group identity as well. As clearly shown in Table 1, the partner's group identity affected the subject's cooperation level substantially (30.69 versus 20.50, the difference of 10.19 yen) when the partner knew of the subject's group identity, but not much when the partner did not have that knowledge (23.69 versus 19.04, the difference of 4.65 yen). The former difference was significant, and the latter was not. The analysis reported in Jin and Yamagishi (1997) indicates that the cooperation level was significantly higher in the first condition than in the other four conditions, and the cooperation levels in the other conditions did not significantly differ from each other.

While the results shown in Table 1 thus support our hypothesis based on the expectations of reciprocity, skeptics might challenge our interpretation of the result. While the group identity of the partner had a much greater impact on the cooperation level of the subject when the partner knew that the subject was an ingroup member than when the partner did not know the subject's group identity, the cooperation level in the ingroup/unilateral knowledge condition was higher, though not statistically significantly higher, than the other three conditions. The statistically nonsignificant latter difference might suggest the existence of the pure group identity effect. An alternative interpretation of the pattern shown in Table 1 may then be possible: both the effect of expectations of reciprocity and the pure group identity effect existed, the latter being responsible for slightly higher cooperation level in the ingroup/unilateral knowledge condition than in the control or the two outgroup conditions. Yamagishi and Kiyonari (1998) conducted a replication experiment to eliminate the remnant of higher level of cooperation in the ingroup/unilateral knowledge condition by improving instructions. They improved the instructions so that subjects could understand the nature of the knowledge manipulation more clearly than in the original instructions. For example, more readable fonts were used and important points were more effectively highlighted. Seventy-two students selected from a large subject pool at a major national university participated in this experiment (Experiment 7). As in the sixth experiment, they were first categorized into Klee group and Kandinski group following the standard picture preference task. They then played the same prisoner's dilemma game four times, each representing a within-subject condition. The four conditions were created by crossing the knowledge the subject had about the partner's group membership (ingroup or unknown) and the knowledge the partner had about the subject's group membership (ingroup or unknown). In each prisoner's dilemma game, the subject decided how much of the endowment of 200 yen to contribute for the partner. The amount contributed by the subject was doubled and was given to the partner.

The result of this replication experiment clearly supported the expectations of reciprocity prediction, and clearly did not support the pure group identity prediction. The average cooperation level in the ingroup/mutual knowledge condition was 79.50 (sd = 60.02) yen. This amount was significantly higher than the cooperation level in the ingroup/unilateral knowledge condition in which subjects contributed an average of 50.47 (sd = 51.60) yen. It was again demonstrated that the knowledge the partner has about the partner's group identity matters. The primary purpose of this experiment, however, was to see if the partner's group identity has any effect even when the partner has no information about the subject's group identity. The effect is not predicted in the expectations of reciprocity approach, since the subject cannot expect a higher level of cooperation from an ingroup partner when the partner does not know that the subject is in the same group. In contrast, at least some, though maybe weak, effect of group identity of the partner is predicted in the social identity theoretic approach since what matters, according to this approach, is whether the subject shares the same social category with the partner. The result was clear cut. When the partner did not know the group identity of the subject, knowledge about the partner's membership *per se* did not affect the subject's cooperation level (an average of 50.47 yen with the ingroup partner versus 55.11 yen with the partner of unknown membership); the statistically insignificant difference was in the opposite direction to the social identity theoretic prediction. It was thus shown that the slightly higher cooperation level in the ingroup/unilateral knowledge condition in Experiment 6 could have been the result of a lack of clarity in the instructions about the nature of knowledge manipulations. In sum, the results of Experiment 7 clearly demonstrate that the partner's group identity affects the subject's cooperation level in the prisoner's dilemma when and only when the subject is aware that the partner also has information about the subject's group identity.

The results of Experiments 5, 6, and 7 indicate that whether the partner is an ingroup member or an outgroup member does not matter unless the partner knows the subject's membership as well and thus are in sharp conflict with the view that categorization alone is sufficient to cause people to act in a favorable manner to ingroup members and in a discriminatory manner to outgroup members. It is impossible to conclude, based on those results, that subjects cooperated with an ingroup member more strongly than with an outgroup member because they wanted to make their own group positively distinct or they derived happiness in seeing an ingroup member prosper. Our interpretation that they cooperated more strongly with an ingroup member because they had expectations that the ingroup member were more likely to reciprocate is consistent with the experimental results. As has been pointed out in the prisoner's dilemma and social dilemma literature (e.g., Pruitt and Kimmel 1977), people cooperate only when they expect that the partner will cooperate as well. According to Pruitt and Kimmel's (1977) goal/expectation theory, even people who are willing to cooperate fail to cooperate unless they expect that the partner will cooperate as well. The results of the three experiments on prisoner's dilemma presented above indicate that the expectation that the partner will cooperate is higher when the partner is an ingroup member than when the partner is an outgroup member; it is this expectation of the partner's cooperation that encouraged subjects to be more cooperative, rather than fondness of, or psychological closeness to, an ingroup member.

SUMMARY OF THE SEVEN EXPERIMENTS

Let us briefly summarize the major findings of the seven experiments presented, before disussing our account of ingroup favoritism in MGEs in a more systematic manner. The most central finding is that subjects in MGEs do not practice ingroup favoritism in reward allocation unless they expect similar favorable treatment from ingroup members. In Experiment 1, subjects in the original minimal group condition practiced ingroup favoritism, but those in the unilateral allocation condition did not. This finding was replicated in Experiment 2. It was further shown in Experiment 2 that "ingroup boasting" occurs in both conditions, suggesting that categorization alone makes people feel boastful about their group, but does not lead them to practice ingroup favoritism that involves utilitarian consequences. This result of Experiment 2, while rejecting an alternative interpretation of the first experiment, points to the importance of conceptually distinguishing ingroup favoritism from ingroup boasting. Watching American athletes win gold medals at Olympic Games may make Americans feel proud of themselves, but would not make them behave in discriminatory ways toward foreigners. Group identity may play an important role in how people feel about themselves, but how people feel about themselves plays only a limited role in how people behave in the social world. The results of Experiments 3 and 5 show that only those who expected reciprocal favor from ingroup members practice ingroup favoritism in reward allocation (Experiment 3) or cooperate more with ingroup members (Experiment 5). Finally, the result of Experiments 6 and 7 shows that players of the prisoner's dilemma game cooperate more with an ingroup member than with a partner of unknown group identity when the partner knew the subject's group identity. These results are also consistent with the results of experiments conducted by Rabbie and his colleagues (1989) and Ng (1980, 1986). The overall conclusion that can be derived from these experiments is that ingroup favoritism is not fundamentally a matter of mere categorization. It occurs when subjects expect reciprocation of their favor only from ingroup members, not from outgroup members. The second major conclusion comes from Experiment 4. The result of that experiment unambiguously indicated that motivation to maximize intergroup difference in allocated reward in the minimal group situation is extremely weak, if it exists at all. The previous studies by Brewer and Silver (1978), Locksley and associates (1980) and Bornstein and associates (1983) have challenged the validity of the maximization motivation proposition in MGEs, and the responses to such criticisms from the social identity approach were that the measurement of that motivation requires a highly sophisticated tool. However, if the motivation is of critical importance in producing ingroup favoritism, it should reveal itself in a wide variety of situations. In Experiment 4, in which subjects clearly understood what they were doing, practically no one wanted to give outgroup members less than what the ingroup member was given. An important implication of the finding is that outgroup discrimination is a result of ingroup favoritism that occurs only in the constant sum situation, which necessarily involves conflict of interest.

BOUNDED GENERALIZED RECIPROCITY

Expectations of Generalized Reciprocity

The seven experiments consistently indicate that ingroup favoritism in MGEs is based on the expectation that favors given to ingroup members are more likely to be reciprocated than favors to outgroup members. Karp and his colleagues (1993) called this expectation the "illusion of control," but the expectation seems to be wider in its content than that term as defined by Karp and his coworkers (1993). As they defined it, it is the expectation that one's action will be directly reciprocated even when there is no interaction basis for the expectation. We now think that this conception of the "illusion of control" is too narrow, especially in that it is based on "restricted exchanges" rather than "generalized exchanges" (Ekeh 1974). In other words, we argue that reciprocation of the favor given to a particular ingroup member is expected to come from any ingroup member rather than directly from that particular member. Remember that Karp and his associates' subjects were a target of the allocation decision by an unknown ingroup member rather than the particular ingroup member they allocated money to. Thus, the expectation of reciprocal favors in such a situation must have a more defused form. That is, exchanges of favors must not be limited to a particular dyad or "restricted exchange"; rather, they should take a more diffused form usually called "generalized exchange."

Seen from this wider perspective, the subjects who exhibited ingroup favoritism in the above experiments seem to have expected that a system of generalized exchange was operating in the group. In a system of generalized exchanges, people receive favors (intangible as well as tangible), but not necessarily from the ones to whom they provided favors. For example, you help a stranded driver on your way home, and later you are helped by someone when your car breaks down in a remote town. When a generalized exchange system exists, each member gives favor to another with the expectation that someday he/she will receive a favor from someone in the system, but not necessarily from the person to whom he/she gave a favor. Thus, in a group where a system of generalized exchanges exists, members can expect favorable treatment from any member of the group provided that he/she is accepted as a member of the system. The acceptance of membership in such a system often presupposes that he/she is a full participant in the system. That is, one can expect to receive favor from other members only insofar as he/she grants favor to the others. In such a situation, people will naturally develop the expectation of *generalized* reciprocity, the expectation of reciprocation not directly from the same person but from someone in the system. This expectation of generalized reciprocity, we argue, is the source of ingroup favoritism in MGEs.

It is no surprise that people have such expectations of generalized reciprocity and act upon such expectations even in the minimal group situation. The defining feature of a minimal group is the *lack of restricted exchanges*. This does not prevent people from seeing it as a place in which *generalized exchanges* take place. We do not expect that the particular stranded driver we help on a road will later reciprocate in kind. In this respect, a system of generalized exchanges is similar to the minimal group situation. It is of critical importance to realize that *a system of generalized exchanges did in fact exist in the minimal groups in the experiments presented earlier*. That is, those who expected to be favorably treated by ingroup members are the ones who gave favor to an ingroup member. On average, their expectations were substantiated. They did in fact receive favor from other ingroup members more than from outgroup members. The lack of opportunity for direct reciprocation in MGEs did not prevent generalized exchanges from taking place. When Tajfel and his colleagues created the minimal group, what they eliminated is direct reciprocity. Generalized exchanges can occur, and did in fact occur, in the MGE.

Jin and Yamagishi (1997) provide evidence from analysis of the postexperimental questionnaire in Experiment 6 that their subjects in fact had expectations of generalized reciprocity. They asked their subjects how much contribution their own group members and members of the other group would provide. The results shown in Table 2 indicate that they expected a higher level of cooperation from own group members than from the other group members; this means that they expected generalized exchanges to take place at a higher level inside their own group than across groups. Furthermore, they expected that members of the other group would cooperate more among themselves than with members of the subject's group. That is, they expected generalized exchanges to take place in the other group as well. They expected that both their own group members and members of the other group would cooperate within their own respective groups at

Table 2. Average Expected Cooperation Level (in Yen) for Ingroup and Outgroup Members (Jin and Yamagishi, 1997)

	With Members of the Subject's Own Group	With Members of the Other Group
Members of the subject's own group would cooperate	37.86 (sd = 21.31)	23.57 (sd = 16.04)
Members of the other group would cooperate	22.29 (sd = 17.27)	37.14 (sd = 22.52)

about the same level, and, furthermore, that those two groups would be about as uncooperative toward each other. It is clear from these results that subjects in this experiment had expectations that people, whether they are ingroup or outgroup members, cooperate more with their own group members than with outsiders. That is, they had the "generic norm" of group behavior. Results of the fifth experiment reported earlier indicate that ingroup favoritism in reward allocation disappears once this expectation of a higher level of cooperation from ingroup members is statistically controlled.

Bounded Generalized Reciprocity

Some systems of generalized exchanges, such as the example of helping stranded drivers, have practically no boundaries—you help a driver in Oklahoma in the United States, and are helped in Nagano, Japan. However, most systems of generalized exchanges have system boundaries. That is, most generalized exchanges take place within more or less demarcated groups. In this sense, most generalized exchanges are *bounded* generalized exchanges, taking place within group boundaries. And, reflecting this boundedness of generalized exchanges, expectations of generalized reciprocity will take the form of expectations of bounded generalized *reciprocity*—expectations that the favor given to own group members would be reciprocated, but not the favor given to outgroup members. As shown in the experiments presented earlier, people often entertain the belief that the favor given to ingroup members will not be a waste; such a favor is generally considered to be a good investment for receiving favor in the future.

Karp and his colleagues (1993) called such expectations illusion of control. As discussed earlier, the term, "illusion of control," is misleading. This is because the expectation is not illusory in the group in which the majority shares the same expectation. In such a group, members prefer ingroup members to outgroup members as recipients of their favor, expecting that they themselves will be treated in a similar manner. And, they are in fact treated favorably by other members of their own group. For example, subjects in the last three experiments on prisoner's dilemmas in fact received more from ingroup members than from outgroup members. Their expectations that they would receive more from ingroup members were thus not illusory. In other words, the expectation of bounded generalized reciprocity creates a situation in which the expectation itself is the reality—it is a self-fulfilling prophesy. It is an illusion to think that one can change the behavior of others in the minimal group situation. However, it is not an illusion to expect favorable treatment from ingroup members.

Group Heuristic and Two Types of Errors

The conclusion of the last section implies that a system of generalized exchanges can be generated and sustained among people who share such an expectation. If subjects of the second experiment, for example, did not have such expectations and gave nothing, they would have ended up earning the original 200 yen instead of 299 yen (the average amount they earned in the ingroup condition; they gave an average of 99.20 yen and thus received an average of 99.20 times 2 or 199.40 yen, resulting in the payoff of 200 − 99.2 + 199.4 x 2 = 299 yen). This, however, does not necessarily give full advantage to the entertainers of such an expectation because people who do not have such an expectation can free ride. Free riders would not give their own resources even to ingroup members, while receiving resources from other ingroup members.

Whether "free riders" are better off than due-paying members of a generalized exchange systems (those who give favor to other ingroup members) would depend on how likely it is that free riders are detected and punished. In a situation in which practically no free riders are detected, free riders are better off than due-paying members. On the other hand, free riding would not be a gainful strategy when all free riders are immediately detected and punished. Human societies have developed various means to monitor and sanction free riders, ranging from formal institutions, such as the police and IRS, to informal practices in communities and workplaces. Cosmides (1989) even claims that humans have a special module in their brain for detecting free riders. Given the arsenal of such means for monitoring and sanctioning free riders, it would be difficult for free riders in most generalized exchange systems to go undetected unless generalized exchanges involve a mammoth system that appeared only in modern societies. Villagers of some traditional societies know who did not appear on the joint labor for maintaining communal irrigation systems. Families would know who did not do dishes.

Given certain chances of being detected of free riding behavior in generalized exchange systems, entertaining expectations of generalized reciprocity *can* be adaptively advantageous. To the degree that free riding is detected and the offender is expelled from the system, paying dues to retain good standing in a system of generalized exchanges (and thus to qualify for receiving benefits from "ingroup members") would be a wise choice. We are fully aware that this advantage of paying dues does not exist in MGEs. In MGEs, free riders (those who did not practice ingroup favoritism in reward allocation in the first three experiments and those who did not give their money to ingroup members in the last three experiments) faced no chance of being detected. If the expectation of bounded generalized exchange is in fact the driving force of ingroup favoritism in those experiments, a question still remains: Why did they fail to see that the chance of being caught free riding did not exist in those experiments? It seems that the best strategy is to pay dues when free riders are likely to be caught and not pay when they are not likely to be caught. Are not those who pay dues even when the chances of being caught are practically zero naive and foolish?

In answering this question, we argue that the subject's willingness to pay dues with the expectation of generalized reciprocity is based on a "group heuristic." The heuristic is triggered by the perception that one faces a group situation. Once triggered, it works to make people overlook the successful possibility of free riding. We argue that people come to be endowed with this heuristic decision rule because the decision prompted by this heuristic is more likely to make one type of error than the other in group situations. We can think of two types of errors when we face a situation involving potentiality for generalized exchanges, including the minimal group situation. The first type of error—let us call it Type I Error, following the practice used in statistical reasoning—occurs when one erroneously assumes that free riding will be detected when free riding is not detected (i.e., the true null hypothesis is that free riding is not detected). When one commits Type I Error, one pays dues that are not really required to receive the fruit of a generalized exchange system. The maximum cost for committing this error is limited to the amount of dues. The other type of error—let us call it Type II Error—occurs when one erroneously assumes that free riding will not be detected when in fact it is detected (i.e., when the null hypothesis is not true). When one commits a Type II Error, there is practically no limit to the cost. It is often the case that the one who commits a Type II Error and is thus caught free riding is expelled from the group. How serious the consequences are of being expelled depends on how important benefits obtained from the generalized exchange system are. Sometimes, the consequences are deadly. Whether or not the group heuristic as defined above is adaptively advantageous should depend on the relative seriousness of committing these two types of errors—committing a Type I Error and paying unnecessary dues versus committing a Type II Error and being frowned at (a relatively mild consequence) or being expelled (a relatively serious consequence).

Because the cost of committing a Type I Error is the amount of dues, the relative seriousness of committing the two types of errors depends on how serious committing a Type II Error is. In a society where groups are relatively closed to outsiders, consequences of committing a Type II Error can be serious. One who commits a Type II Error and is expelled from the group may have nowhere else to go for the benefit he/she has received from the generalized exchange system. In such a situation, the group heuristic would provide an adaptive advantage, since it protects people from committing a Type II Error at a cost of increasing the chances of committing a Type I Error. In contrast, in a society in which groups are relatively open to outsiders and to newcomers, consequences of committing a

Type II Error would not be as serious. Then, the group heuristic would not provide an adaptive advantage; rather, such a heuristic decision making can be adaptively disadvantageous because it increases the chance of committing a Type I Error. We thus expect that the group heuristic operates heavily (i.e., ingrained in people's decision schemes) in a collectivist society in which groups and relations are more or less closed to outsiders. In a cross-societal experiment using sequential prisoner's dilemma, Hayashi and associates (1998) found that the group heuristic (or the expectation of bounded generalized reciprocity) has a stronger effect among Japanese subjects than among American subjects. They predicted this difference based on the reasoning that the collectivist nature of social relations in Japan makes a Type II Error more deadly to commit in Japanese society than in American society.

Group Heuristic, Generic Norm, and Interdependence of Interest

The idea of group heuristic presented above is similar to the idea of "generic" social norm of ingroup-outgroup behavior, idea originally proposed by Tajfel and coworkers (1971) and later discarded. It is even closer to the idea of social script proposed by Wilder (1986), which he developed as a theoretical offshoot of the generic social norm. On the other hand, group heuristic is distinct from such predecessors as generic group norm or social script in that *it emphasizes the existence of real generalized reciprocity* in the minimal group. Members of the minimal group are not simply following a norm or script that is implanted in them from outside as an abstract principle. The idea of group heuristic is based on the understanding that people's behavior in the minimal group reflects the nature of interdependence of interest actually existing in the group. Generalized exchanges do take place even in the minimal group as explained above—*ingroup favoritism itself produces and maintains generalized exchanges*. We argue that ingroup favoritism is not simply a product of abstract norm or script, but rather it sustains itself by producing a social interaction basis that makes the group heuristic adaptive.

The idea of group heuristic is also similar to Rabbie and his colleagues' idea that actual interdependence with utilitarian consequences is the critical factor for the emergence of ingroup favoritism in MGEs. We differ from them in making the distinction explicit between generalized exchanges and restricted exchanges and by assigning the former the status of the focal player in the interdependency game. In the "restricted" sense, choices of one member can have no utilitarian consequence to him/herself. However, in the "generalized" sense, members can create an environment in which generalized exchanges do in fact take place. In the minimal group, it is not an illusion for the members to expect bounded generalized reciprocity. The idea of group heuristic combines the two predecessors in a productive manner, and offers an alternative explanation of ingroup favoritism in MGE that has wider theoretical and practical implications.

BRINGING INTERDEPENDENCY
BACK INTO SOCIAL PSYCHOLOGY

The results of the experiments presented in this paper illuminate the large schism between "ingroup boasting" (Jin et al. 1996) or favorable perception of ingroup members and ingroup favoritism and outgroup discrimination in reward allocation with utilitarian consequences. Past research in intergroup conflict in the social identity tradition has prematurely closed this schism by overlooking the indirect or generalized type of interdependency that exists even in the minimal group situation. How people perceive and evaluate ingroup and outgroup members is an interesting research topic in itself, but perceiving ingroup members favorably does not necessarily mean that one will practice ingroup favoritism in reward allocation. Social identity theorists define social interdependency too narrowly, that is, as interdependency of direct nature, which Ekeh (1974) calls the restricted exchange, and thus discount the importance of social interdependency in intergroup conflict in particular and in social psychology at large. We believe that we have demonstrated the role that indirect or a generalized type of interdependency plays even in the minimal group situation. It is time to bring back social interdependency with utilitarian consequences into social psychology.

According to the group heuristic approach, ingroup favoritism is an implicit "game strategy" people use in socially interdependent situations including the minimal group situation. Thus, people do not practice ingroup favoritism when it is made salient that the strategy does not work (such as in the first and the second experiments). This basic finding will provide a ground for future work aimed at reducing intergroup conflict and promoting intergroup harmony. Ingroup favoritism that supposedly underlies intergroup conflict can be reduced by making it salient that the "boundedness" of the bounded generalized reciprocity need not be as strong as people intuitively perceive. This avenue for the reduction in intergroup conflict will be more fruitful than the avenue that is recommended by the social identity approach. According to the social identity approach, reduction in ingroup favoritism should be based on reduction in identification with the social category. Even when this is possible, the reduction in group identification can create a side effect of lowered group cohesion. According to the social identity approach, a world without ingroup favoritism would be where groups have no binding power. This solution seems to be impracticable. Our recommended solution is stretching out the perceived boundaries of generalized exchanges. We prefer that people keep paying dues to join generalized exchange systems. That is how societies function better. Generalized exchange systems are not to be blamed for ingroup favoritism; what is to be blamed is excessively narrowly perceived boundaries of such generalized exchange systems. As an example of applying this avenue, we may teach teenage gangs that their perception that they can expect favorable treatment only from within their group is not necessarily true—that they do not need to restrict the circle of mutual ingroup favoritism to their narrow gang groups.

ACKNOWLEDGMENTS

The series of studies reported in this paper has been supported by the Japanese Ministry of Education Scientific Research Grants. We would like to thank Norbert Kerr and Alan Miller for their helpful comments on earlier drafts of this paper, and Motoki Watabe, Nobuyuki Takahashi, Yoriko Watanabe, Yohsuke Ohtsubo, Motoko Kosugi, and other students at Hokkaido University for providing help in conducting studies presented in this paper. All correspondence concerning this article should be addressed to Toshio Yamagishi, Faculty of Letters, Hokkaido University, N10 W7 Kita-ku, Sapporo, Japan 060-0810, Fax +81 (11) 706-3066, Email Toshio@let.hokudai.ac.jp.

NOTES

1. According to the revised version of social identity theory proposed by Tajfel and Turner (1979), ingroup-outgroup bias occurs through the three steps of categorization, identification, and comparison.

2. More recently, Wilder (1986) proposed the conceptualization of such "generic" norms of group behavior as a social script that is automatically triggered in an intergroup situation.

3. According to a footnote, their experiment was conducted in or before 1992.

4. Rabbie et al. (1989), who drew the same conclusion as we did, used money as the resource to be allocated.

5. Another way to express the idea of Karp and colleagues (1993) is the subjective transformation of mutual fate control into bilateral behavior control.

6. We will later present the differences in the design between this and Experiment 2 by Jin et al. (1996).

7. The experiment is reported in Jin et al. (1996) in Japanese.

8. The experiment is partially reported in Jin (1995) in Japanese.

9. The experiment is partly reported in Jin and Shinotsuka (1996) in Japanese.

10. Different experimenters conducted the "first" and the "second" experiments.

11. See Dawes (1980); Edney and Harper (1978); Kollock (1998); Komorita and Parks (1995, 1996), Messick and Brewer (1983); Orbell and Daws (1981); Pruitt and Kimmel (1977); Stroebe and Frey (1982); Yamagishi (1995) for reviews of this literature.

REFERENCES

Axelrod, R. 1984. *The Evolution of Cooperation.* New York: Basic Books.

Berkowitz, N.H. 1994. "Evidence That Subjects' Expectancies Confound Intergroup Bias in Tajfel's Minimal Group Paradigm." *Personality and Social Psychology Bulletin* 20: 184-195.

Bettelheim, B., and M. Janowitz. 1949. "Ethnic Tolerance: A Function of Social and Personal Control." *Americal Journal of Sociology* 55: 137-145.

Billig, M. 1973. "Normative Communication in Minimal Intergroup Situation." *European Journal of Social Psychology* 3: 339-344.

Billig, M., and H. Tajfel. 1973. "Social Categorization and Similarity in Intergroup Behaviour." *European Journal of Social Psychology* 3: 27-55.

Bornstein, G., L. Crum. J. Wittenbraker, K. Harring, C.A. Insko, and J. Thibaut. 1983. "On Measurement of Social Orientations in the Minimal Group Paradigm." *European Journal of Social Psychology* 13: 321-350.

Brewer, M.B., and R.M. Kramer. 1986. "Choice Behavior in Social Dilemmas: Effect of Social Identity, Group Size, and Decision Framing." *Journal of Personality and Social Psychology* 50: 593-604.

Brewer, M.B., and M. Silver. 1978. "Ingroup Bias as a Function of Task Characteristics." *European Journal of Social Psychology* 8: 393-400.

Brown, R.J. 1988. *Group Processes: Dynamics Within and Between Groups.* Oxford: Basil Blackwell.

Byrne, D. 1969. "Attitudes and Attraction." Pp. 35-89 in *Advances in Experimental Social Psychology*, Vol. 4, edited by L. Berkowitz. New York: Academic Press.

Cook, K.S., and T. Yamagishi. 1983. "Social Determinants of Equity Judgments." In *Equity Theory: Psychological and Sociological Perspectives*, edited by D.M. Messick and K.S. Cook. New York: Praeger.

Cosmides, L. 1989. "The Logic of Social Exchange: Has Natural Selection Shaped How Humans Reason? Studies with the Wason Selection Task." *Cognition* 31: 187-276

Dawes, R.M. (1980. "Social Dilemmas." *Annual Review of Psychology* 31: 169-193.

Dawes, R.M. 1989. "Statistical Criteria for Establishing a Truly False Consensus Effect." *Journal of Experimental Social Psychology* 25: 1-17.

Dollard, J., L. Doob, N. Miller, O. Mowrer, and R. Sears. 1939. *Frustration and Aggression.* New Haven: Yale University Press.

Edney, J.J., and C.S. Harper. 1978. "The Commons Dilemma: A Review of Contributions from Psychology." *Environmental Management* 2: 491-507.

Ekeh, P. 1974. *Social Exchange Theory: The Two Traditions.* Cambridge, MA: Harvard University Press.

Gagnon, A., and R. Bourhis. 1996. "Discrimination in the Minimal Group Paradigm: Social Identity or Self-Interest?" *Personality and Social Psychology Bulletin* 22: 1289-1301.

Gerard, H.B., and M.F. Hoyt. 1974. "Distinctiveness of Social Categorization and Attitude Toward Ingroup Member." *Journal of Personality and Social Psychology* 29: 836-842.

Hayashi, N., L. Ostrom, J. Walker, and T. Yamagishi. 1998. "Reciprocity, Trust, and the Illusion of Control: A Cross-Societal Study." *Hokkaido Behavioral Science Report* No. SP-4.

Hogg, M.A. 1992. *The Social Psychology of Group Cohesiveness: From Attraction to Social Identity.* New York: Harvester.

Hogg, M.A., and D. Abrams. 1988. *Social Identifications: A Social Psychology of Intergroup Relations and Group Processes.* London: Routledge.

Horwitz, M., and J.M. Rabbie. 1982. "Individuality and Membership in the Intergroup System." In *Social Identity and Intergroup Relations*, edited by H. Tajfel. Cambridge: Cambridge University Press.

Jin, N. 1995. "Social Identity Theory and the Group Cooperation Heuristic." Pp. 70-73 in *Proceedings of the 36th Annual Meetings of the Japanese Social Psychological Association.* (In Japanese)

Jin, N., and H. Shinotsuka. 1996. "Perception of Interdependency and the Cooperative Tendency." Pp. 154-155 in *Proceedings of the 37th Annual Meetings of the Japanese Social Psychological Association.* (In Japanese)

Jin, N., and T. Yamagishi. 1997. "Group Heuristics in Social Dilemma." *Japanese Journal of Social Psychology* 12: 190-198. (In Japanese)

Jin, N., T. Yamagishi, and T. Kiyonari. 1996. "Bilateral Dependency and the Minimal Group Paradigm." *Japanese Journal of Psychology* 67: 77-85. (In Japanese)

Karp, D., N. Jin, T. Yamagishi, and H. Shinotsuka. 1993. "Raising the Minimum in the Minimal Group Paradigm." *Japanese Journal of Experimental Social Psychology* 32: 231-240.

Kelley, H.H., and A.J. Stahelski. 1970. "Social Interaction Basis of Cooperators' and Competitors' Beliefs about Others." *Journal of Personality and Social Psychology* 16: 66-91.

Kerr, N.L., and E. Stone. 1993. "In Search of the Elusive Minimal-group Effect." Paper presented at the Sixteenth International Nags Head Conference on Groups, Networks, and Organizations.

Kollock, P. 1997. "Transforming Social Dilemmas: Group Identity and Cooperation." Pp. 186-210 in *Modeling rational and moral agents*, edited by P. Danielson. Oxford: Oxford University Press.

Kollock, P. 1998. "Social Dilemmas: The Anatomy of Cooperation." *Annual Review of Sociology* 24: 183-214.

Komorita, S.S., and C.D. Parks. 1995. "Interpersonal Relations: Mixed-Motive Interaction." *Annual Review of Psychology* 46: 183-207.

Komorita, S.S., and C.D. Parks. 1996. *Social Dilemmas*. Boulder: Westview Press.

Kramer, R.M., and M.B. Brewer. 1984. "Effect of Group Identity on Resource Use in a Simulated Commons Dilemma." *Journal of Personality and Social Psychology* 46: 1044-1057.

Kuhlman, D.M., C. Camac, and D. Cunha. 1986. "Individual Differences in Social Orientation." In *Experimental Studies of Social Dilemmas*, edited by H. Wilke, C. Rutte, and D.M. Messick. Frankfurt: Peter Lang.

Kuhlman, D.M., and A.F.J. Marshello. 1975. "Individual Differences in Game Motivation as Moderators of Programmed Strategy Effects in Prisoner's Dilemma." *Journal of Personality and Social Psychology* 32: 922-931.

Liebrand, W.B.G. 1984. "The Effect of Social Motives, Communication and Group Size on Behavior in an n-Person Multi-Stage Mixed-Motive Game." *European Journal of Social Psychology* 14: 239-264.

Locksley, A., V. Ortiz, and C. Hepburn. 1980. "Social Categorization and Discriminatory Behaviour: Extinguishing the Minimal Intergroup Discrimination Effect. *Journal of Personality and Social Psychology* 39: 773-783.

McClintock, C.G., and W.B.G. Liebrand. 1988. "The Role of Interdependence Structure, Individual Value Orientation, and Other's Strategy in Social Decision Making: A Transformational Analysis." *Journal of Personality and Social Psychology* 55: 396-409.

Messick, D.M., and M.B. Brewer. 1983. "Solving Social Dilemmas: A Review." In *Review of Personality and Social Psychology*, Vol. 4, edited by L. Wheeler. Beverly Hills, CA: Sage Publications.

Messick, D.M., and D.M. Mackie. 1989. "Intergroup Relations." *Annual Review of Psychology* 37: 602-607.

Messick, D.M., and C.S.G. McClintock. 1968. "Motivational Bases of Choice in Experimental Games." *Journal of Experimental Social Psychology* 4: 1-25.

Ng, S.H. 1980. "Equity Theory and the Allocation of Rewards Between Groups." *European Journal of Social Psychology* 11: 439-443.

Ng, S.H. 1986. "Equity, Intergroup Bias and Interpersonal Bias in Reward Allocation." *European Journal of Social Psychology* 16: 239-255.

Orbell, J., and R.M. Dawes. 1981. "Social Dilemmas." In *Progress in Applied Social Psychology*, Vol. 1, edited by G. Stephenson and J.H. Davis. New York: Wiley.

Pruitt, D.G., and M.J. Kimmel. 1977. "Twenty Years of Experimental Gaming: Critique, Synthesis and Suggestions for Future." *Annual Review of Psychology* 28: 363-392.

Rabbie, J.M., and M. Horwitz. 1969. "Arousal of Ingroup-Outgroup Bias by a Chance Win or Loss." *Journal of Personality and Social Psychology* 13: 269-277.

Rabbie, J.M., and H.F.M. Lodewijkx. 1994. "Conflict and Aggression: An Individual-Group Continuum." *Advances in Group Processes* 11: 139-174.

Rabbie, J.M., J.C. Schot, and L. Visser. 1989. "Social Identity Theory: A Conceptual and Empirical Critique from the Perspective of a Behavioural Interaction Model." *European Journal of Social Psychology* 19: 171-202.

Rokeach, M. 1960. *The Open and Closed Mind*. New York: Basic Books.

Sherif, M., O.J. Harvey, B.J. White, W.R. Hood, and C.W. Sherif. 1961. *Intergroup Conflict and Cooperation: The Robbers Cave Experiment.* Norman: Institute of Group Relations, University of Oklahoma.

St Claire, L., and J.C. Turner. 1982. "The Role of Demand Characteristics in the Social Categorization Paradigm." *European Journal of Social Psychology* 12: 307-314.

Stroebe, W., and B.S. Frey. 1982. "Self-Interest and Collective Action: The Economics and Psychology of Public Goods." *British Journal of Social Psychology* 21: 121-137.

Tajfel, H. 1982. "Social Psychology of Intergroup Relations." *Annual Review of Psychology* 33: 1-30.

Tajfel, H., and M. Billig. 1974. "Familiarity and Categorization in Intergroup Behavior." *Journal of Experimental Social Psychology* 10: 159-170.

Tajfel, H., M. Billig, R. Bundy, and C. Flament. 1971. "Social Categorization in Intergroup Behaviour." *European Journal of Social Psychology* 1: 149-178.

Tajfel, H., and J.C. Turner. 1979. "An Integrative Theory of Intergroup Conflict." In *The Psychology of Intergroup Relations*, edited by W.G. Austin and S. Worchel. Monterey, CA: Nelson-Hall.

Thibaut, J.W., and H.H. Kelley. 1959. *The Social Psychology of Groups.* New York: Wiley.

Turner, J.C. 1983a. "Some Comments on…'the Measurement of Social Orientations in the Minimal Group Paradigm.'" *European Journal of Social Psychology* 13: 351-367.

Turner, J.C. 1983b. "A Second Replay to Bornstein, Crum, Wittenbaraker, Harring, Insko and Thibaut on the Measurement of Social Orientations." *European Journal of Social Psychology* 13: 383-387.

Turner, J.C., M.A. Hogg, P.J. Oakes, S.D. Reicher, and M.S. Wetherell. 1987. *Rediscovering the Social Group: A Self-Categorization Theory.* Oxford: Blackwell.

Wilder, D.A. 1986. "Social Categorization: Implication for Creation and Reduction of Intergroup Bias." Pp. 291-355 in L. Berkowitz (Ed.) *Advances in Experimantal Social Psychology*, Vol. 19, edited by L. Berkowitz. New York: Academic Press.

Wilson, W., N. Chun, and M. Kayatani. 1965. "Projection, Attraction, and Strategy Choices in Intergroup Competion." *Journal of Personality and Social Psychology* 2: 432-435.

Wit, A.P., and H.A. Wilke. 1992. "The Effect of Social Categorization on Cooperation in Three Types of Social Dilemmas." *Journal of Economic Psychology* 13: 135-151.

Yamagishi, T. 1986a. "The Structural Goal/Expectation Theory of Cooperation in Social Dilemmas." *Advances in Group Processes* 3: 51-87.

Yamagishi, T. 1986b. "Interpersonal Conflicts in Reward Allocation and Their Resolution." *Japanese Journal of Psychology* 58: 78-83 (In Japanese)

Yamagishi, T. 1990. "Factors Mediating Residual Effects of Group Size in Social Dilemmas." *Japanese Journal of Psychology* 61: 162-169 (In Japanese)

Yamagishi, T. 1995. "Social Dilemmas. Pp.311-335 in *Sociological Perspectives on Social Psychology*, edited by K.S. Cook, G. Fine, and J. House. Boston: Allyn and Bacon.

Yamagishi, T., and T. Kiyonari. 1998. *Matrix Transformation and Expectation as Mediators of Group Identity Effect in a Prisoner's Dilemma.* Unpublished experiment report, Hokkaido University, Japan. (In Japanese)

STATUS ORDERS IN TASK
DISCUSSION GROUPS

John Skvoretz, Murray Webster, and
Joseph Whitmeyer

ABSTRACT

This chapter reports the results of research designed to test a model for the emergence of status structures in face-to-face discussion groups. The model is a stochastic process model proposed by Skvoretz and Fararo (1996). It is grounded in expectation states theory and proposes solutions to several problems of enduring interest, among them, the search for a theoretically based account of inequality structures that develop in groups, an explanation of individual level who-to-whom participation data, and the development of both fully and partly transitive inequality structures. The data are coded discussions of four person groups. The groups vary in status composition. Analysis of speech duration distributions provides basic support for the model and the effects it hypothesizes to influence the formation of status orders.

Advances in Group Processes, Volume 16, pages 199-218.
Copyright © 1999 by JAI Press Inc.
All rights of reproduction in any form reserved.
ISBN: 0-7623-0452-9

INTRODUCTION

This chapter builds on three research programs developed since the 1950s and early 1960s. The first is the mathematical modeling of the behavior of members of task-oriented small groups (Bales et al. 1951; Bales 1953; Stephan and Mishler 1952; Coleman 1960; Horvath 1965; Leik 1965, 1967; Skvoretz 1981, 1985, 1988; Balkwell 1991a; Fişek, Berger, and Norman, 1991). The second and third are strands of the expectation states framework that until recently have been separate (Wagner and Berger 1993; Webster and Foschi 1988). One strand, power and prestige (or behavior-expectation) theories, describes the development of power and prestige hierarchies in task-oriented small groups of initially undifferentiated persons. The other strand, status characteristics theories, describes how people's attributes organize interaction in status-heterogeneous groups. Recently, Skvoretz and Fararo (1996) have advanced a dynamic model for the emergence of status orders in task groups that integrates these three lines of research. Our proposed research evaluates and extends this model and thus contributes to all three long-standing research programs.

Efforts to model behavior by participants in task-focused small groups began with Bales, and the setting still is known as Bales groups (Bales et al. 1951; Bales 1953). A most reliable finding is that, after an initial acquaintance phase, the groups develop an enduring structure of inequality that is reflected in, among other things, differential rates of participation in the group. Bales hoped to develop a behavioral model to describe his data. The first attempt, the "harmonic model," supposes that, after ranking participants by amount of participation, the ratio of adjacent group members' participation rates takes the form of increasing ratios of adjacent integers: 2:1 then 3:2 then 4:3 and so forth. That model's fit was disappointing (Bales et al. 1951). As an alternative, Bales (1953) proposed algorithms to simulate interaction. About the same time, Stephan and Mishler (1952) developed an "exponential model," proposing that (for all participants except the group leader, whose participation rate is determined independently) after ranking, the ratio of adjacent participation rates is a constant, r, $0 \leq r \leq 1$.

Further attempts at modeling participation rates were presented in the 1960s by Coleman (1960), Horvath (1965), and Leik (1965, 1967). Horvath (1965) was the first to derive a model from theoretical assumptions about interaction. These were that each participant has an equal probability of initiating an act and that each participant exercises that probability in turn, passing from top to bottom of the group hierarchy. A version of Stephan and Mishler's exponential model follows from those assumptions. Although it too is empirically unsatisfactory (Kadane, Lewis, and Ramage 1969), it is important because it points the way to future development of behavioral models that are theoretically based, rather than ad hoc modeling exercises.

Power and prestige theories explain how the structure of expectations for task performance in a task-oriented small group can determine the power and prestige hierarchy that emerges (Berger 1958; Berger and Conner 1969). Researchers develop mathematical models to describe the process by which unit evaluations of specific performances lead to expectations, and expectations determine the inequality structure (Berger, Conner, and McKeown 1969). Status characteristics theories explain how status differentiation external to a group can influence the interaction between group members (Berger, Cohen, and Zelditch 1966, 1972; Balkwell 1991b). Researchers here focus on influence in dyads, and how differential status affects an actor's probability of accepting influence. Formal models describe the process by which status dimensions are activated and become relevant to task outcomes (Berger, Fişek, Norman, and Zelditch 1977).

In these two research programs, efforts to explain the development of participation hierarchies in task groups either have been restricted to status homogeneous groups, as in the Markov chain model of Fişek (1974), or have not been based on dynamic models of the process of group interaction (Skvoretz 1985; Fişek, Berger, and Norman 1991). The model we evaluate, the e-state structuralist model of Skvoretz and Fararo (1996), is not restricted to homogeneous groups and is based on a dynamic formulation of the group interaction process.

THE THEORETICAL METHOD OF E-STATE STRUCTURALISM

E-state structuralism models proposed by Fararo, Skvoretz, and colleagues (Fararo and Skvoretz 1986, 1988; Fararo, Skvoretz, and Kosaka 1994) integrate the abstract core of expectation states theories (Berger, Wagner, and Zelditch 1985) with social network imagery. The core of expectation states theory holds that actors' behavior toward others depends on the performance expectations they hold for themselves and for others. There are many different ways that performance expectations may form. For instance, in the status-characteristics branch of expectation states theory, differentiation on external status may be used to form performance expectations even if the characteristic is not obviously task relevant. In this research tradition, "expectations" refer to unobservable states of relational orientation to self and others; the states themselves are "expectations" in a functional, not necessarily phenomenological, sense; actors need not have cognitive awareness of them. In fact, in e-state structuralism, actors may not even be human. e-state structuralism adopts a broad interpretation of this idea of expectations that includes the possibility of nonhuman organisms having "e-states" in relation to one another—for example, dominant-submissive e-states "held" by chickens in a barnyard pecking order.

In e-state structuralism the power and prestige hierarchy in a task group is represented as a social network and the concern is with how such networks emerge. States of relational orientation among actors are characterized as a type of social tie. Pairs of actors are connected by such ties in an overall network of relational orientations. The analytical concern is how this network of ties is created and maintained over time. An e-state structural model proposes specific ways in which such ties are created or changed and, therefore, how the "state" of the actor system changes over time. In general, e-state models follow two basic principles: First, ties may be created through the behavior of actors in relation to one another or through the observation of the interaction between two actors. Second, the network of ties existing at a particular point in time stochastically determines which behaviors may occur and how they may be interpreted by actors. Specific e-state models differ in how they conceptualize relevant behavior events and the specific mechanisms and parameters that govern how events may create specific ties of relational orientation.

The merger of the actor-situation framework of expectation states theory with the system focus of social network imagery is the essence of e-state structuralism (described in detail in Fararo and Skvoretz 1986, 1988). In those articles, a specific e-state model is proposed to explain data gathered by others on the emergence of dominance hierarchies in animal groups (Chase 1982). Axioms define a dynamic model with two major parameters: π, the probability that an e-state called dominance orientation forms following the occurrence of a particular behavior, and θ, a similar probability involving bystanders to the behavioral event. Analysis examines the equilibrium probability of an emergent hierarchy of dominance as a function of the two parameters.

Skvoretz and Fararo (1996) develop an e-state model for interaction in human task-oriented groups. The model integrates three specific lines of research. First, Fişek and coworkers (1991) conception of the status structure of a task group is abridged and welded to the conceptual apparatus of the e-state structuralism models. Second, Balkwell's (1994) log-linear model translates expectation states into participation differentials consistent with often observed regularities in the who-to-whom matrix of directed participation. Finally, the e-state model for dominance hierarchies in nonhuman groups is modified to reflect the particular context of application, participation in task groups. It is this model we evaluate. We presenting its details in the next section.

A DYNAMIC MODEL FOR THE EMERGENCE OF STATUS ORDERS IN TASK GROUPS

Figure 1 diagrams the Skvoretz and Fararo (1996) e-state model for the emergence of status orders. At the structural level, e-states that actors hold in relation to one another are represented as directed ties between them. These are called precedence ties, to signify that a tie from x to y means that x has precedence or is ascendant over y in the group's evolving status order. (They are not called dominance ties since "dominance" has a particular meaning of aggressiveness in related expectation states research, see Ridgeway and Diekma 1989). A particular configuration of ties, representable as a directed graph, determines each actor's

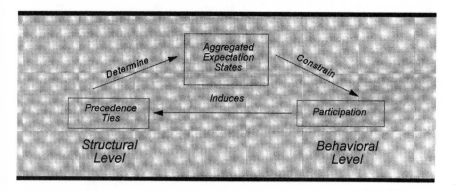

Figure 1. Schematic Diagram of Model

aggregated expectation state. These states, in turn, stochastically constrain the occurrence and interpretation of behavioral events, (e.g., directed acts of participation) in task group discussion. Behaviors feed back to the structural level governing chances that new precedence ties will form. The model's assumptions account for each step of the process.

The set of precedence ties formed by a particular point in the discussion constitutes the group's status order. The existence of a tie between actors x and y and its direction condition the dynamic meaning of an act that one actor directs to another. If no tie exists (denoted xNy), an act x directs to y is a claim by x to superiority over y. The claim succeeds with a probability that depends on the relative standing of x and y on any external status characteristics (see below). If x is ascendant over y in the group's emerging status order (denoted xPy), the x to y act simply expresses x's ascendancy; concretely, suggestions, guidance, and so on, typical of higher status actors. If y is ascendant over x (denoted $xP^{-1}y$), the x to y act expresses x's deference to y; concretely, expressions of agreement or acceptance of guidance typical of lower status actors. The ties are mutually exclusive and, furthermore, xPy holds if and only if $yP^{-1}x$ holds.[1]

Five axioms listed in Table 1 define the model (Skvoretz and Fararo 1996). The first two are the simplest: (1) there are no preestablished ties of precedence in the group and (2) once formed, ties of precedence are stable. The fifth axiom is also relatively simple. It specifies how positions of actors in an evolving status order condition the probability that one of them, x, addresses another, y. A modification of a log-linear function proposed by Balkwell (1994) translates actors' aggregated expectation states into probabilities of directed participations.

Axioms (3) and (4) specify mechanisms by which precedence ties can form in response to acts that one actor, x, directs to another, y. Both mechanisms take account of the external status of group members. Axiom (3), the interactant

Table 1.   Axioms of the E-State Structuralism
Model for the Emergence of Status Orderss

Axiom 1 (Initial State): At t=0, every pair of actors is in state N.

Axiom 2 (The Stability): For any x and y, if xPy at t then xPy at t+1.

Axiom 3 (Interactant): At any t, if xNy holds and x directs a participation to y and the diffuse statuses of x and y are denoted by sx and sy, then the probabilty xPy forms is:

$$Pr(xPy) = \begin{cases} \eta + (1-\eta)\pi, & \text{if } sx > sy \\ (1-\eta)\pi, & \text{if } sx < sy \\ \pi, & \text{if } sx = sy \end{cases}$$

Axiom 4 (Bystander): Let x direct a participation to y and let z be a bystander where sx, sy, and sz are the diffuse statuses of x, y, z. Then

$$Pr(xPz) = \begin{cases} \eta + (1-\eta)\theta, & sx > sz \ \& \ xPy \text{ or } xNy \\ (1-\eta)\theta, & sx < sz \ \& \ xPy \text{ or } xNy \\ \theta, & sx = sz \ \& \ xPy \text{ or } xNy \end{cases} \quad Pr(zPx) = \begin{cases} (1-\eta)\theta, & sx > sz \ \& \ yPx \\ \eta + (1-\eta)\theta, & sx < sz \ \& \ yPx \\ \theta, & sx = sz \ \& \ yPx \end{cases}$$

and

$$Pr(zPy) = \begin{cases} \eta + (1-\eta)\theta, & sz > sy \ \& \ xPy \text{ or } xNy \\ (1-\eta)\theta, & sz < sy \ \& \ xPy \text{ or } xNy \\ \theta, & sz = sy \ \& \ xPy \text{ or } xNy \end{cases} \quad Pr(yPz) = \begin{cases} (1-\eta)\theta, & sz > sy \ \& \ yPx \\ \eta + (1-\eta)\theta, & sz < sy \ \& \ yPx \\ \theta, & sz = sy \ \& \ yPx \end{cases}$$

where $0 \le \theta, \eta \le 1$.

Axiom 5 (Behavior): The probability that x directs a participation to y, denoted xAy, is given by the formula:

$$P(xAy) = \frac{\exp(\gamma_x + \delta\gamma_y)}{\displaystyle\sum_{i \ne j} \exp(\gamma_i + \delta\gamma_j)}$$

where $\delta > 1$, $\gamma_i + (e_i - \Sigma e_i/n)$, and e_i, I's aggregate expectation state, is a function of the number of precdence ties linking I to other actors j.

---

axiom, pertains to just the two actors involved in the behavioral event, while Axiom (4), the bystander axiom, pertains to the bystanders to that event.

Axiom (3) introduces two parameters that affect the probability that a precedence tie will form between x and y when x directs an act to y. The first parameter η applies when x and y are differentiated on external status. The second parameter π applies regardless of status position and refers to an inference of ascendancy based on immediate interaction, namely, the "behavior interchange patterns" of Fişek, Berger, and Norman (1991). The intuitive content of this axiom can be described as follows: (a) If x has higher external status than y, then with probability η, the external status characteristic is activated and *xPy* forms with probability 1. Social psychologically, actors interpret the interaction through the lens of differential status and accord higher internal rank to x automatically. If external status is not activated (probability 1–η), then xPy may form through a behavior interchange interpretation with probability π.[2] (b) If x has lower external status than y, then with probability η, the differentiating characteristic is activated but *xPy* never forms. Here, actors interpret a precedence claim through the lens of status and refuse to accord higher internal rank to x. However, if external status is not activated, then xPy may form via a behavior interchange interpretation with probability π. Finally, (c) if x and y are status equals, status is not activated with probability 1 and thus *xPy* can form *only* via a behavior interchange interpretation, with probability π.

The bystander axiom (4) describes how the orientation of bystanders to x and y may change as a result of an act that x directs to y. The axiom has two parts. The first part describes contingencies that affect the formation of a precedence tie (either *zPx* or *xPz*) between a bystander z and the initiator x. The second part describes contingencies for the formation of a precedence tie between z and the receiver y. It uses two parameters to describe this process. First is the external status activation parameter η. Its role in the formation of ties between z and x, and z and y, is similar to its role in formation of ties between x and y; namely, it enhances or inhibits tie formation depending on the relative external status of x and z and z and y. The second parameter θ plays a role similar to the π in bystander tie formations. It controls the formation of ties between x and z, and z and y based on interpretations of interaction.

These axioms describe a Markov chain process by which the status order of a group of strangers evolves from the initial state of all N ties between actors, through a set of intermediate states in which precedence ties exist between some pairs of actors, to a set of absorbing states in which a precedence tie exists between every pair of actors. The number of states in the state space is a function of group size and diffuse status heterogeneity. For instance, homogeneous four-person groups have a state space of 42 different structures. This number increases if the four actors differ in external status. The dynamics of the model play themselves out through transitions from one state to another in such state spaces. The model's parameters determine the transition probabilities.

E-state structuralism has much to recommend it from a scientific point of view. It brings together power and prestige theory and status characteristics theory, two theories sharing a common theoretical base whose development has proceeded separately. The model considerably advances one of the original goals of research on task-oriented small groups—namely, explaining participation rates. This particular model for status orders incorporates several highly desirable features:

- It treats expectation states as *theoretical constructs*, in line with their actual position in status generalization theories, rather than as empirical quantities.

- It describes the *process* of status evolution in the group as well as the eventual power and prestige structure; previous models (Skvoretz 1988; Fişek et al. 1991; Balkwell 1991a) only describe the eventual inequality structure.
- It considers both *status* and *behavior* information in predicting the power and prestige hierarchy of the group, an advance over the simple "behavior interchange pattern" in Fişek and coworkers (1991) and a similar behavioral element in Balkwell's (1991a) model.
- It exploits the idea of *bystanders*, individuals not immediately engaged in interaction, in predicting effects on their own expectations and subsequent behavior and on the expectations and behavior of interactants.
- It is *stochastic*—a strong advance over previous models—explaining the development of complete and incomplete hierarchies, and fully or partly transitive structures.

To illustrate these points, consider a typical "realization" of the Markov process described by the model. Table 2 displays the results for a four-person group differentiated by external status into two high status members, A and B, and two low status members, c and d. The narrative accompanying the state transitions puts into words the outcomes of the various stochastic events that compose the overall process. For instance, the first event is a participation directed from A to c, the external status characteristic is activated for this initiator-receiver pair and, as a result, a precedence tie forms from A to c. Both B and d are bystanders to this event and so potentially could, via bystander effects, develop precedence ties in relation to A and c. However, none of these possibilities materialize after the first interaction. The second event is a directed participation from c to A. Because a precedence tie has already formed from A to c, this interaction simply confirms the internal ordering of these two actors. The third event is a directed participation from B to d. In this case, the external status difference is not activated, but a precedence tie forms from B to d through a "behavior interchange" interpretation. In addition, bystander effects occur: a precedence tie forms from A to d as the external status difference between A and d happens to be activated and one forms from c to d, but here the mechanism is a "behavior interchange" interpretation. At this point in the discussion, four of the six ties possible between pairs of actors have formed: in the internal ranking of the group, A is seen as more competent that both c and d, and B and c are seen as more competent than d. The internal orderings of A and B and B and c have yet to be determined. The fourth interaction, B directing a participation to A, occasions the formation of these last two ties: first, B gains precedence over A via a "behavior interchange" interpretation, and second, B gains precedence over c via a bystander effect. The internal status order of the group is now complete. The order happens to be a fully transitive linear hierarchy, although this is but one of several possible outcomes. Also, for the purposes

Table 2. A Realization of the Model for Status Order Emergence

Participation	State of Network	Explanation
A to c	A, B, c, d (A→c)	A and B have High external status, c and d have Low external status; A gains precedence over c via external status activation in the context of a initiator-receiver pair.
c to A	A, B, c, d (A→c)	No change in the structure of the status order.
B to d	A, B, c, d (A→d, B→d, c→d)	B gains precedence over d via behavior interchange interpretation in the context of initiator-receiver pair; A gains precedence over d via external status activation in the context of a bystander-receiver pair; c gains precedence over d via a behavior interchange interpretation in the context of a bystander-receiver pair.
B to A	A, B, c, d (B→A, A→c, B→d, A→d, c→d)	B gains precedence over A via behavior interchange interpretation in the context of initiator-receiver pair; B gains precedence over c via external status activation in the context of a bystander-receiver pair.

of illustration, the status order has emerged very rapidly. In actual groups and, of course, depending on the values of the model's parameters, emergence is not expected to be nearly as swift.

EMPIRICAL METHODS

Perhaps surprisingly, few large-scale data collection efforts using discussion groups have been undertaken since Bales' program. One reason undoubtedly is operational complexity: discussion groups, incorporating aspects of both controlled and natural situations, present several design challenges. The most thorough of recent studies are the 31 6-person groups on which Smith-Lovin, Skvoretz, and Hudson collected data in 1980. Those data have been used for empirical evaluations of several earlier models, including all three described above (Fişek et al. 1991; Balkwell 1991a; Smith-Lovin, Skvoretz, and Hudson 1986). In addition, those groups have been a valuable resource for secondary analyses. But they have limitations that preclude using them for much further analysis, particularly the analyses we need to evaluate the e-state model.

Among the problems: (1) the groups were videotaped with two cameras from behind one-way mirrors. Details such as eye gaze that may signal an action opportunity are impossible to observe. (2) The tapes have deteriorated and now may be unplayable. What remain are transcripts, lacking nonverbal behaviors. (3) The number of groups in each condition is small, making the data subject to fluctuation from the normal variability of uncontrolled discussions. In general, data recording technology has developed beyond where it was in 1980; new observational measures including nonverbal behavior and the "deference cycle" coding developed by Shelly and Munroe (1994) are more complex; and interactional models are considerably more precise than earlier models.

Our completed research uses four-person groups. Subjects are paid volunteers recruited from classes at the University of North Carolina. They include women and men and representatives of the various ethnic groups. Groups are equated so far as possible on gender, skin color, and unfamiliarity with the task. A single status dimension is salient in each group. Like the six-person groups used earlier by Smith-Lovin and associates (1986), ours permit all combinations of status: all high, all low, majority high and low, and equal-size subgroups. Our data are from three conditions that are most informative for model testing: all low, one high and three low, and two high and two low.

The groups must meet certain theoretical and operational conditions. Scope conditions require group members to be task focused and collectively oriented. Task focus means that their primary purpose is to work on a problem or a set of problems, rather than to experience interaction itself (which would be process focus). A committee is task focused; members of a 12-step group are process focused. Collective orientation means it is both legitimate and necessary to take each group member's ideas into account, rather than working alone (individual orientation). A jury must be collectively oriented; students taking the SAT should be individually oriented.

Initial and interactional conditions likewise constrain the design. First, there must be a status dimension that may differentiate (in heterogeneous conditions) or equate members (in homogeneous conditions). In heterogenous conditions, the status distinction must remain salient throughout the session. For later work, multiple status dimensions must be possible. Second, individuals must believe the task has better and worse outcomes; it must not be one in which anyone's opinion may be as good as anyone else's, and individuals must believe that others outside their group can assess outcome quality. This means the task must look complicated, but not so difficult that nobody could tell what the best outcome would be. Asking students to pick a new school mascot or devise a cure for cancer would not qualify. Third, interaction must be free for the model's processes to display themselves. Many controlled experimental designs useful for other purposes, and some variable manipulations that would be desirable for this project, are impossible

with free interaction. Fourth, the discussion must last long enough for status structure evolution and stability. Therefore, the task must hold group members' attention, and it must not permit them to reach closure about a solution too quickly.
Our design addressed these problems as follows.

We created a status distinction having both natural and artificial aspects. The
natural aspect is that the heterogeneous groups mix first-year and fourth-year students; the artificial aspect is that we link year at school to measures of skills such
as SAT scores and GPA. For status-heterogenous groups, we tell individuals we
are composing groups of people having different characteristics, and that their
group will contain both first-year and fourth-year students. First-year students are
instructed separately from fourth-year students. We tell first-year students that
their partners will be fourth-year who happen to have extremely high scores on
several measures of academic performance. Fourth-year students are told their
partners happen to have low scores. Both groups are told their own scores are
about average for their student body. Typically this creates a status distinction,
"academic achievement," composed of year in school linked to ability. (We
learned through pretesting that merely identifying first-year and fourth-year students does not reliably create a status difference for these participants. Hence we
developed an elaborate status induction procedure, using charts of purported
"standards" and other props.) When individuals enter the group discussion room
together, they sit at a table identifying each by a letter label (e.g., A, B, C, or D)
and year in school, to keep status information salient during discussion. Postin-
duction and postsession questionnaires assess success of the manipulations and
other aspects of the experiment.

The task we use is an adaptation of "fallout shelter," in which members rank
order 15 items in terms of usefulness for surviving in a hostile environment.
Among its attractions are that individuals are equally (un)skilled at it, it is involving and complex such that discussions are prolonged, and subjects believe there
are better and worse ideas and final choices. (Johnson and Johnson 1995 describes
many other group tasks.) The survival task is explained and participants are given
45 minutes to reach the best ranking they can of items. Video and audio recording
equipment is identified for the participants, who are told their deliberations are to
be recorded for later study by observers.

Coding uses a new software/hardware package from NOLDUS Information
Technology, called the *Observer's Video Tape Analysis System* for Windows
3.11. The hardware includes a time code generator, a time code reader, and a
video overlay board. The time code generator adds time stamp to each frame
(1/30th second) of a video tape. We added the stamp by copying the original
tape. The advantage of the generator is that all coding now has a common time
reference. Thus multiple coding runs can be made on a particular tape and all
the coding sequenced with reference to the common time stamp. For instance,
we have made multiple passes through a tape to code duration of speech for
each actor and then to code "acts," speeches that express a single complete

Table 3.   Distributions of Performance Outputs

Group	Composition	Rank 1	Rank 2	Rank 3	Rank 4	Total
1	1H/3L	122	47	42	31	242
2	1H/3L	150	125	93	61	429
3	2H/2L	168	144	96	84	492
4	1H/3L	139	127	99	39	404
5	1H/3L	126	63	52	44	285
6	1H/3L	164	156	114	58	492
7	4L	107	86	78	64	335
8	2H/2L	166	116	101	39	422
9	1H/3L	211	155	121	106	593
10	2H/2L	98	79	51	47	275
12	1H/3L	177	96	87	69	429
13	1H/3L	166	140	107	87	500
15	2H/2L	156	61	54	50	321
16	4L	198	152	103	58	511
17	4L	110	109	94	67	380
19	2H/2L	138	94	30	20	282
20	1H/3L	121	78	65	47	311
21	2H/2L	188	165	106	22	481
22	1H/3L	101	92	87	59	339
23	2H/2L	109	82	61	40	292
24	2H/2L	203	127	121	70	521
25	4L	173	151	149	129	602
26	2H/2L	184	101	68	56	409
27	2H/2L	152	104	40	31	327
28	1H/3L	111	104	85	64	364
29	4L	117	114	63	38	332
31	2H/2L	118	111	84	41	354
33	4L	143	101	75	65	384
34	4L	163	156	76	46	441
36	4L	106	82	59	31	278
38	4L	82	73	54	30	239
39	4L	104	90	78	36	308
40	4L	147	117	103	95	462
41	2H/2L	87	86	75	44	292
42	1H/3L	151	144	121	73	489
43	2H/2L	146	81	68	59	354
44	1H/3L	161	88	55	45	349
45	2H/2L	89	72	61	26	248
46	2H/2L	62	61	59	45	227
47	2H/2L	170	88	79	74	411
48	2H/2L	125	89	78	43	335
49	4L	128	118	70	57	373
50	4L	181	142	120	108	551
51	1H/3L	160	68	55	38	321
53	1H/3L	162	108	62	36	368
54	4L	108	78	75	29	290
55	1H/3L	95	86	71	62	314
57	1H/3L	109	66	42	7	224
59	1H/3L	118	89	77	64	348
60	4L	72	45	44	17	178
61	4L	84	78	44	37	243
		6927	5158	3952	2688	18752
Total proportion		.37	.28	.21	.14	

thought. Additional runs can easily be made to code nonverbal aspects of inter-action or to classify the content of an act. The time code reader is a PC card that enables the software to read the time stamp on each frame. The video overlay board allows the videotape to be played in a window on the monitor. The software includes routines to control the playback of the VCR, to define coding protocols, to map keys to codes, to enable the coder to view and code video tapes, and basic data analysis routines such as reliability analysis.

EVALUATION OF THE MODEL

In this section, we offer an evaluation based on a coding of 51 groups using *performance outputs (participation acts) by each actor* as our primary dependent variable. The distributions of these performance outputs are given in Table 3. These participation acts are counted using a 1.5 seconds pause rule, that is, speech acts by a single subject that are separated by a pause of less than 1.5 seconds are counted as one act. This rule was followed in the coding of Fişek (1974) and Smith-Lovin et al. (1986). In addition, we drop speech acts that are so brief (<.33 seconds) that they are unlikely to be meaningful utterances. The number of per-formance outputs varies from a maximum of 591 to a minimum of 178. In terms of clock time, group discussions varied from 20 to almost 45 minutes. We code behavior as long as the group remains task focused.

To coordinate these results with the model, we need to consider how perfor-mance outputs would be distributed in absorbing states of the e-state model. Recall that an absorbing state is any state of the network of precedence ties in which there is a tie between each pair of persons. Once a group enters such a state, there can be no further change because precedence ties are assumed to be stable once formed. In four person groups there are exactly four absorbing states of the e-state process. They are depicted in Figure 2. Only one of the four states, state T (for transitive hierarchy), has no intransitive triples, that is, triples of actors in which i has precedence over j and j over k, but k has precedence over i. There are two distinct ways to realize one intransitive triple, I3/1 and I1/3, and one way to realize two intransitive triples, I2/2. How groups will distribute themselves over these four absorbing states depends on the parameters of the process. In general, of course, we expect the T state to occur at much greater than chance levels. The model predicts as much so long as the bystander effect is nonzero. The absorbing states refer to (unobserved) configurations of precedence ties, and not to observed rates of participation. Clearly, observed rates are, of course, always transitive, that is, if A's rate is greater than B's and B's is greater than C's, then A's is always greater than C's.

Each absorbing state maps to a different vector of paths connecting actors to task outcomes via bases of differentiation. In the model, each precedence tie cor-responds to a basis of differentiation between the two actors such that the actor

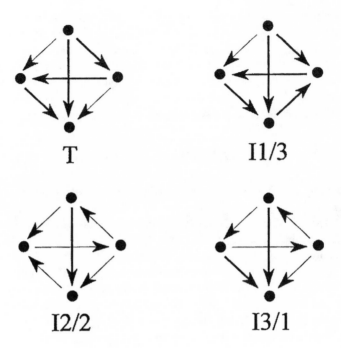

T   **I1/3**

I2/2   **I3/1**

Figure 2. Absorbing States

with precedence receives credit for one 4 path and one 5 path to positively evaluated task outcomes, with the actor subject to the tie is credited with one 4 path and one 5 path to negatively evaluated outcomes. The same counts hold regardless of the precise basis of differentiation, that is, external status or behavior interchange pattern. The basis of differentiation can be ignored because both external status and behavior interchange differences connect to similarly signed task outcomes with paths of length 4. However, if one of these bases were an instrumental characteristic directly task-relevant and so linked to task outcomes by shorter paths, then we would need to distinguish different types of precedence ties. The different types would then credit actors connected by those types with different lengths of paths and so change the calculation of expectation advantage.

The path vectors determine the aggregate expectation states for each actor in the group. Actors with identical path vectors have identical aggregate states. Furthermore, in the e-state model, participation is determined entirely by one's aggregate state relative to the aggregate expectation states of all actors in the group. Therefore, regardless of the particular function by which aggregate states are mapped into probabilities of participation, the e-state model predicts that *only four participation distributions will be observed*. These four are: (a) a distribution in which all are differentiated from one another; (b) one actor participates much more than the other three, all of whom participate at the same level; (c) three actors participate at the same level and the fourth much less than these three; and (d) two actors participate at the same level but noticeably more than the other two who participate at the same, lower level. Of course, because participation is stochastic, there will be some random fluctuation around these patterns, but nevertheless we should be able to identify them in observations. Note that intransitivity at the unobserved level of the network of ties does not mean observed intransitivity at the level of participation rates (an impossible outcome). Rather, intransitivity at the network level "translates" into predictions of roughly equal rates of participation. Because of stochastic fluctuation, exactly equal rates cannot be reasonably expected and so we should observe a complete ranking in any group based on rates alone. The question is whether subsets of these rates are sufficiently different that the various hypotheses of equality, corresponding to the absorbing states with intransitivities, can be rejected.

The number of different absorbing states expands for conditions in which actors differ on some external, diffuse, or specific status characteristic. For instance, if the group consists of one high status actor and three low status actors, there are four different forms of state T, and two different forms of each of the other two states, depending on where the high status actor is located. With two high status and two low status actors, there are six different forms of state T, two different forms of states I3/1 and I1/3, and three different forms of state I2/2. Within a state, the distribution of groups over form is governed by the status effect parameter in the e-state model. This parameter governs the probability that external status is activated when two actors involved in a participation occupy different states of the characteristic. The greater the parameter the more likely it is that the groups are absorbed in the forms that have high status actors on top of the participation hierarchy. How the groups are distributed over these forms and the four states yields information valuable to the estimation of parameters.

Table 4 identifies which of the absorbing states each group in Table 3 has attained. We use likelihood ratio chi-square to evaluate whether or not the distribution of performance outputs in a group is consistent with one of the three constrained distributions, that is, I3/1, I1/3, or I2/2.[3] Distributions that are inconsistent with all three are identified as T distributions. The order of the actors is listed in the last column with the high status actors in a group placed in upper case. Table 5 then presents the distribution of groups over tournament outcomes while Table 6 compares the participation ranks of high and low status actors in mixed status groups.

To explain in more detail how absorbing states are identified, consider the first group. From Table 3, the actual rates of participation in this group are 122, 47, 42, and 31. The rates of the last three actors are clearly very close to one another and very different from the rate of the top ranked actor. The distribution looks like what would be predicted if the status order of the group was absorbed into state

Table 4.   Classification of Distributions Using Likelihood Ratio χ^{2*}

Group	I1/3	I2/2	I3/1	Type	Order
1	1.50	15.69	23.10	I1/3	Deab
2	9.76	3.90	5.89	T	cbDa
3	7.82	1.15	8.94	I2/2	AdBc
4	22.16	11.95	3.08	T	bAdc
5	1.49	9.59	16.31	I1/3	Abdc
6	20.37	8.15	4.50	T	cdAd
7	1.44	1.59	2.12	I1/3	badc
8	19.20	16.22	7.65	T	BcAd
9	4.23	4.17	10.95	T	Acbd
10	4.29	0.96	6.63	I2/2	BcdA
12	2.00	11.50	16.84	I1/3	cbAd
13	5.53	1.86	5.61	I2/2	cAbd
15	0.49	18.76	29.09	I1/3	cBAd
16	18.95	8.17	13.25	T	adbc
17	4.51	1.98	0.68	I3/1	cdab
19	27.42	4.52	33.00	T	BcAd
20	3.40	5.33	8.19	T	Adcb
21	54.21	26.70	10.67	T	BAdc
22	3.63	2.53	0.47	I3/1	dAbc
23	6.41	3.57	6.00	T	BAdc
24	8.62	13.66	11.54	T	BcAd
25	0.91	1.27	0.96	I1/3	cdab
26	6.11	11.16	25.67	T	BdAc
27	22.10	4.43	30.44	T	ABdc
28	4.18	1.39	1.61	I2/2	bdcA
29	17.97	2.73	8.1	T	bcda
31	14.78	6.65	2.77	T	dABc
33	3.65	3.47	9.54	T	abdc
34	29.50	3.30	16.93	T	bcda
36	10.40	5.18	5.90	T	dcba
38	8.07	3.25	2.62	I3/1	cabd
39	11.32	7.32	1.62	I3/1	acdb
40	1.02	1.62	3.53	I1/3	cadb
41	6.42	3.55	0.47	I3/1	ABcd
42	10.67	5.28	1.57	I3/1	Adcb
43	1.52	8.47	14.69	I1/3	BdAd
44	6.77	9.87	24.77	T	dAbc
45	10.53	7.07	2.32	I3/1	AcBd
46	1.24	0.82	0.03	I3/1	BcAd
47	0.54	11.59	18.36	I1/3	BcAd
48	7.70	7.10	5.24	T	AcBd
49	10.55	0.76	8.46	I2/2	cdab
50	2.07	2.32	5.55	I1/3	adcb
51	3.76	17.95	28.32	T	Adbc
53	16.79	7.75	20.13	T	Abdc
54	12.25	11.26	3.22	T	cbda
55	1.73	0.46	1.54	I2/2	Abdc
57	24.14	16.68	13.74	T	dAcb
59	1.78	2.29	4.00	I1/3	dcbA
60	7.03	8.11	3.90	T	abcd
61	7.52	0.36	6.33	I2/2	abcd

Note: *Rejection level set at 2.71 for $p < .10$. High-status actors are upper cased in last column.

Table 5. Observed vs. Expected Number of Tournament Types

Tournament	Observed	Expected
T	25	19.1
I1/3	11	6.4
I2/2	7	19.1
I3.1	8	6.4

Note: Percent Transitive Triples = 83 percent

Table 6. Precedence Score in Mixed Status Groups

Status	Average Score (n)
High	1.98 (52)
Low	1.22 (88)

I1/3, that is, one actor having precedence over the other three, with the other three having precedence over just one other person in the group. In fact, we can test this hypothesis via a likelihood ratio chi-square test with one degree of freedom. The predicted rates would be 122, 40, 40, and 40. The likelihood ratio chi-square value is quite small, 1.50, indicating that this hypothesis cannot be rejected. An alternative hypothesis, that the underlying absorbing state is I2/2, would predict the rates 84.5, 84.5, 36.5, and 36.5, but this hypothesis can be clearly rejected because it produces a likelihood ratio chi-square value of 15.69. Each of the three hypotheses tested to identify the absorbing state has 1 df. We set a liberal rejection level for the hypotheses (p<.10) which works against the e-state model's overall predictions that the transitive state will occur more frequently than chance and that actors of high external status will more often occupy higher ranks in the internal status order of the groups. Thus our test of the model's predictions is a conservative one.

First, in the absence of any external status effect or a bystander effect, the T state would occur 37.5 percent of the time, whereas it occurs 49 percent of the time. Overall 83 percent of the triads are transitive as compared to the chance expectation of 75 percent. These findings provide evidence for both effects. Second, in the absence of an external status effect, placement of high status actors in the performance output distribution is random. In particular, high status actors should have no greater precedence scores (i.e., number of others over whom precedence is attained) than low status participants. Table 6 shows this expectation to be false. High status actors do have higher precedence scores, on average. The effect is about .75 of a rank. Thus the data display exactly the kinds of effects the model leads us to expect. Furthermore, these effects are not deterministic, but reflect the underlying probabilistic nature of the process.

CONCLUSION

This initial evaluation of the e-state model for status order emergence is quite favorable. Triads are more transitive than expected by chance, indicating a bystander effect at work, and high status actors rank higher in the participation hierarchy than low status actors, indicating a status activation effect at work. The next step in the model's evaluation is to consider in detail the estimation of effect parameters and then to derive certain over time consequences that can be further used to evaluate the theory.

In particular, there is a need to evaluate the portion of the model that links aggregate expectation states to rates of participation. Our examination of the distributions of performance outputs simply looked at their form rather than the amount of inequality they represent or other parameters of the distribution. Consequently we cannot say for certain that the underlying process by which aggregate expectation states are translated into participation differentials can adequately account for the extent of differentiation in the performance output distribution.

ACKNOWLEDGMENTS

Research was supported by National Science Foundation Collaborative Research Grants SBR-9511514 and SBR-9511127. For their assistance in data collection and coding we thank Tracy Burkett, Kevin Childers, Brad Edwards, and Katrina Kuhns.

NOTES

1. In reality, the e-state of x toward y might not complement that of y to x, as assumed. Fararo and colleagues (1994) explore models in which such complementarity is contingently related to behavioral events. To avoid unnecessary complication, we present only the basic model.

2. According to status characteristics theory (Wagner and Berger 1993), activation will take place if either of two conditions holds: actors notice that some status characteristic differentiates them, or they believe that one or more statuses actors possess are relevant to task completion. A mixed gender group ordinarily is sufficient to meet the first condition; a group of mothers with a task involving child care would meet the second condition.

3. The likelihood ratio statistic is given by the formula

$$G^2 = -2\sum_i x_i \ln\frac{m_i}{x_i}$$

where x_i is the number of observed and m_i, the number of expected participations for the ith person.

REFERENCES

Bales, R.F. 1953. "The Equilibrium Problem in Small Groups." Pp. 111-165 in *Working Papers in the Theory of Action*, edited by T. Parsons, R.F. Bales, and E.A. Shils. Glencoe, IL: Free Press.

Bales, R.F. 1970. *Personality and Interpersonal Behavior*. New York: Holt, Rinehart, and Winston.

Bales, R.F., F.L. Strodtbeck, T.M. Mills, and M.E. Rosenborough. 1951. "Channels of Communication in Small Groups." *American Sociological Review* 16: 461-468.

Balkwell, J. 1991a. "From Expectations to Behavior: An Improved Postulate for Expectation States Theory." *American Sociological Review* 56: 355-369.

Balkwell, J. 1991b. "Status Characteristics and Social Interaction: Assessment of Theoretical Variants." *Advances in Group Process* 8: 135-176.

Balkwell, J. 1995. "Strong Tests of Expectation-States Hypotheses." *Social Psychology Quarterly* 58: 44-51.

Berger, J. 1958. *Relations Between Performance, Rewards, and Action-Opportunities in Small Groups*. Unpublished Ph.D. dissertation, Harvard University.

Berger, J., B.P. Cohen, and M. Zelditch, Jr. 1966. "Status Characteristics and Expectation States." Pp. 26-46 in *Sociological Theories in Progress*, Vol. 1, edited by J. Berger, M. Zelditch, Jr., and B. Anderson. Boston: Houghton-Mifflin.

Berger, J., B.P. Cohen, and M. Zelditch. 1972. "Status Characteristics and Social Interaction." *American Sociological Review* 37: 241-255.

Berger, J. and T. Conner. 1969. "Performance Expectations and Behavior in Small Groups." *Acta Sociologica* 12: 189-198.

Berger, J., T. Conner, and W. McKeown. 1969. "Evaluations and the Formation and Maintenance of Performance Expectations." *Human Relations* 22: 481-502.

Berger, J., M.H. Fiçek, R.Z. Norman, and M. Zelditch, Jr. 1977. *Status Characteristics and Social Interaction: An Expectation States Approach*. New York: Elsevier.

Berger, J., D.G. Wagner, and M. Zelditch, Jr. 1985. "Introduction: Expectation States Theory: Review and Assessment." Pp. 1-72 in *Status, Rewards, and Influence: How Expectations Organize Behavior*, edited by J. Berger and M. Zelditch, Jr. San Francisco: Jossey-Bass.

Coleman, J.S. 1960. "The Mathematical Study of Small Groups." Pp. 7-149 in *Mathematical Thinking in the Measurement of Behavior*, edited by H. Solomon. Glencoe, IL: Free Press.

Fararo, T.J., and J. Skvoretz. 1986. "E-State Structuralism: A Theoretical Method." *American Sociological Review* 51: 591-602.

Fararo, T.J., and J. Skvoretz. 1988. "Dynamics of the Formation of Stable Dominance Structures." Pp. 327-350 in *Status Generalization: New Theory and Research*, edited by M. Webster, Jr. and M. Foschi. Stanford, CA: Stanford University Press.

Fararo, T.J., J. Skvoretz, and K. Kosaka. 1994. "Advances in E-state Structuralism: Further Studies in Dominance Structure Formation." *Social Networks* 16: 233-265.

Fişek, M.H. 1974. "A Model for the Evolution of Status Structures in Task-Oriented Groups." Pp. 53-83 in *Expectation States Theory: A Theoretical Research Program*, edited by J. Berger, T.L. Conner, and M.H. Fiçek. Cambridge, MA: Winthrop.

Fişek, M. H., J. Berger, and R.Z. Norman. 1991. "Participation in Heterogeneous Groups: A Theoretical Integration." *American Journal of Sociology* 97: 114-142.

Fişek. 1995. "Evaluations and the Formation of Expectations." *American Journal of Sociology* 101: 721-746.

Horvath, W.J. 1965. "A Mathematical Model of Participation in Small Group Discussion." *Behavioral Science* 10: 164-166.

Johnson, D.W. and F.P. Johnson. 1994. *Joining Together: Group Theory and Group Skills*, 5th ed. Boston: Allyn and Bacon.

Kadane, J.B., G. Lewis, and J.G. Ramage. 1969. "Horvath's Theory of Participation in Group Discussions." *Sociometry* 33: 348-361.

Leik, R.K. 1965. "Type of Group and the Probability of Initiating Acts." *Sociometry* 28: 57-65.

Leik, R.K. 1967. "The Distribution of Acts in Small Groups." *Sociometry* 30: 280-299.

Reynolds, P.D. 1972. "Comment on 'Distribution of Participation in Group Discussions' as Related to Group Size." *American Sociological Review* 36: 704-706.

Ridgeway, C.L., and D. Diekma. 1989. "Dominance and Collective Hierarchy Formation." *American Sociological Review* 54: 79-93

Shelly, R., and M. Webster. 1997. "How Formal Status, Liking, and Ability Status Structure Interaction: Three Theoretical Principles and a Test." *Sociological Perspectives* 40: 81-107.

Skvoretz, J. 1988. "Models of Participation in Status-Differentiated Groups." *Social Psychology Quarterly* 51: 43-57.

Skvoretz, J. 1985. "Status Characteristics, Expectation States and Participation in N Person Task Groups." Pp. 163-188 in *Status, Rewards and Influence*, edited by J. Berger and M. Zelditch, Jr. San Francisco: Jossey-Bass.

Skvoretz, J. 1981. "Extending Expectation States Theory: Comparative Status Models of Participation in N Person Groups." *Social Forces* 59: 752-770.

Skvoretz, J., and T.J. Fararo. 1996. "Status and Participation in Task Groups: A Dynamic Network Model." *American Journal of Sociology* 101: 1366-1414.

Smith-Lovin, L., J.V. Skvoretz, and C.G. Hudson. 1986. "Status and Participation in Six-Person Groups: A Test of Skvoretz's Comparative Status Model." *Social Forces* 64: 992-1005.

Stephan, F., and E.G. Mishler. 1952. "The Distribution of Participation in Small Groups: An Exponential Approximation." *American Sociological Review* 17: 598-608.

Strodtbeck, F.L., R.M. James, and C. Hawkins, 1957. "Social Status in Jury Deliberations." *American Sociological Review* 22: 713-19.

Wagner, D.G., and J. Berger, 1993. "Status Characteristics Theory: The Growth of a Program." Pp. 23-63 in *Theoretical Research Programs: Studies in the Growth of Theory*, edited by J. Berger and M. Zelditch, Jr. Stanford, CA: Stanford University Press.

Webster, M., and M. Foschi. Editors. 1988. *Status Generalization: New Theory and Research.* Stanford, CA: Stanford University Press.

INSTITUTIONAL LOGICS AND GROUP ENVIRONMENTS:
TOWARD AN OPEN SYSTEM PERSPECTIVE ON GROUP PROCESSES

Lisa Troyer and Steven D. Silver

ABSTRACT

The environment of groups has long been recognized as a critical factor affecting and affected by groups, although it has received little conceptual elaboration in the recent study of group processes. We propose that the concept of institutional logics found in organization theory may be a useful theoretical mechanism that can help us better conceptualize the role of the environment in group processes. New institutional theory posits that an actor's environment is composed of a variety of institutional logics (repertoires of behavior that are tied to and rationalized by existing social institutions). Organizational theorists note that (1) particular institutional logics may be mobilized by actors to determine action and even gain advantage in interaction and (2) different logics may conflict in terms of the behavior patterns and rationales they offer for social action. Groups may similarly mobilize one or more logic(s) to guide their interaction. However, it is important to note that groups are often embedded in and beholden to a broader social environment. The logic(s) mobi-

Advances in Group Processes, Volume 16, pages 219-252.
ISBN: 0-7623-0452-9

lized by a group may or may not be consonant with the logic(s) that dominates that group's external environment. When the logic of the group is not consonant with that of its external environment, the group may experience conflict with external actors and difficulty acquiring the resources it needs to sustain itself. We illustrate these arguments in a case study of organizational work teams.

In some respects, the focus of the theory and research offered here is not so much an "advance" in group processes, but rather a call to return to the roots of theoretical traditions in group dynamics. More specifically, we propose that it is timely to heed the insights of a founding theorist of group dynamics, Kurt Lewin (1951), who emphasized the importance of attending to the fact that groups are social systems, situated within a broader social environment, and offered methods of conceptualizing the effects of environments on groups and groups on environments. In returning to these founding principles of group dynamics, we propose that ideas from new institutionalism in organization theory (e.g., Powell and DiMaggio 1991) can facilitate the elaboration of Lewin's ideas on groups as situated social systems. This leads us to propose an "open system" framework for the study of group processes, which we then employ in a case study of two organizational teams.

In fact, importing concepts from organization theory to the study of group processes is not such a strange proposal. Sociological studies of groups and organizations share a common lineage that is perhaps most well recognized in work that occurred at the Research Center for Group Dynamics (initially at the Massachusetts Institute of Technology and later at the University of Michigan), as a result of the Hawthorne studies (Mayo 1933, 1945; Roethlisberger and Dickson 1939), and from the Tavistock Institute for the Study of Human Relations (e.g., Bion 1961; Emery 1949; Trist 1960; Trist and Bamforth 1951), all of which cemented the importance of the social group as a key unit in organizations. The importance of the organization to the group and the group to the organization was an insight that was explicitly celebrated in edited volumes resulting from conferences at the University of Oklahoma's Institute of Group Relations emphasizing the interdisciplinary nature of the study of group dynamics (Rohrer and Sherif 1951; Sherif and Wilson 1953). However, since these important early trends in the study of group processes, theoretical development and research on group processes (even on organizational work groups) has largely remained distinct from theoretical development and research on organizations. Yet, within organizations, groups have become no less important. In fact, a revolution of sorts has occurred in recent decades, as the landscape of organizational work design has become populated by various group-based interventions including, teams, self-managing work teams, and semi-autonomous teams (e.g., Drucker 1988; Glaser 1992; E. E. Lawler, Mohrman, and Ledford 1995).

The sections that follow begin by briefly outlining early developments in the study of group processes arising within the context of organizational research. This outline traces interest in group dynamics as an important factor in the evolution of organizational development, which, in turn, facilitated the rise of the team as a fundamental component of organizational work design. However, this article also provides evidence that a team design for work has not always lived up to the expectations of managers, consultants, and social scientists. In part, such failures may be attributed to the fact that researchers who have focused on work groups have attended to theory and research on group processes, but have not adequately attended to the relation between teams and their organizational environments. Within the field of group processes, there have been few attempts to develop theoretical frameworks that adequately represent the effect of the external environment on groups (for exceptions, see Ancona 1993; O'Connor 1980). To address this gap in knowledge and advance theory on group processes, arguments from new institutionalism (e.g., Meyer and Rowan 1977; DiMaggio and Powell 1983; Powell and DiMaggio 1991) in organization theory may enhance our understanding of the role that environmental influences may have on an organizational collective like a team. The article then examines arguments representing an "open system" framework for the study of group process that incorporates the concept of institutional logics from new institutional theory in a case study of two organizational teams. It concludes with a discussion of the implications of this synthesis for theory and research on group processes.

THE DEVELOPMENT OF THEORY AND RESEARCH ON GROUP PROCESSES: EARLY TIES TO ORGANIZATION THEORY[1]

As noted above, early studies of group processes were an important component of research on organizations. Eventually, two branches of group processes research seem to have emerged from the early studies. One of these (a more applied branch) is directed at improving work design by attending to interaction processes occurring in work groups. This branch is best developed today in the area of organization development (e.g., Burke 1994; French and Bell 1990; Schein 1988) and the human relations school of organization theory (e.g., Mayo 1945; Roethlisberger and Dickson 1939). The other branch (a more formal theoretical branch) is directed at identifying theoretical principles governing the operation of social processes in groups. This branch is perhaps most well recognized in contemporary theoretical research programs representing such areas as exchange theories (e.g., Cook 1987; Markovsky, Willer, and Patton 1988), expectation states theories (e.g., Berger, Conner, and Fiçek 1974)), distribution justice (Jasso 1980; Markovsky 1985), and bargaining (Bacharach and E. J. Lawler 1981). A dichotomy like this is admittedly somewhat of an oversimplification as researchers working in applied areas have offered important theoretical advances (e.g., Fiedler 1971; Hackman and Morris 1975; Hackman and Oldham 1980), researchers working in formal theory have developed applied interventions (e.g., Cohen and Roper 1972), and some research has consistently spanned both application and theory development (e.g., Bales and Cohen 1979). Even so, an inspection of the literature does seem to identify these as two rather distinct branches of research on group processes, as well as an increasing gap between the branches over time. In this section, we focus primarily on the applied branch, which initially paid explicit attention to environments within groups. Later, we demonstrate how a reconceptualization of this early attention to include attention to the external environments of groups may facilitate both applied and theoretical advances in the study of group processes.

Although social scientists have long recognized the important role of groups in society, the establishment of group dynamics as a distinct area of scientific study is generally attributed to Kurt Lewin's work in the 1930s and 1940s. In 1945, Lewin established the Research Center for Group Dynamics (RCGD) at the Massachusetts Institute of Technology, which would bring together legendary theorists of group dynamics, including Robert Freed Bales, Kenneth Benne, Dorwin Cartwright, Leon Festinger, John French, Rensis Likert, and Ronald Lippitt. Lewin's research, and the work that was conducted through the RCGD based on Lewin's research, would give rise to the application of theory on group dynamics to organizations. This would eventually evolve as "organizational development" and would draw on Lewin's well-recognized work on intergroup conflict, leadership, and the development of field theory (Lewin 1936, 1947, 1948, 1951; Lewin, Lippitt, and White 1939). These interrelated programs of research have influenced key strategies in organizational development, including T-group methods (e.g., Bradford, Gibb, and Benne 1964), and survey feedback methods (e.g., Mann 1961).

In particular, Lewin's field theory (Lewin 1951) has had a particularly strong impact on studies of organizations involving groups, and subsequent applied research related to organizations. Field theory is one of the early arguments recognizing the effect of environments (physical and social) on social actors. According to field theory the person and the environment together comprise a single system or "life space" (Lewin 1951). For Lewin, an actor's life space is comprised of the activities available to the actor. These activities, in turn, are the result of the actor's psychological past and future. Thus, to understand behavior, one must understand the forces in the environment that affect psychological states, subsequently leading to behavioral change. Lewin argued that both physical forces (like the spatial distribution of resources) and social forces (like interaction with others) affect needs and attempts to satisfy needs. Lewin's approach emphasized the equilibrium-seeking tendencies of social actors. He argued that needs create tensions in actors, which they attempt to reduce by satisfying the needs. Also, though, people experience conflicts (largely arising from choices and the juxtaposition of different needs) in their attempts at satisfying needs. Attitudinal and behavioral change in this model come about as a result of the actions individuals take to resolve conflicts in the course of meeting needs. From an applied standpoint, Lewin and his students argued that by diagnosing the forces acting on individuals (which emanate from the environment), a researcher could pinpoint the confluence of factors that generate particular behaviors and attitudes. By intervening to weaken these forces (by either eliminating or adding to them to throw them into a state of disequilibrium), researchers could invoke behavioral and attitudinal change. The notion of intervention subsequently became known as "action research"—attempts to change work environments on the basis of systematic analysis and application of theory. Action research, like other developments motivated by Lewin's work, has remained an important component of organization development.

Lewin also made a key insight on the importance of the group as a unit of change. He argued that change was most effective when it occurs at the group level, rather than individual level. This is because the group represents part of the individual's social environment (and hence is an influential force acting on the individual). Attempts to change individual attitudes (without changing group attitudes), for example, would generate conflict because the changed individual would be considered a "deviant," and thus be subject to either rejection or pressures toward conformity from the group. The key ideas that have been picked up by subsequent researchers from in this line of inquiry are that (1) the forces acting on individuals are multiple and complex, emanating from both the physical and social environment, (2) action occurs within a system of forces, (3) the system is itself dynamic, changing in response to the actions taken within it, (4) the system may be more or less open to external influence, and (5) the level of intervention that is most effective for generating change is the level of the group.[2]

In the same era that Lewin's early work on group dynamics was being conducted (Lewin 1936), researchers from Harvard University had begun conducting the famous Hawthorne Studies (e.g Mayo 1933, 1945; Roethlisberger and Dickson 1939). Initially, the Hawthorne Studies involved investigations of Frederick Taylor's then-popular principles of Scientific Management (Taylor 1911). Contrary to the predictions of "Taylorism," though, the research team found that work production was not guided by formal structure directed at motivating and controlling individual behavior. Rather, they found that what occurs in an organization depends largely on informal structures arising from processes that occur in social groups. In a spectacular departure from the planned program of research, these scientists astutely turned to development of arguments on the social organization of work groups, motivation in groups, and informal norms that arise in group settings. As Cartwright and Zander (1968) note, the historical emphasis of organization theory on individuals was irretrievably shifted to recognition of the importance of social collectives.

The Hawthorne Studies were not the only benchmark in the history of group dynamics that occurred at Harvard. With the founding of the Department of Social Relations at Harvard in 1946 and the arrival of Robert Freed Bales, important strides were being made in the analysis of group processes.[3] Bales, influenced by the work of Lewin and Mead, also saw the group as an interdependent system.[4] To examine and understand the dynamics of groups, he developed Interaction Process Analysis (IPA), a method of systematically documenting behavior patterns and roles as they emerged in interactive groups. This work was mostly experimental, relying on laboratory groups to refine both method and theory. Eventually, though, Bales turned his attention back to the point that Lewin had made on how "fields" affect groups, paying particular attention to the notion of countervailing forces and the effect of these forces on interaction patterns within groups.[5] This line of research gave rise to a second method of group analysis, System for Multiple Level Observation of Groups (SYMLOG) (Bales and Cohen 1979). SYMLOG, a combination of method and theory, can be used to examine individuals, groups, intergroup, and even group-organization relations (though thus far there is little empirical research using SYMLOG to examine group-organization relations; for an example of group-organization research using the SYMLOG paradigm, see Farrell, Schmitt, and Heinemann 1988). The SYMLOG method plots group members' observations and ratings of self and others in order to gain a more complete picture of how individuals relate to one another and to the group. By providing feedback to group members regarding the results of a SYMLOG analysis, consultants using the approach are able to help actors understand and adjust their behavior to enhance group work. That is, SYMLOG is used by consultants to as a tool of organizational development to intervene in work groups whose members seek to improve the group interaction and performance.

Lewin's research and theory had wide-reaching effects that extend beyond studies of group dynamics in the United States. Researchers at the Tavistock Institute in England had close ties and scholarly contact with Lewin, Likert, and others from the RCGD. The influence of group dynamics research is evident in the classic studies conducted by Eric Trist and colleagues from the Tavistock Institute on work group processes in coal mines (e.g., Trist and Bamforth 1951). In this comprehensive analysis of alternative methods of coal mining, Trist and Bamforth observed that changes in the technology coal miners used affected the social system by reorganizing work relations (i.e., new technology led to a new division of labor, which segmented work groups, led to increased specialization among workers, and generated a redistribution of incentives according to the tasks that individuals performed within the new system). These changes created problems in morale among workers and an increased rate of absenteeism. Trist and colleagues reasoned that the restructuring of work around the new technology created a psychological and social distance between groups that decreased coordination, increased competition, and de-skilled workers (who previously were responsible for a variety of different tasks). These changes, in turn, generated lower levels of satisfaction.

Interestingly, the technology was introduced in more than one coal mining pit, and the Tavistock researchers found that despite the new technology, work had not been so drastically restructured in some of the pits. In some of the coal pits, the old work group structure was still largely intact. This afforded the opportunity for a quasifield experiment to systematically test the hypothesis of the Tavistock researchers, and determine whether it was the technological change itself or the work restructuring that resulted from the new technology that was generating the declines in worker morale and increased absenteeism. Trist and Bamforth (1951) found that among the workers who did not confront changes in work design (but did experience technological change), satisfaction was higher, absenteeism was lower, and productivity was higher compared to workers who were subjected to work redesign. On the basis of these insights (and the influence of Lewin), the Tavistock researchers developed "sociotechnical systems theory." According to this theory, organizations are composed of both social and technical systems. Each system operates under different principles (technical systems adhere to principles of the physical and natural world, while social systems adhere to principles of social interaction). Moreover, an effective (and hence successful) organization is one that meets both the demands of the technical and social systems in its design. Furthermore, the Tavistock researchers argued that the work group is the organizational unit best suited to meet the demands of both systems. The notion that multiple systems influence organizational process and structure would become a key feature of contemporary organization theory.

Lewin's field theory and other developments like those arising from the Hawthorne studies, the research of Bales and his colleagues, and the Tavistock studies have had a lasting impact on theory and research on group processes and organizations in two respects. First, this line of research identified the group as a critical source of social forces. This led researchers interested in organizational work to begin focusing their attention increasingly on processes and dynamics occurring within groups, and to treat the group itself as a social system. For instance, such topics as conformity, social control, social roles, leadership, power, communication, conflict resolution, and motivation are today easily recognized as key substantive areas within the study of group processes that have continued to receive attention and elaboration. Within the context of research on organizational work, the study of group processes has remained the domain of organization development and human relations, leading to contemporary interventions and applications that import knowledge on the aforementioned substantive areas to the design of work groups. In contemporary research, this has emerged as the basis of "team building" (e.g., Dyer 1987; Katzenbach and Smith 1993; Reddy and Jamison 1988). However, as we later emphasize, there is not clear empirical evidence on the consistent performance advantages of teams.

Second, the systemic arguments developed in the thread of research originating with the study of work groups have directed social scientists to pay special attention to environments, as well as the systemic and dynamic nature of social action. It is interesting to note, though, that organization theory has continued to elaborate systemic and dynamic character of organizations as well as the nature and influence of environments. However, these conceptual advances have received virtually no attention in contemporary theory and research on group processes in organizations. That is, studies focusing on groups within the domain of organization development and human relations (as well as the majority of theoretical developments in the research programs on group processes listed above) have not adequately recognized, much less incorporated, the conceptual advances regarding systems and environments that have recently been made in organization theory.[6] We turn now to a brief overview of how contemporary organization theory has elaborated the concepts of systems and environments. This discussion is followed by an integrated model of groups that explicitly imports ideas from contemporary organization theory.

SYSTEMS AND ENVIRONMENTS
IN ORGANIZATION THEORY

The study of organizations has a long history of focusing on the systemic nature of action. However, as noted by Scott (1998), until about 1960, most research and theory on organizations represented them as "closed systems." That is, the primary focus of researchers prior to 1960 was on the internal structures and processes of organizations, while little attention was paid to how external environments affected those structures and processes. Scott traces the beginnings of an "open system" perspective on organizations to the rise of general systems theory (e.g., Bertalanffy 1969), an intellectual movement that permeated a variety of scholarly disciplines (including engineering, biology, physics, and the social sciences). A key feature of systems theory is its attention to how systems (physical, organic, social) affect and are affected by their external environments. With respect to organizations, an open system perspective holds that organizations are constantly interacting with, and hence influenced by, their technical, social, cultural, and political environments. In fact, all organizations to a greater or lesser extent, rely on their external environment (e.g., Pfeffer and Salancik 1978); although at times, organizations may try to insulate themselves or parts of their operations from their environments (e.g., Thompson 1967). The key insight from this development in the conceptualization of organizations is the influential role that external environments may play in shaping the processes within and outcomes of organizations.

What is an "external environment?" Following on the arguments of general systems theorists, early conceptions of external organizational environments paid particular attention to technical demands and constraints arising from outside the boundaries of an organization. That is, environments represented a kind of external warehouse from which organizations extracted resource inputs (like raw materials) and return outputs (like finished products). From this perspective, organizational effectiveness depends on whether the organization has a structure that is optimally able to meet the demands and constraints of the technical environment (e.g., Lawrence and Lorsch 1967; Hannan and Freeman 1977). However, in recent years, Meyer and his colleagues (e.g., Meyer and Rowan 1977; Meyer and Scott 1983; Scott and Meyer 1994) have increasingly pointed to the importance of processes emanating from the "institutional environment." According to this provocative line of theory and research, organizations must respond not only to the technical demands of external actors and conditions, but also to cultural components arising from the social context in which organizations are embedded, their institutional environments (e.g., Meyer and Rowan 1977; Scott 1991). This insight suggests that organizations respond to and are constrained by not only the technical demands but also to normative demands placed upon them by external actors (e.g., DiMaggio and Powell 1983). Recent attempts to integrate notions of technical and institutional environments assert that an organization's ability to survive and manage its technical environment depends in part on how well it meets the demands of its institutional environment (e.g., Scott 1983, 1991, 1994). This is because legitimacy (i.e., the extent to which an actor, action, or process is viewed as appropriate by others) is itself a key resource which enables organizations to extract other resources from the environment. Legitimacy, in turn, arises from meeting the demands of the institutional environment.

In an analysis that has been gaining increasing attention in recent years, Friedland and Alford (1991) assert that in Western society there are at least five key institutions that influence social action: the capitalist market, the bureaucratic state, democracy, the nuclear family, and Christian religion. These theorists propose that patterns of behavior with meaning and value arise from our history and experiences with these institutions. From this viewpoint, institutions are conceptualized generally as:

> supraorganizational patterns of activity through which humans conduct their material life in time and space, and symbolic systems through which they categorize that activity and infuse it with meaning...[shaping] individual preferences and organizational interests as well as the repertoire of behaviors by which they may attain them. These institutions are potentially contradictory and hence make multiple logics available to individuals and organizations (Friedland and Alford 1991, p. 232).

According to Friedland and Alford, then, each institution provides actors with an alternative logic on which to base patterns of action. Moreover, they assert that actors may be more or less skilled at manipulating or reinterpreting action in light of these logics. Logics, then, are repertoires of action, which are legitimated by social institutions and serve as resources that individuals, groups, and organizations may mobilize and exploit to gain advantage in a social situation (see also Stryker forthcoming, and Scott, Mendel, and Pollack forthcoming).

Friedland and Alford (1991) note that the logic of bureaucracy is embodied in hierarchical relations defining actors' rights in a system along with the routinization, rationalization, and formal regulation of human activities through such hierarchical relations in the social system. They contrast this with (among other logics) the logic of democracy, which they portray as characterized by equality among individuals with respect to rights, autonomy of individuals in defining their social roles and action, participation of individuals in public life, and popular control over human activity. On the one hand, the bureaucratic state provides a logic that legitimizes regulation of human activity through legal and hierarchical means and the rational removal of individual, idiosyncratic behavior. On the other hand, the logic of democracy legitimizes action that involves participation, egalitarianism, personal responsibility to the collective, and collective control over human activity. Because they offer different scripts and rationales for action, bureaucracy and democracy may represent conflicting logics that guide social activity. To the extent that they are discretely mobilized (i.e., invoked at different times, in different spheres of social life), the contradictions between them may pose little problem. However, when they are concurrently mobilized, as we argue may occur in the case of organizational teamwork and other contexts, then the stage is set for an institutional contest of sorts. We turn now to the elaboration of a conceptual argument that integrates these insights from new institutional theory with Lewin's and others' concern for the life space of group interaction.

TEAMWORK IN ORGANIZATIONS: THE CONSEQUENCES OF DEMOCRATIC LOGIC IN A BUREAUCRATIC SYSTEM

As elaborated earlier, the emergence of teams as a basic unit of organizational work design reflects not only understanding of the advantages that collective interaction may offer in the workplace, but also acknowledgment of the importance of social processes in generating effective interaction. Teams are not simply groups, but rather are groups whose members are collectively oriented to the same goals and who aspire (more or less) to egalitarian ideals for interaction. In this respect, we propose that the term "team" is often used by managers, consultants, and social scientists to refer to a unit that represents (at least in theory) the institutional logic of democracy.[7] As such, the arguments we propose that describe the relation between organizations and teams are limited to groups/teams whose members attempt to invoke the logic of democracy. When organizations make an explicit attempt to implement teamwork, an appeal is being made to base interaction on a logic that corresponds with the institution of democracy. At the same time, it is important to note that these appeals are being made within a system that may be heavily imbued with a bureaucratic logic.

Managers, consultants, and social scientists are not blind to the inherent conflict that a team design poses in a complex, formal organization. In fact, the many of the strategies of organizational development and team building (e.g., Dyer 1987, Reddy and Jamison 1988) represent explicit recognition of the fact that organizations are traditionally hierarchically organized systems composed of formal rules and positions. For example, it is not unusual for team building strategies to involve ritualistic interventions directed at instilling a defined set of individuals with an alternative logic for work-based interactions, that of democracy. Much of the work at team building involves re-patterning interaction among members of a bureaucratic organization so that members not only understand *how* to interact according to egalitarian principles, but also come to *value* those principles (e.g., Dyer 1987; Katzenbach and Smith 1993; Reddy and Jamison 1988). Successful team building, then, occurs when members of a collective mobilize a democratic logic as the basis of work interaction. Research indicates that teams whose members undergo formal team-building training, particularly as a collective, are more likely to adopt such a logic than teams whose members do not undergo such training or undergo it individually (e.g., French and Bell 1990, Troyer 1995).

However, organizational teams whose members successfully adopt a repertoire for behavior that is consistent with a democratic logic are not always successful (e.g., Bowers 1973; Bowers and Seashore 1966; Kaplan 1979; Porras 1979; Troyer 1995; Woodman and Sherwood 1980). Research findings that call into question the success of teamwork seem at odds with research and theory on group processes. Research on group processes indicates that egalitarian based styles of interaction (e.g., open communication, reduced conflict, high levels of participation, and equal valuing of member contributions) often (though not always) generate high levels of productivity, creativity, and satisfaction in task-based groups (e.g., Collins and Guetzkow 1964; Dunnette, Campbell, and Jaastad 1963; Hollenbeck, Williams, and Klein 1989; Kelley and Thibaut 1954; Levine and Moreland 1990; Lamm and Trommsdorff 1973; McGrath 1984; Osborn 1957; Shaw 1932; Steiner 1972). Consequently, it is somewhat paradoxical that a team design for organizational work does not seem to offer clear and consistent advantages over alternative bureaucratic-based organizational work design.

We propose that a key to unlocking this paradox is in acknowledging the environment in which teams exist, and further, that this acknowledgment can come through more explicit integration of insights from organization theory described above. That is, it is important to note that just as an organization is embedded in the broader environment of a society, a team is embedded in the broader environment of the organization, an environment that may be comprised of alternative conflicting logics. More specifically, the inculcation of a democratic logic may become problematic when the team embracing that logic is embedded in an organization that is more generally characterized by a bureaucratic logic. This is because the two logics legitimize and prescribe alternative repertoires of action. As previously noted, the repertoire of bureaucracy involves hierarchy, authority, formal rules, and responsibility to one's office, while the repertoire of democracy involves broad participation, egalitarian decision making, autonomous action, and collective responsibility to the unit as a whole. When enacted in discrete life spaces (i.e., domains of social life that do not overlap) the coexistence of the two logics may not be problematic.[8] However, the life space of the organization is not compartmentalized. Rather, action for team members and others in the organization occurs in a collective life space. As such, the conflict between the two logics may come to the surface with detrimental outcomes for the team, the organization, or both. Such conflict will most likely be manifested in interactions that implicate both the team and the organization. That is, we propose that conflict will become evident (and instrumentally problematic) when the team is engaged in interactions with other nonteam actors in the organization. Examples of such interactions might be when the team is attempting to secure resources for its work or when it is being evaluated by nonteam actors in the organization. It is at these interfaces that actors are often held accountable not only for *what* they do, but also (and perhaps more importantly) for *how* they act and *why* they take particular actions.[9] The "how and why" of action is often based on the institutional logic to which an actor or collective subscribes and is manifested in the *way* actors behave.

To summarize, we propose that one reason for the failure of teams to consistently live up to the theoretical advantages that democratic-based interaction offers is that the designers of teams (i.e., consultants and managers), as well as social scientists (upon whose work the designs are based) have not adequately acknowledged the external environment of teams. (An exception is found in the work of Ancona (Ancona 1990, 1993; Ancona and Caldwell 1992), who argues for more explicit development of "external strategies" by teams.) The more a team's actions correspond to a democratic logic and the more bureaucratic the organization in which the team is embedded, the greater the likelihood that the team will be unsuccessful its attempts to acquire resources and support from the organization (i.e., the team's "external" environment). As this line of reasoning suggests, we are proposing that consistency between the team and the organization with respect to the logics that are invoked may play a key role in determining team efficacy. From a theoretical standpoint, acknowledgment of the external environment of groups may offer not only insight into what factors contribute to group outcomes, but also understanding of the alternative sources of group structure and processes. As such, reconceptualizing group dynamics as embedded in institutional environments will advance our understanding of group processes. We will return to a discussion of the potential contributions of this reconceptualization. First, though, we examine these arguments in a case study of two teams embedded in a bureaucratic organizational environment.

A CASE STUDY OF CONFLICTING LOGICS IN
TWO TEAMS IN A BUREAUCRATIC ORGANIZATION

This case study involves the examination of two construction project teams engaged in a $300 million reconstruction program for a west coast municipality. Team A was responsible for the extensive structural repairs to a city hall building, while Team B was responsible for extensive structural repairs to four performance halls managed by the city. The two teams were both embedded in a highly bureaucratic department of a municipal government. In addition, the two teams manifested vastly different repertoires of behavior. This research setting provided a unique opportunity to examine the effects of the contrasting institutional logics manifested in these teams on both within-team interactions and interactions of the teams with the city bureaucracy in which they were embedded.

Data Collection

Data collection for this study included observation and videotaping of team meetings for both Team A and Team B throughout the conceptual design phase of their respective projects. We observed and videotaped five meetings of Team A, totaling 3.05 hours, and eight meetings of Team B, totaling 8.47 hours. These meetings spanned four months. After all observations were complete, we coded the videotapes for the amount of time each team member spoke in each meeting. Twelve members comprised Team A and four members comprised Team B.

In addition to team meetings, we observed team members in the course of their daily work outside of the formal meetings. Although all members were observed at least once for at least one hour, the amount of observation time per member varied from one to eight hours. All observations were made with full awareness and consent of members. Field notes were taken during and subsequent to these observations to facilitate the analysis and interpretation of the data.

Additionally in the final month of observation, we asked all members of both teams to complete a voluntary questionnaire. Only one of the 16 members on the two teams (a member of Team A) declined to complete the questionnaire, yielding a response rate of 93.75 percent. This member was not included in the analyses we offer here. The questionnaire included items requesting members' assessments of the nature and organization of their work, the amount and content of their interaction with other employees (both within and across teams), modes and domains of decision making in the team, problems encountered both within the team and within their division of the city government, and descriptive information regarding themselves (e.g., age, ethnicity, education, length of employment, civil service occupational classification).

Finally, lengthy discussions with the program director, team leaders, team members, and other employees of the office also constituted an important aspect of the data collection. The program director was instrumental in organizing this reconstruction program under a team structure. Our discussions with him yielded critical background information regarding the history of teams in this division of the city, the impetus for the use of teams in this particular program, descriptions of the program and its component projects, and insights on the alternative organization of other work within this and other divisions of the city. Team leaders, team members, and other employees also provided important insights on their work within their respective teams, as well as their work experiences in this bureau of the city. These alternative sources of data allow insight on the institutional logics enacted within the teams, the institutional environment in which the teams were embedded, and the problems experienced by the teams in their work.

Institutional Logics of Team A and Team B

The teams that we observed were created at the same time, were involved in similar tasks (conceptual and preconstruction design tasks), with similar budgets, both funded by public bonds. In additional, the project managers of both teams had been employees in city government for nine years, both with thorough knowledge of the idiosyncrasies of this particular city office. However, despite these similarities, Team A and Team B assumed very distinct repertoires of behavior. Differences between the patterns of behavior were apparent in both the within- and extrateam interactions of the members of both teams.

In the meetings of Team A, members closely followed an agenda that varied little between meetings and was written by the team leader and senior team members. The meetings of this team consisted of status reports on aspects of the project and the giving of directions for what, how, and by whom work should be done. The directions followed a distinct hierarchy within the team, with each successive individual providing assignments and instructions to his or her subordinates within the team, in turn, down the membership hierarchy. These assignments reflected a high division of labor among the membership. For example, certain members were assigned to oversee building permit processes, others were engaged exclusively in design tasks, and only the senior members of the team handled scheduling and budgetary issues. There was very little discussion of the subtasks that members were engaged in, and members were not encouraged to share the problems they were encountering in their daily work. Additionally, the meetings of this team rarely included the dissemination of information regarding other operations within this bureau of the city government.

In contrast, Team B members enjoyed a more democratic normative system within their team. This was exemplified during team meetings in which members contributed freely to the articulation and solving of problems confronting both individual members and the team as a whole. This shared problem-solving in Team B mirrored the division of labor within the team. All members participated in all phases of the team's reconstruction project, including design, analyses of

Table 1. Proportion of Membership in Teams A and B
Reporting Shared Participation in Six Decision Domains

Decision Domain	Team A	Team B
Work Assignments	.46	1.00
Work Scheduling	.46	1.00
Whether to Hire Personnel	.09	.25
Whom to Hire	.09	.50
Procedures for Work	.55	1.00
Meeting Agendas	.64	.50
Mean	.38	.71
Standard Deviation	.23	.33

existing structures, permit acquisition, scheduling, and budget management. In additional, Team B meetings included discussions of business within the bureau that was not necessarily specific to the team's project.

These observations on the institutional logics manifested in the teams are corroborated with two more systematic measures of the manifestation of a democratic logic; one that is behavioral, and one that is self-reported. First, we examined the actual distribution of participation of members in team discussions through the videotape records of team meetings to provide a systematic behavioral measure of egalitarianism. For each member, we assessed the proportion of total meeting time she or he held the floor over all meetings (Team A = 5 meetings, Team B = 8 meetings). We then assessed the coefficient of variation (CV) (see, Blalock 1979) for each meeting to determine the extent to which participation was shared across the membership. For Team A, the mean CV over team meetings for proportion of time spent talking was 1.29, while for Team B, it was .92, indicating more equally distributed participation among members of Team B.

Although the distribution of floor time in team meetings evidenced greater egalitarianism in Team B, it is possible that channels other than team meetings existed whereby members could participate in the team. One such channel is decision making. Although many decisions are made in the context of the team meetings, we also sought to capture team interaction outside of the meetings. Toward this end, we administered a questionnaire to all members of both teams. Included on the questionnaire were questions regarding participation in six different domains of decision making (work assignments, work scheduling, whether to hire additional personnel, whom to hire, work procedures, meeting agendas).

For each decision domain, members were asked to indicate whether they made such decisions alone, with other team members, or did not participate at all in such decisions. Members indicating that they did not participate or that they made such decisions alone were coded as "0," and members indicating participation with other members (i.e., shared decision making) were coded "1."[10] We then examined the proportion of the membership reporting shared decision making in each domain. As indicated in Table 1, Team B showed a higher proportion of the membership reporting shared decision making in all types but agenda setting. For Team A, the mean proportion of members indicating shared decision making across all decision domains was .38 (sd = .23), while for Team B, the mean across the six decision domains was .71 (sd = .33).[11] Thus, the observations, behavioral indicator, and self-report measures of the enactment of a democratic logic in these teams uniformly suggest that Team B was more democratic than Team A.

In interactions reaching beyond their own teams, members seemed to follow the normative scripts representing their respective teams. Team A members closely followed official channels and procedures. This adherence to bureaucratic rules was especially evident in their use of equipment. When in need of a particular shared resource, rather than approach the current user, members of Team A would send formal requisition papers to acquire the item. This would occur even when their estimated use of the item was temporary. Likewise, they were reluctant to release items without receiving the appropriate requisition forms. In another manifestation of bureaucracy, if problems arose for a member of Team A on the project, the member would seek advise only from his/her within-team superior. The superior, if unable to resolve the problem, would consult with his/her respective superior. This "chain of command" was strictly adhered to, even if a member knew that direct resolution by his/her own immediate superior was unlikely.

Team B members showed a markedly different approach in their extrateam interactions. These individuals frequently sought informal consultations with team and nonteam employees of the bureau who were both junior and senior to themselves to resolve difficulties they were experiencing in their work. Members of Team B also indicated explicit awareness of the relation of their own project to that of other teams working within the same reconstruction program. They often initiated informal contact with other teams and individuals in an attempt to inform them on Team B's progress, preempt conflict other units or individuals in their work, and to "borrow" shared resources for work.

These two teams, thus, seem to have adopted distinct institutional logics. Team A can be conceptualized as a bureaucratic unit with emphases on formal and explicit lines of authority, as well as strict adherence to formal procedures. The bureaucratic logic of Team A was evident in the interactions of members both with other team members and with nonteam individuals. In contrast, Team B can be conceptualized as a more democratic unit, emphasizing shared participation, cooperation, and openness. The fact that this was the first time that this division in the city had adopted a team organization for its work may, in part, explain the potential for divergence in the institutional logics of these two teams. The project managers, serving as team leaders, were not instructed in traditional team-building techniques (see, for example, Dyer 1987; French and Bell 1990; Reddy and Jamison 1988). Rather, they were each permitted autonomy in the hiring and recruitment of team members and the development of the day-to-day routines, meeting formats, and other procedural rules for their respective teams. The lack of explicit guidance in the development of the teams, along with the increased size and differentiation evident in Team A relative to Team B may explain the different evolution of the institutional logics characterizing the two teams.

The Institutional Environment of the Teams: The Municipal Bureaucracy

Another important point for the purposes of our study, is the fact that both of these teams are embedded in a highly bureaucratic organization, municipal government. As previously noted, this was the first time this division of the city government had organized its projects in terms of teams. Before this program, employees were assigned to projects out of "pools." For example, one draftsperson might be asked to update structural aspects of blueprints for a number of different projects simultaneously, while another draftsperson would be responsible for incorporating landscape changes into blueprints across different projects. However, in this new team organization, each team would instead have members explicitly dedicated only to their projects. Moreover, these individuals were not necessarily required to limit their work to such highly specialized areas. It is important to note that the concept of teamwork was relatively new throughout this city government. Most divisions of the city (and, in fact, other projects within this office and division) were still using pools to organize their work, though teams were beginning to become more evident. Despite the growing interest in teams, though this division of the city government was still highly bureaucratic in its day-to-day operations.

The organization clearly embodied the logic of bureaucracy that we described earlier. The bureaucratic character of this division of the city was perhaps most evident in its heavy reliance on two manuals: (1) bureau operating procedures and (2) civil service guidelines. Both of these documents were placed prominently on public shelves in the office for the reference of all employees. The bureau operating procedures manual (often referred to by employees as "The Bible") was the definitive reference for inquiries on issues including (but not limited to) office maintenance, equipment use, permit acquisition criteria and procedures, budget analysis and accounting, and architectural standards. Questions regarding job responsibilities, lines of authority, hiring procedures and criteria, promotions and evaluations, and work ethics were generally resolved by consulting the civil service guidelines manual (commonly referred to by employees as "The Commandments"). These two reference manuals together articulated the authority structure within the bureau (and the city government, in general), the procedures for the movement of people and work through the organizational structure, the expectations and requirements for work, and advancement within the system.

Although many employees acknowledged the arduous and confining nature of this highly bureaucratic system, they also espoused the belief that the entire system functioned more efficiently because of it, even if it meant extra paperwork and time for some individuals. One clerical staff member within the bureau (who was not a member of either team we observed) noted that if anyone failed to adhere to the procedural guidelines it would cause others difficulty in their work, and could even result in legal repercussions for the entire bureau. She noted that it was not so much that documentation and adherence to procedures made a difference in the actual work. Rather, it was important to the *flow* of work through the system. She further related that the failure of a particular individual on Team B to leave appropriate "paper trails" (related to the hiring process and overtime hours worked by team members) had created considerable difficulty and extra work on occasion for the clerical staff.

Likewise, the program director chastised team leaders when they failed to submit appropriate documentation for their work or missed deadlines for submitting the required monthly project progress reports. It is interesting to note that in rationalizing the need for the these items, he did not invoke the importance to the work itself, but rather referred to the fact that his own superiors were upset with him over the fact that these items were missing from the records. In one particular incident a team leader (not one of the two we observed) noted that there had been absolutely no change in the status of his project (which was currently on hold), and thus the project report was equivalent to the one submitted the previous month. He argued that he should not have to submit a new report, given that there had been no change. The Program Director, angrily replied, "It doesn't matter! It has to be done! Those are the rules! If you guys can't handle this, then I'll find someone who can!" When the team leader retreated and said that he would get the project assistant on his team to complete the report, the program director advised him that it was not the project assistant's responsibility, but rather was a duty of the project manager (team leader). He further instructed this team leader that, "It's a Commandment! [reference to the civil service guidelines] Look it up!"

Clearly, this bureau was characterized by well-defined authority lines, formally prescribed roles, and formal operating procedures as manifested by the documentation and rationales that were frequently invoked and relied upon in day-to-day operations and conversation. Thus, this setting offered a unique opportunity to observe two teams with different internal institutional logics operating within an external institutional environment that was characterized by a bureaucratic logic. The institutional logic of one of the teams, Team A, resembled the institutional environment of the city bureaucracy in its formal division of labor, formal lines of authority, and the emphasis it placed upon hierarchy and well-defined procedures. The democratic institutional logic of the second team, Team B, with its shared work organization and egalitarian norms and values, stood in sharp contrast to the traditional city bureaucracy.

Table 2.   Mean Problem Levels Reported by Members of
Teams A and B for Six Internal and Six External Problems[a]

Problem	Team A	Team B
Internal Problems		
Insufficient Communication Between Team Members	98.91	42.50
Insufficient Communication Between Members and Leader	87.55	49.25
Inadequate Clarification of Work Assignments within Team	94.18	30.75
Failure of Team Members to Adhere to Deadlines	108.27	40.50
Failure of Team Members to Convey Information to Team	101.09	33.75
Conflicting Procedural Directions within Team	84.46	48.75
Mean	95.74	40.92
Standard Deviation	8.09	6.93
External Problems		
nsufficient Communication Between Teams	53.91	75.50
Failure of Non-Team Members to Convey Info. to Team	77.91	95.75
Inconsistencies Between Teams in Operating Procedures	85.91	95.25
Competition Between Teams for Resources	60.73	113.75
Inadequate Supply of Personnel from City	88.82	119.50
Inadequate Supply of Equipment from City	65.09	104.25
Mean	72.06	100.67
Standard Deviation	13.00	14.29

Note: [a]Scale for each response was from 0 = not at all problematic to 150 = highly problematic. For Team A,
$n = 11$; for Team B, $n = 4$.

Consequences of the Enactment of the Institutional Logics of
Teams in the Institutional Environment of the Organization

The opportunity to observe two teams embedded in the same institutional environment that seemed to appeal to opposing institutional logics offers an important initial investigation of how theory and research on group processes can be advanced by arguments from organization theory. As noted in research on group dynamics, the more apparent egalitarianism (i.e., corresponding to a democratic logic) is in team interactions, the less the membership should experience within-team problems. In contrast, drawing on arguments from organization theory, for teams such as these, embedded in highly bureaucratic organizations that are essentially antithetical to a democratic logic, increased egalitarianism may lead to increased problems in extrateam interactions. Thus, we might expect that Team B would evidence lower levels of within-team problems, but increased problems when interacting with individuals and units outside of the team, relative to Team A.

Both within-team (i.e., internal) and extrateam (i.e., external) problems were assessed through a questionnaire. Members were asked to indicate the extent to which 12 types of problems confronted their teams. The response method for members' judgments of the these questions required that members make a vertical stroke on a line of 150 millimeters, with "Not at All Problematic" as the anchor of the line at the minimum (i.e., left-hand endpoint of the line), and "Highly Problematic" as the anchor at the maximum (i.e., right-hand endpoint of the line). Thus, we report results on a scale of 1 = "Not at All Problematic" to 150 = "Highly Problematic." Six of the questions addressed internal problems for team members, and six addressed problems that the team might encounter in working with the city government. These questions and the mean responses for each team are presented in Table 2. As indicated in the table, for internal problems, the mean for Team A was 95.74 (sd = 8.09), and for Team B the mean was 40.92 (sd = 6.93). In contrast, for external problems, the mean for Team A was 72.06 (sd = 13.00) and the mean for Team B was 100.67 (sd = 14.29).[12] Thus, there is some evidence that the logic of democracy appears effective within the team, but corresponds to problems when the external actions of the team are examined.

It is important to note that these teams differed in respects other than the institutional logics that characterized them. While their tasks were similar both in scope and budget, discussions with the program director indicated that, because of its high visibility and the clients of the project, Team A's project (central offices of city officials) assumed greater status within the city, relative to the structures for which Team B was responsible (several entertainment venues managed by the city). However, it is unlikely that project status would alone lead to the consistent differences across the entire range of problems encountered by the two teams. In fact, it might be argued that the greater importance attributed to Team A's project could have created greater external problems for that team in its interactions with the city government via increased monitoring of the project by city officials.

Yet, it is conceivable that the two projects may have varied in other ways corresponding to the types of problems reported in the two groups. For instance, increased uncertainty in the project demands might lead members to perceive greater internal problems of the kind we examined. That is, for example, high uncertainty might make task assignments more difficult to clarify or information transfer more difficult to efficiently accomplish within a team. Likewise, the two projects may have varied in the interdependence of members' work. Increased interdependence could exacerbate any existent within-team problems, leading to higher reports of internal problems in one team than the other (see, for example, Thompson 1967; Tjosvold 1986). The questionnaire allowed us to test both these possible alternative explanations.

Members were asked to report the extent to which uncertainty was problematic in their work. The same response method used in assessing member judgments of internal and external problems confronting the team was used for this question, again generating a response scale of 0 = "Not at All Problematic" to 150 = "Highly Problematic." Members of Team A did report a slightly higher level of uncertainty in their project than did members of Team B ($M_{Team\ A}$ = 104.09, sd = 22.99; $M_{Team\ B}$ = 100.50, sd = 44.79; ns). This result provides little support for the hypothesis that project uncertainty corresponds to a heightened perception of internal problems within a team. The magnitude of the difference between the two teams in uncertainty was quite small (less than four percent) and not statistically significant, while the magnitude of the difference between the two teams with respect to internal problems was quite large (exceeding 130 percent). It seems unlikely that such a small difference in uncertainty could generate such large differences in internal problems. Moreover, it is quite possible to posit that the causal relation between uncertainty and internal problems is opposite; that internal problems generate uncertainty.

The questionnaire also enabled us to assess the possibility that interdependence generates internal problems. Members were asked (1) how often they exchanged information or physical products with other members in contributing to the team's work; and (2) how often they supplied information or a physical product to the team that constituted a final product itself, independent of the work of other members. For both questions, responses were made on a scale of 0 = "Never" to 150 = "Always," using the same response method cited for internal problems, external problems, and uncertainty. The first question provides an indication of the level of interdependence members experienced, while the second question conveys members' perceptions of independence in their work. Comparisons of the team means of member responses for these two questions indicates no significant difference in either levels of interdependence or independence. For the first question, indicating interdependence, the mean for Team A was 89.55 (sd = 46.94), and for Team B, the mean was 90.00 (sd =35.97). Means for the second question, indicating levels of independence were 93.55 (sd = 43.13) and 93.50 (sd = 54.68), for Team A and B, respectively. Thus with respect to interdependence, Team B, the more egalitarian team with lower levels of internal problems, had only slightly higher levels of interdependence. Teams A and B were virtually equivalent with respect to independence. These observations do not support the competing explanation that interdependence generates increased internal problems.

Turning now to alternative explanations for the differences between the two teams regarding external problems, it may be that length of employment of a team's members may affect the degree of difficulty members experience in the organization. That is, one could argue that length of employment represents a proxy for an employee's bureaucratic experience, and hence bureaucratic acumen. Employees with greater bureaucratic experience should be more effective at navigating the bureaucracy of the organization. Yet, differences in length of employment across the two teams were small, not statistically significant, and favored Team B (mean number of months employed: Team A = 35.09, sd = 62.99;

Team B = 38.25, sd = 47.59). Thus, member experience does not appear to be an adequate explanation for the differences in the level of external problems reported by members across the two teams.

However, leader experience and influence within the city bureaucracy might account for differences in external problems. As previously noted, though, both leaders had been employed by the city for nine years, providing each with sufficient understanding of and experience with the routines and channels of the municipal bureaucracy. The leaders did, though, differ in their tenure with this particular office. The leader of Team B had been an employee of this particular office for nine years, while the leader of Team A had only been associated with the office for 2.5 years. The leader of Team A transferred to the office after spending seven years in a different office of this division of the municipality. Nonetheless, Team B experienced greater external problems, despite the greater experience of its leader with the bureaucratic routines of this particular office of the municipality. As such, experience does not represent a viable alternative explanation.

Could differential influence within this particular division of city government on the part of the two leaders affect the external problems experienced by the teams? Shortly after observations of these two teams were completed, the leader of Team B was promoted to the position of Assistant Program Director. By all indications, the leader of Team B was both more experienced, and of higher status within this office, relative to the leader of Team A. If leader characteristics account for the degree of inter- and extra-team problems encountered by the teams, one would expect that Team B would experience *fewer* extra-team problems, in contrast to the empirical evidence.[13]

The above analyses of the internal and external problems confronting these two teams are corroborated by observations of these two teams in their extra-team interactions. Furthermore, these observations also support the contention that the institutional logics characterizing interaction within the teams were exported to extra-team interactions. For Team B, whose democratic logic conflicted with its institutional environment (the municipal bureaucracy), the use of egalitarian norms and values in extra-team interactions resulted in striking disadvantages for this team. This is especially apparent in the following three incidents in which Team A and Team B sought similar outcomes.

In the first incident, a member of Team B related the following hiring problem, which exemplifies the contrasting norms that members of Team B and Team A relied on in their interactions. It seems that a member of Team B contacted a member of Team A to tell him that Team B had recently interviewed a particularly well-qualified candidate, who could conceivably fill vacancies on either team. The Team B member suggested it would be a good idea for Team A to interview the individual as well, to see if they agreed. This member of Team B also rationalized her disclosure to Team A by stating, that it would be in the best interest of the entire program if each team had members that were "exchangeable," even if their membership was primarily to one team. Before Team B was able to arrange a second interview for the candidate, Team A had interviewed and hired her for itself.

It is interesting to note that Team A and Team B had targeted their memberships to be similar in size (12 and 10 members, respectively, at some future date). Additionally, both teams began the hiring process at the same time, competing for personnel that were identified as candidates through civil service screening processes. On several occasions, Team A and Team B would both express a desire to hire the same candidate. However, Team A always succeeded in acquiring the individual, either through incidents similar to the one reported above or by arguing that the new employee was better suited to their project. Members of Team B complained about the injustice of this repeated outcome in the hiring process, citing the reputed equal project demands across the two teams. Yet, Team B was never able to compete successfully with Team A for personnel during the period of these observations.

In a second incident, members of Team B knew that in the coming two weeks they would be approaching a blueprint deadline on their project. They also knew that Team A was confronting the same deadline. Both teams would require intensive use of the office's limited Computer-Aided Design (CAD) resources, in the week prior to the deadline. Generally, these resources were reserved by an employee by indicating on a weekly sign-up sheet (referred to as the "reserve sheet") when the employee was planning to use the computer and software in the designated week. Equipment reserved on the sign-up sheet was allocated on a "first come-first served" basis. In a meeting of Team B, a member noted the impending conflict over CAD resources between the two teams. It was agreed that this member of Team B should approach Team A and point out the potential conflict. He did so, suggesting that he and a member of Team A meet over coffee the next day to work out a schedule for use of the CAD resources. Upon receipt of this information the member of Team A promptly requested the reserve sheet for the deadline week from the clerical staff and signed himself up on behalf of Team A for that week. This precluded Team B from gaining access to the CAD resources during regular office hours in the deadline week. As a result, members of Team B had to come in after-hours during that week to use the CAD resources and meet the deadline.

Similar differences in interaction styles and subsequent inequalities were evidenced in a third incident involving the allocation of office space. During the time of these observations, plans were being made to relocate this bureau of the city government. Members of Team B expressed feelings of injustice over the fact that Team A was given the most desirable location in the new office (near conference rooms and computer clusters). In probing members of Team A about how these allocations arose, we found that prior to moving an unofficial "office layout committee" was organized within the office. Members of both teams were represented on this committee, but a member of Team A was also charged with contacting the Fixtures and Equipment Department of the building lease company to convey the city's technical requirements for its new offices. Working through official bureaucratic channels, this individual succeeded in conveying the team's preference for a central location in the office to the lease company. Portable walls and wiring configurations were set up by the leasing company in the region of the office that corresponded to Team A's needs and preferences. Although the office layout committee arrived at an allocation configuration that would have placed Team A elsewhere, it was apparent that this would require re-locating walls and wiring, which had already been put in place. Because of the cost and inconvenience of doing this, the office layout committee acquiesced and granted the space to Team A. As noted by a member of Team A, "You gotta work through the right channels to get anything accomplished...they [the office layout committee] weren't an official committee anyway."

These events provide important insight on how the institutional logics enacted within the two teams (1) were imported into extrateam negotiations, and (2) interacted with the bureaucratic institutional environment in which the teams were situated. These incidents document the extra-team difficulties experienced by Team B, and the role that conflict between the institution logic adopted by Team B and that of its institutional environment (i.e., the municipal bureaucracy) played in leading to these problems. In contrast, the correspondence between the bureaucratic institutional logic Team A adopted and the bureaucratic institutional environment appeared to provide an important advantage for this team.

Because this analysis represents a case study, we urge caution in the interpretation of the results. Clearly, further research needs to be conducted on groups in organizations and in other contexts in order to elaborate and substantiate the effects we have described. Nonetheless, the observations we made of these teams (along with member self-reports) suggests that theory and research on group processes will be advanced if scholars attend more closely to groups as open systems with both internal and external environments. We turn now to a discussion of the implications of our arguments for both work teams and the general study of group processes.

IMPLICATIONS OF INSTITUTIONAL ARGUMENTS FOR THEORY AND RESEARCH ON GROUP PROCESSES

As the case study we presented indicates, organizational work teams are embedded within a broader organizational environment. The logic that pervades that environment may or may not correspond to the democratic logic that is often held up as the standard to which organizational teams are encouraged to aspire. When the democratic logic the team embraces conflicts with the logic(s) more commonly found in the organization (i.e., the team's external institutional environment), it is not surprising that the team encounters problems in its work. Organizational theorists have long noted the dependency of organizations on their environments for resources (i.e., both material resources, like raw materials; and social resources, like legitimacy). When an organization is unable to secure either or both resources, effectiveness suffers (e.g., Meyer and Rowan 1977; Pfeffer and Salancik 1978). We are proposing that the same dependencies operate with respect to teams and the organizational environments in which they are embedded, and more generally, to groups and their external environments. Recognition of groups as "open systems" engenders an appreciation for the fact that groups are engaged in exchanges with other actors in their environments. Attention to these exchanges necessarily requires examining the environment in which they occur. The advances in organizational theorizing on conceptualizing the environment, then, can be imported into theory and research on group processes. This integration has implications for both applied studies of teams as well as general theorizing on group dynamics.

First, with respect to applied studies of teamwork, acknowledgment of the organizational environment of teams suggests that consultants and managers should pay more attention to the strategies teams deploy in their interactions with non-team actors. Toward these ends, Ancona and her colleagues have already made strides (e.g., Ancona 1990, 1993; Ancona and Caldwell 1992). She asserts that teams need to develop strategies to bridge their work with the organization. This can be accomplished by incorporating an "external perspective" on teamwork. As an alternative to Ancona's arguments, some researchers have suggested that teams be granted greater license in the organization, thereby reducing their dependencies (and presumably the importance of the institutional environment characterizing the organization) (e.g., McGregor 1960; Weisbord 1987). Under this model, discrepancy between the logic the team adopts and the logic that more generally characterizes the organization would become less problematic. However, we believe it is unrealistic to entirely divorce the team from the organization in which it is situated. At some point, interaction at the team-organization interface is inevitable and could potentially be hindered by conflicting logics. A third alternative, sensitizing key organizational players to the discrepant logic of democratic teamwork, may hold some promise. Along these lines, SYMLOG-based interventions focusing on providing feedback key organizational players in a position to evaluate teams and govern resources allocated to them may help teams and organizations avoid the debilitating effects of conflict in institutional logics on team effectiveness.

Second, with respect to advances in theory and research on group processes, the integration of insights from organization theory on institutional environments may provide the conceptual tools that allow researchers to more systematically develop Lewin's and others ideas regarding groups as systems. As so many of the founders of the scientific study of group processes have recognized, groups do not develop and act in a vacuum. They are a human creation (more or less purposefully), with ongoing ties to actors outside their membership boundaries. To ignore this history and these ties is to ignore a key influence on group processes. The concept of an institutional environment draws attention to the history and external social ties of groups. As Friedland and Alford (1991) note, institutional logics are consistently available to actors in order to mobilize to gain advantage in an organizational context. However, the concept of institutional logics may be more generally applied to social collectives, and as such may help advance understanding of a wide array of research programs related to the study of group processes and social psychology. We turn now to a few examples of how the concept might relate to such work.

Recent advances in expectation states theory have turned attention to how legitimation processes affect status organizing processes (e.g., Berger, Ridgeway, Fisek, and Norman 1998; Ridgeway 1989; Ridgeway and Berger 1988). This development focuses on how shared cultural beliefs in the external environment of a group shape group members' patterns of deference behaviors. Legitimacy arises when others in the group either react overtly in support of the behaviors or fail to act in a manner that contradicts them (thereby implying the appropriateness of the patterns). It may be that "cultural beliefs" correspond to sets of institutional logics (as described by Friedland and Alford 1991). Cues in the environment of the group may make alternative logics more or less salient, thereby determining which sets of beliefs will or will not be honored in the group. For instance, calling attention to the work orientation of a task group (e.g., "We've got our work cut out for us here"), may invoke a bureaucratic logic, lending legitimacy to the rapid organization of a status hierarchy. In contrast, explicit references to the ideology of a group (e.g., "We're one big happy family"), even in the context of work, may evoke an alternative logic (e.g., the logic of the institution of the family), which may delegitimate actions corresponding to an explicit status hierarchy. If this is the case, then it will be important to investigate the factors that affect the mobilization of institutional logics in collectives.

Likewise, researchers studying procedural and distributive justice, particularly the multilevel theories offered by Jasso (1980) and Markovsky (1985), may find the concept of institutional logics useful. An empirical and theoretical problem within this area of research has to do with identifying the sources and processes leading to "allocation rules" (e.g., whether distributions will be based on equality, equity, or need (Deutsch 1975). A variety of factors have been posited as important determinants of allocation principles including structural factors (e.g., Cook and Hegtvedt 1986), self-interest (e.g., Cohen 1982), cultural ideology (e.g., Bond 1984; Major and Deaux 1982), and affective ties (e.g., Austin 1980). The problem for theories of justice is in developing a theoretical framework that can adjudicate among these factors. The concept of institutional logics may help such a development. More specifically, increased understanding of the processes leading to the mobilization of institutional logics may be critical to a theory of allocation principles in justice processes.

Arguments derived from symbolic interactionism (e.g., Mead 1934; Goffman 1959) might be particularly useful in examining how institutional logics are mobilized through a process of exchange and negotiation. As is well recognized, symbolic interactionists pay special attention to the social construction of reality (a point also related to the roots of institutional theory in the important work of Berger and Luckmann (1967)). Goffman (1959) describes the process whereby the nature of the situation and actors' roles within it are negotiated through the offering of cues regarding each actor's claims regarding the situation. The resolution of this process, the "working consensus," may represent the settling of the interactants on a particular institutional logic that becomes the frame for subsequent interaction (see also, Goffman 1974).

Another line of research that holds a great deal of promise for understanding the processes by which institutional logics become mobilized by actors is recent work by Knottnerus (1997). In his theory of structural ritualization, Knottnerus argues that the environments in which groups are situated are characterized by sets of "ritualized symbolic practices" (RSPs) and that these practices are cognitively represented as actors' schemata. The concept of an RSP (i.e., a schema-driven action repertoire) corresponds closely with the notion of an institutional logic. The advantage of Knottnerus' framework is that he offers a systematic theoretical argument detailing how a particular RSP becomes enacted in a collective. Enactment is determined by an RSP's ranking in the social setting. The rank of a RSP (i.e., its dominance in a group) depends on its salience (i.e., how central it is to action being taken in the group), repetitiveness (i.e., how frequently the set of practices is performed), homologousness (i.e., how similar it is to other RSPs), and resource availability (i.e., the materials and social characteristics needed to engage in RSPs). The theory of structural ritualization, then, offers a systematic explanation of how institutional logics (or RSPs) become mobilized in a collective.

It is interesting to note that organizational theorists have commented little on how institutional logics become represented among actors. In addition to insights from symbolic interactionism and the theory of structural ritualization, theory and research on group development, socialization, and evolution (e.g., Gersick 1988; Tuckman 1965) may be instructive. The key point we are emphasizing here is that the intellectual flow of concepts need not be one-way; organization theory may benefit from the insight social psychologists and group theorists can offer on how actors come to hold and enact particular repertoires of behavior that correspond to broader sociocultural ideologies.

In conclusion, our knowledge of group processes can be advanced by crossing intellectual boundaries and importing concepts like institutional logics from organization theory, which are useful to the elaboration of systems and environments. And, as we have noted, there are gains to be made in the study of organizations by such a strategy. In addition, though, we are proposing that this intellectual journey should be made in a manner that not only crosses the boundary between organizational scholars and scholars studying group processes, but also crosses the boundary of time. That is, we propose that with our bags packed with conceptual ideas borrowed from new institutional theory in organizations, we are in a position to attend to the early insights on the systemic nature of group dynamics. Perhaps Whyte's sagacious summons to researchers of group dynamics best captures the spirit of the integration we are proposing:

> Studies of groups, I feel, need to be placed in a perspective of larger organizational structures. Ours is a society of large and complex organizations. The most difficult human relations problems are found within these organizations. We cannot afford to lose sight of the small group, but neither can we afford to study it in isolation...we need to learn how to tie our small group and large organizational studies together in the same general framework of theory (Whyte 1951, p. 297).

ACKNOWLEDGMENT

We gratefully acknowledge the Center for Integrated Facilities Engineering (CIFE) at Stanford University, which provided a grant to support the empirical research we report. Also, we appreciate the helpful comments from two anonymous reviewers and the editors that vastly improved this manuscript.

NOTES

1.   We provide only a brief overview of developments in the study of group processes as they relate to organizational work design. Students of group processes will note the omission of details related to a host of important early scholars including Bavelas (1950), Heider (1958), Homans (1950), Sherif (1936), Whyte (1943). A more comprehensive discussion of the background of group dynamics can be found in Cartwright and Zander (1968) or in Forsyth (1983).

2.   As Back (1990) notes, Lewin's approach can be applied to social units (e.g., groups, households) other than indivuals. Yet, little work has been done explicitly extending Lewin's arguments to such units.

3.   We pieced together information from a variety of sources for this discussion, primarily Strodtbeck (1984), Bales (1984), Bales and Cohen (1979), Burke (1994), and Cartwright and Zander (1968). and also, the Harvard Psychology Department Web Site (http://wjh-www.harvard.edu/psych, 1998) and SYMLOG Web Site (http://www.symlog.com/, 1998).

4.   In fact, Bales participated in an early workshop held by the RCGP in Bethel, Maine. At this workshop, he taught participants the Interaction Process Analysis (IPA) method for studying groups.

5.   Bales's interest in the context of groups is also apparent in his Masters Thesis (Bales 1940), in which he analyzes the sociological concept "situation," paying particular attention to Mead's use of this concept, and arguing that "situation" implied actor, action, values, and environment.

6.   The lack of attention to the development of the concept of environments in the study of organizational work groups is somewhat ironic, given the fact that scholars studying work groups recognize the importance of external environments to advancing a research agenda relating to teamwork in organizations (e.g., Burke 1994; French and Bell 1994; Sundstrom, de Meuse, and Futrell, 1990). At the same time, these scholars acknowledge that a key problem they are confronting is the lack of an adequate theoretical framework that captures the mechanisms whereby external environments affect groups. The conceptual arguments we offer here are a step in bridging this conceptual chasm.

7.   The logic of the nuclear family (Friedland and Alford 1991) may also represent a culturally accepted rationale that legitimizes the components of interpersonal acceptance and obligation to the

collective that commonly characterize teams and provides a repertoire for action (e.g., Dyer 1987). However, in the present exposition, we limit our discussion to the logic of democracy as a basis for patterns of behavior within teams.

8. Although the coexistence of competing logics may not itself be problematic, the training of team members to adopt an alternative competing logic is recognized as difficult. That is, re-training actors to ascribe to a different set of behaviors and rationale for those behaviors is not a simple task. For this reason, specialists in team building training often advocate removing the team members from the organizational setting for a period of time (ranging from a few hours to several days) in order to obviate the environmental cues that bring to the forefront conflicting logics like bureaucracy (e.g., Dyer 1987; French and Bell 1990; Pearce and Ravlin 1987; Reddy and Jamison 1988). A more drastic alternative involves rebuilding the human resources of the team by selecting workers as team members who presumably have not developed strong ties to a bureaucratic logic, and as such are more easily socialized to the logic of democracy (e.g., Kochanski 1992).

9. In previous research (Troyer 1995) it is shown that evaluations of group effectiveness may reflect the procedures members use, rather than the outcomes they produce (see also, Dornbusch and Scott 1975; Scott 1977; Suchman 1967).

10. Multiple items for each of these decision categories were not included. We did, however, discuss the aggregate results with team leaders who corroborated the reports of members. That is, team leaders indicated that members' reports of participation in these decision domains were accurate.

11. Although a t-test of the difference between the two means is significant (one-tailed p<.01), we present these statistics as descriptive rather than inferential statistics because of the small number of observations ($n = 11$ and $n = 4$ for Team A and Team B, respectively).

12. As in the case of the statistics on participation in decision making reported earlier, t-tests of the differences between team means for these values are significant (one-tailed $p < .01$). Again, though, we present these as descriptive statistics because of the small number of observations.

13. Although leadership differences do not appear to explain the difference between the two teams with respect to internal and external problems, they may explain the adoption of alternative logics. For instance, it may be that a leader with longer tenure in an organization is more willing to deviate (or tolerate deviations) from the organization's formal bureaucratic system or is less attentive to the formal bureaucracy than a leader with less tenure. We are grateful to an anonymous reviewer who suggested this possibility.

REFERENCES

Ancona, D.G. 1990. "Outward Bound: Strategies for Team Survival in an Organization." *Academy of Management Journal* 33: 334-365.

Ancona, D.G. 1993. "The Classics and the Contemporary: A New Blend of Small Group Theory." Pp. 225-243 in *Social Psychology in Organizations: Advances in Theory and Research*, edited by J.K. Murnighan. Englewood Cliffs, NJ: Prentice Hall.

Ancona, D.G., and D.F. Caldwell. 1992. "Bridging the Boundary: External Activity and Performance in Organizational Teams." *Administrative Science Quarterly* 37: 634-665.

Austin, W. 1980. "Friendship and Fairness: Effects of Type of Relationship and Task Performance on Choice of Distribution Rules." *Personality and Social Psychology Bulletin* 6: 402-408.

Bacharach, S.B., and E.J. Lawler. 1981. *Bargaining: Power, Tactics, and Outcomes.* San Francisco: Jossey-Bass.

Back, K.W. 1990. "Small Groups." Pp. 320-343 in *Social Psychology: Sociological Perspectives*, edited by M. Rosenberg and R.H. Turner. New Brunswick, NJ: Transaction Publishers.

Bales, R.F. 1940. "The Concept 'Situation' as a Methodological Tool." Unpublished Master's Thesis. University of Oregon, Eugene.

Bales, R.F. 1984. "The Integration of Social Psychology." (In response to the presentation of the Cooley-Mead Award for the Social Psychology Section of the American Sociological Association, Detroit, MI August 31, 1983.) *Social Psychology Quarterly* 47: 98-101

Bales, R.F., and S.P. Cohen (with the assistance of S.A. Williamson). 1979. *SYMLOG: A System for the Multiple Level Observation of Groups*. New York: Free Press.

Bavelas, A. 1950. "Communication Patterns in Task Oriented Groups." *Journal of the Acoustical Society of America* 22: 725-730.

Berger, J., T.L. Conner, and M.H. Fişek, eds.. 1974. *Expectation States Theory: A Theoretical Research Program*. Cambridge, MA: Winthrop.

Berger, J., C. Ridgeway, M.H. Fişek, and R.Z. Norman. 1998. "The Legitimation and Delegitimation of Power and Prestige Orders." *American Sociological Review* 63: 379-405.

Berger, P.L., and T. Luckmann. 1967. *The Social Construction of Reality*. New York: Doubleday.

Bertalanffy, L. von. 1969. *General Systems Theory; Foundations, Development, Application*. New York: Braziller.

Bion, W.R. 1961. *Experiences in Groups*. New York: Basic Books.

Blalock, H.M., Jr. 1979. *Social Statistics*, 2nd ed., rev. New York: McGraw-Hill.

Bowers, D.G. 1973. "OD Techniques and Their Results in 23 Organizations: The Michigan ICL Study." *Journal of Applied Behavioral Science* 9: 21-43.

Bowers, D.G., and S.E. Seashore. 1966. "Predicting Organizational Effectiveness with a Four-Factor Theory of Leadership." *Administrative Science Quarterly* 11: 238-263.

Bradford, L.P., J.R. Gibbs, and K.D. Benne, eds. 1964. *T-Group Theory and Laboratory method: Innovation in Re-education*. New York: Wiley.

Burke, W.W. 1994. *Organization Development: A Process of Learning and Changing*, 2nd ed. Reading, MA: Addison-Wesley.

Cartwright, D., and A. Zander. 1968. *Group Dynamics: Research and Theory*, 3rd ed. New York: Harper and Row.

Cohen, E.G., and S.S. Roper. 1972. "Modification of Interracial Interaction Disability." *American Sociological Review* 37: 648-655.

Collins, B.E., and H. Guetzkow. 1964. *A Social Psychology of Group Processes for Decision-Making*. New York: Wiley.

Cohen, R.L. 1982. "Perceiving Injustice: An Attributional Perspective." Pp. 119-160 in *Equity and Justice in Social Behavior*, edited by J. Greenberg and R.L. Cohen. New York: Academic Press.

Cook, K.S., ed. 1987. *Social Exchange Theory*. Newbury Park, CA: Sage Publications.

Cook, K.S., and K.A. Hegtvedt. 1983. "Distributive Justice, Equity, and Equality." *Annual Review of Sociology* 9: 217-241.

Deutsch, M. 1975. "Equity, Equality, and Need: What Determines What Value Will Be Used as the Basis for Distributive Justice?" *Journal of Social Issues* 31: 137-150.

DiMaggio, P.J., and W.W. Powell. 1983. "The Iron Cage Revisited: Institutional Isomorphism and Collective Rationality in Organizational Fields." *American Sociological Review* 48: 147-160.

Dornbusch, S.M., and W.R. Scott (with the assistance of B.C. Busching and J.D. Laing). 1975. *Evaluation and the Exercise of Authority*. San Francisco: Jossey-Bass.

Drucker, P.F. 1988. "The Coming of the New Organization." Harvard Business Review. January-February: 45-53.

Dunnette, M.D., J. Campbell, and K. Jaastad. 1963. "The Effect of Group Participation on Brainstorming Effectiveness for Two Industrial Samples." *Journal of Applied Psychology* 47: 30-37.

Dyer, W.G. 1987. *Team Building: Issues and Alternatives*, 2nd ed. Reading, MA: Addison-Wesley.

Emery, F.E. 1951. *Characteristics of Socio-Technical Systems*. London: Tavistock Institute of Human Relations.

Farrell, M.P., M.H. Schmitt, and G.D. Heinemann. 1988. "Organizational Environments of Health Care Teams: Impact on Team Development and Implications for Consultation." *International Journal of Small Group Research* 4: 31-53.

Fiedler, F.E. 1971. *Leadership*. Morristown, NJ: General Learning Press.

Forsyth, D.R. *An Introduction to Group Dynamics*. Monterey, CA: Brooks Cole.

French, W.L., and C.H. Bell, Jr. 1990. *Organization Development: Behavioral Science Interventions for Organization Improvement*, 4th ed. Englewood Cliffs, NJ: Prentice Hall.

Friedland, R., and R.R. Alford. "Bringing Society Back In: Symbols, Practices, and Institutional Contradictions." Pp. 232-263 in *The New Institutionalism in Organizational Analysis*, edited by W.W. Powell and P.J. DiMaggio. Chicago: University of Chicago Press.

Gersick, C.J. 1988. "Time and Transition in Work Teams: Towards a New Model of Group Development." *Academy of Management Review* 31: 9-41.

Glaser, R.. Ed. 1992. *Classic Readings in Self-Managing Teamwork*. King of Prussia, PA: Organization Design and Development.

Goffman, E. 1959. *The Presentation of the Self in Everyday Life*. Garden City, NY: Doubleday.

Goffman, E. 1974. *Frame Analysis: An Essay on the Organization of Experience*. New York: Harper and Row.

Hackman, J.R., and C.G. Morris. 1975. "Group Tasks, Group Interaction Process, and Group Performance Effectiveness: A Review and Proposed Integration." Pp. 127-169 in *Advances in Experimental Social Psychology*, Vol. 7, edited by L. Berkowitz. New York: Academic Press.

Hackman, J.R., and G.R. Oldham. 1980. *Work Redesign*. Reading, MA: Addison-Wesley.

Hannan, M.T., and J. Freeman. 1977. "The Population Ecology of Organizations." American *Journal of Sociology* 82: 929-964.

Harvard University Social Psychology Department. 1998. Web Site. http://wjh-www.harvard.edu/psych.

Heider, F. 1958. *The Psychology of Interpersonal Relations*. New York: Wiley.

Hollenbeck, J.R., C.R. Williams, and H.J. Klein. 1989. "An Empirical Examination of the Antecedents of Commitment to Difficult Goals." *Journal of Applied Psychology* 74: 18-23.

Homans, G.C. 1950. *The Human Group*. New York: Harcourt, Brace, and World.

Jasso, G. 1980. "A New Theory of Distributive Justice." *American Sociological Review* 45: 3-32.

Kaplan, R.E. 1979. "The Conspicuous Absence of Evidence That Process Consultation Enhances Task Performance." *Journal of Applied Behavioral Science* 15: 346-360.

Katzenbach, J.R., and D.K. Smith. 1993. *The Wisdom of Teams: Creating the High Performance Organization*. Boston, MA: Harvard Business School Press.

Kelley, H.H., and J.W. Thibaut. 1954. "Experimental Studies of Group Problem Solving and Process." Pp. 735-785 in *Handbook of Social Psychology*, edited by G. Lindzey. Cambridge, MA: Addison-Wesley.

Knottnerus, J.D. 1997. "The Theory of Structural Ritualization." Pp. 257-279 in *Advances in Group Processes*, Vol. 14, edited by B. Markovsky, M.J. Lovaglia, and L. Troyer. Greenwich, CT: JAI Press.

Kochanski, J. 1992. "Hiring in Self-Regulating Work Teams." Pp. 247-257 in *Classic Readings in Self-Managing Teamwork*, edited by R. Glaser. King of Prussia, PA: Organization Design and Development.

Lamm, H., and G. Trommsdorff. 1973. "Group Versus Individual Performance on Tasks Requiring Ideational Proficiency (Brainstorming)." *European Journal of Social Psychology* 3: 361-387.

Lawler, E.E. III, S.A. Mohrman, and G.E. Ledford, Jr. 1995. *Creating High Performance Organizations: Practices and Results of Employee Involvement and Total Quality Management in Fortune 1000 Companies*. San Francisco: Jossey Bass.

Lawrence, P.R., and J.W. Lorsch. 1967. *Organization and Environment: Managing Differentiation and Integration*. Boston, MA: Graduate School of Business Administration, Harvard University.

Levine, J.M., and R.L. Moreland. 1990. "Progress in Small Group Research." Pp. 585-634 in *Annual Review of Psychology*, Vol. 41, edited by M.R. Rosenzweig and L.W. Porter. Palo Alto: Annual Reviews.

Lewin, K. 1936. *Principles of Topological Psychology*. New York: McGraw-Hill.

Lewin, K. 1947. "Frontiers in Group Dynamics." *Human Relations* 1: 26-27.

Lewin, K. 1948. *Resolving Social Conflicts*. New York: Harper.

Lewin, K. 1951. *Field Theory in Social Science*. New York: Harper.

Lewin, K., R. Lippitt, and R.K. White. 1939. "Patterns of Aggressive Behavior in Experimentally Created 'Social Climates'." *Journal of Social Psychology* 10: 271-299.

Major, B., and K. Deaux. 1982. "Individual Differences in Justice Behavior." Pp. 43-76 in *Equity and Justice in Social Behavior*, edited by J.Greenberg and R.L. Cohen. New York: Plenum.

Mann, F.C. 1961. "Studying and Creating Change: A Means to Understanding Social Organization." Pp. 605-613 in *The Planning of Change*, edited by W.G. Bennis, K. Benne, and R. Chin. New York: Holt, Reinhart and Winston.

Markovsky, B. 1985. "Toward a Multilevel Distributive Justice Theory." *American Sociological Review* 50: 822-839.

Markovsky, B., D. Willer, and T. Patton. 1988. "Power Relations in Exchange Networks." *American Sociological Review* 53: 220-236.

Mayo, E. 1933. *The Human Problems of an Industrial Civilization*. New York: Macmillan.

Mayo, E. 1945. *The Social Problems of an Industrial Civilization*. Boston: Graduate School of Business Administration, Harvard University.

McGrath, J.E. 1984. *Groups: Interaction and Performance*. Englewood Cliffs, NJ: Prentice Hall.

McGregor, D. 1960. *The Human Side of Enterprise*. New York: McGraw-Hill.

Mead, G.H. 1934. *Mind, Self, and Society from*The University of *the Standpoint of a Social Behaviorist*, Vol. 1, edited by C.W. Morris. Chicago: University of Chicago Press.

Meyer, J.W., and B. Rowan. 1977. "Institutionalized Organizations: Formal Structure as Myth and Ceremony." *American Journal of Sociology* 83: 340-363.

Meyer, J.W., and W.R. Scott, eds. (with the assistance of B. Rowan and T.E. Deal). 1983. *Organizational Environments: Ritual and Rationality*. Beverly Hills, CA: Sage Publications.

O'Connor, G.G. 1980. "Small Groups: A General System Model." *Small Group Behavior* 11: 145-174.

Osborn, A.F. 1957. *Applied Imagination* (revised edition). New York: Scribner.

Pearce, J.A. II, and E.C. Ravlin. 1987. "The Design and Activation of Self-Regulating Work Groups." *Human Relations* 40: 751-782.

Pfeffer, J., and G.R. Salancik. 1978. *The External Control of Organizations*. New York: Harper and Row.

Porras, J.W.E. 1979. "The Comparative Impact of Different OD Techniques and Intervention Intensities." *Journal of Applied Behavioral Science* 15: 156-178.

Powell, W.W., and P.J. DiMaggio, eds. 1991. *The New Institutionalism in Organizational Analysis*. Chicago: University of Chicago Press.

Reddy, W.B. (with K. Jamison). 1988. *Team Building: Blueprints for Productivity and Satisfaction*. San Diego, CA: University Associates.

Ridgeway, C.L. 1989. "Understanding Legitimation in Informal Status Orders." Pp. 131-159 in *Sociological Theories in Progress: New Formulations*, edited by J. Berger, M.Zelditch, Jr., and B. Anderson. Newbury Park, CA: Sage Publications.

Ridgeway, C.L., and J. Berger. 1988. "The Legitimation of Power and Prestige Orders in Task Groups." Pp. 207-231 in *Status Generalization: New Theory and Research*, edited by M. Webster, Jr., and M. Foschi. Stanford: Stanford University Press.

Roethlisberger, F.J., and W.J. Dickson. 1939. *Management and the Worker*. Cambridge: Harvard University Press.

Rohrer, J.H., and M. Sherif, eds. 1951. *Social Psychology at the Crossroads*. New York: Harper.

Schein, E.H. 1988. *Process Consultation*, Vol. 1: *Its Role in Organization Development*, 2nd ed. Reading, MA: Addison-Wesley.

Scott, W.R. 1977. "Effectiveness of Organizational Effectiveness Studies." Pp. 63-95 in *New Perspectives on Organizational Effectiveness*, edited by P.S. Goodman and J.M. Pennings. San Francisco: Jossey-Bass.

Scott, W.R. 1983. "The Organization of Environments: Network, Cultural, and Historical Elements." Pp. 155-175 in *Organizational Environments: Ritual and Rationality*, edited by J.W. Meyer and W. Richard Scott (with the assistance of B. Rowan and T.E. Deal). Beverly Hills, CA: Sage Publications.

Scott, W.R. 1991. "Unpacking Institutional Arguments." Pp. 164-182 in *The New Institutionalism in Organizational Analysis*, edited by W.W. Powell and P.J. DiMaggio. Chicago: University of Chicago Press.

Scott, W.R. 1994. "Institutions and Organizations: Toward a Theoretical Synthesis." Pp. 55-80 in *Institutional Environments and Organizations: Structural Complexity and Individualism*, edited by W.R. Scott and J.W. Meyer. Thousand Oaks, CA: Sage Publications.

Scott, W.R. 1998. *Organizations: Rational, Natural, and Open Systems*, 4th ed. Upper Saddle River, NJ: Prentice Hall.

Scott, W.R., P. Mendel, and S. Pollack. Forthcoming. "Environments and Fields: Studying the Evolution of a Field of Medical Care Organizations." In *Remaking the Iron Cage: Institutional Dynamics and Processes*, edited by W.W. Powell. Chicago: University of Chicago Press.

Scott, W.R., and J.W. Meyer, eds. 1994. *Institutional Environments and Organizations: Structural Complexity and Individualism*. Thousand Oaks, CA: Sage Publications.

Shaw, M.E. 1932. "A Comparison of Individuals and Small Groups in the Rational Solution of Complex Problems." *American Journal of Psychology* 44: 491-504.

Sherif, M. 1936. *The Psychology of Social Norms*. New York: Harper and Row.

Sherif, M., and M.O. Wilson, eds. 1953. *Group Relations at the Crossroads*. New York: Harper.

Steiner, I.D. 1972. *Group Process and Productivity*. New York: Academic Press.

Strodtbeck, F.L. 1984. "Difficult Decisions behind the Originality of SYMLOG." (Presentation of the Cooley-Mead Award for 1983.) *Social Psychology Quarterly* 47: 95-98.

Stryker, R. 1998. "Legitimacy Processes as Institutional Politics: Implications for Theory and Research in the Sociology of Organizations." In *Research in the Sociology of Organizations: Organizational Politics*, Vol. 15, edited by S.B. Bacharach and E.J. Lawler. Greenwich, CT: JAI Press.

Suchman, E.A. 1967. *Evaluation Research*. New York: Russell Sage Foundation.

Sundstrom, E., K.P. de Meuse, and D. Futrell. 1990. "Work Teams: Applications and Effectiveness." *American Psychologist* 45: 120-133.

SYMLOG Consulting Group. 1998. Web Site. http://www.symlog.com.

Taylor, F.W. 1911. *The Principles of Scientific Management*. New York: Harper.

Thompson, J.D. 1967. *Organizations in Action*. New York: McGraw-Hill.

Tjosvold, D. 1986. "The Dynamics of Interdependence in Organizations." *Human Relations* 39: 517-540.

Trist, E.L. 1960. *Socio-Technical Systems*. London: Tavistock Institute of Human Relations.

Trist, E.L., and K.W. Bamforth. 1951. "Some Social and Psychological Consequences of the Long Wall Method of Coal-Getting." *Human Relations* 4: 1-8.

Troyer, L. 1995. "Team Embeddedness: The Relations between Team Social Structures, Organization Social Structures, and Team Performance." Unpublished Ph.D. Dissertation. Stanford University, Stanford.

Tuckman, B.W. 1965. "Developmental Sequence in Small Groups." *Psychological Bulletin* 63: 384-399.

Weisbord, M.R. 1987. *Productive Workplaces: Organizing and Managing for Dignity, Meaning, and Community*. San Francisco: Jossey-Bass.

Whyte, W.F. 1943. *Street Corner Society*. Chicago: University of Chicago Press.
Whyte, W.F. 1951. "Small Groups and Large Organizations." Pp. 297-312 in *Social Psychology at the Crossroads*, edited by J.H. Rohrer and M. Sherif. New York: Harper.
Woodman, R.W. and J.J. Sherwood. 1980. "The Role of Team Development in Organizational Effectiveness: A Critical Review." *Psychological Bulletin* 88: 166-186.